# The Singer's Debussy

# The Singer's Debussy

Edited, with Introductions
and Translations
by
**Marie-Claire Rohinsky**

PELION PRESS
An Imprint of The Rosen Publishing Group, Inc.
New York

Published in 1987 by Pelion Press, Inc.
29 East 21st Street, New York City, New York 10010

First Edition
Copyright 1987 by Marie-Claire Rohinsky

**Library of Congress Cataloging-in-Publication Data**

Debussy, Claude, 1862–1918.
  The Singer's Debussy.

  Song texts.
  Includes original French texts, with pronunciations,
and English translations.
  Bibliography: p.309
  Includes indexes.
  1. Songs—Texts.  I. Rohinsky, Marie-Claire.
II. Title.
ML54.6.D42R62  1985        784.3′05        85-12368
ISBN 0-8239-0671-X

Manufactured in the United States of America

# Contents

Preface
    I.  French Pronunciation and Diction     1
   II.  Debussy and His Time     23
  III.  Debussy and the Poets     33
  IV.  Songs     47

Appendixes
   A.  Correspondences between Spelling
       and Sound     293
   B.  Chronology     298
   C.  Catalogue of Songs     304

Notes     306

Bibliography     309

Index of Titles     311

Index of First Lines     312

General Index     313

# Preface

The purpose of *The Singer's Debussy* is twofold: first, to present relevant background information that will help the singer to interpret the texts of Debussy's fifty-nine published songs for voice and piano; and second, to provide the translation and pronunciation of the French texts as accurately as possible. No book can claim to replace the primary source of knowledge for a singer, the lessons of a master. This book must be used as a complement and a resource.

The first chapter deals with the general principles and mechanics of French diction and pronunciation. The language used is standard contemporary Paris-educated speech, conventionally and for practical purposes transcribed by the International Phonetic Alphabet. Since French is essentially a language of open syllables, the notation has been arranged in syllabic units ending with vowel sounds. This will allow the singer not only to identify and match syllables and music notes but to reproduce the natural flow of the French legato.

The second chapter describes in general terms the artistic and intellectual environment of Debussy's time, with emphasis on the people, places, and aesthetic ideas that were most influential on him. The third chapter treats of the poets who inspired Debussy, from Charles d'Orléans to Mallarmé. Details have been chosen in the light of Debussy's selection of poems. Space has been apportioned accordingly: for example, more pages are devoted to Verlaine, nineteen of whose poems were set to music by Debussy.

The fourth chapter (by far the largest) examines the songs themselves, which are organized chronologically by date of composition after François Lesure's and Margaret Cobb's catalogues of Debussy's works. For each song is presented first, an introduction to the poem; second, the text of the song (as it appears in contemporary score editions) along with its IPA transcription and word-for-word English version; third, the entire text of the song in French and finally, an English version in free verse syntactically close to the French.

The titles and numbers of the songs are those seen in the latest editions of Debussy's vocal works. Titles and epigraphs are meant to be said, not sung, and therefore are transcribed in IPA according to the principles of spoken French diction. The IPA transcriptions of the song texts reflect the tendency of contemporary French singers to update and minimize the rhetoric of "poetic" diction: to this effect, some of the schwas and optional linking sounds have been put in parentheses, suggesting a lighter, almost inaudible voicing.

Because of misinterpretations arising from the many variants and errors in spelling and punctuation carried by both French and non-French editions—whether originals or reprints—the English verse versions of the French poems given here result also from a close reading of the poetic source of the song texts. Comparing the song texts with the original poems reveals textual variants and changes, where Debussy edited and added, repeated, or omitted words or, at times, whole sentences; only these textual differences have been pointed out and incorporated in the footnotes.

Providing supplementary help and insight into the first two chapters, three appendixes offer an alphabetical list of correspondences between French spelling and sound, a chronology of Debussy's life and time, and a catalogue of his songs.

Footnotes are grouped together following the appendixes. The bibliography is selective and includes the various editions of Debussy's songs used here. Three indexes—Titles, First Lines, and General—complete the book.

I wish to express my sincere gratitude to my publisher, Roger Rosen, whose trust, assistance, and encouragement have been invaluable in this project. My appreciation for gracious help goes to the Bibliothèque Nationale staff, particularly to François Lesure, head of the Music Library, who gave me access to an out-of-print early song of Debussy's; and to Joel Fauquet, musicologist, and Jocelyne Chamonin, Jacques Lilisech, and Michel Hamel, artists and voice teachers. I also wish to thank my family and friends who have helped me in many ways.

———

# The Singer's Debussy

# Chapter I

## French Pronunciation and Diction

A mong French composers of art songs, Claude Debussy stands out as the poets' musician for both artistic interpretation of the poems and technical mastery of the French language. The integration of text and music in his songs is so thorough that to achieve excellence in production depends as much on the singer's pronunciation and diction as on his or her musical skill and sensibility. The acquisition of good diction and pronunciation in a foreign language cannot come only from a book, but demands continuous practice under expert supervision. This chapter does not by any means attempt to teach a singer how to sound French—excellent books have been written on the subject—but rather to refresh memory on various aspects and problems of French pronunciation and diction.

In view of the natural evolution of styles in the French language, the question arises as to how, in the 1980's, to pronounce the texts of Debussy's settings without sounding either affected or over-technical or, conversely, informal. Contemporary professional French singers tend to favor a diction closer to normal speech than was prevalent half a century ago. A French singer does not fall into the informality characteristic of casual-to-normal speech,[1] but reproduces the formal style of the educated Parisian, that is, with vocalic differentiation and a fairly good amount of liaisons. The desired effect is an altogether light, unaffected though refined diction, free of some of the mannerisms of nineteenth-century poetic reading. Pre-Classical texts, on the other hand, have additional problems of spelling variants and word obsolescence, and the accuracy of their pronunciation can only be guessed. It is therefore advisable to update the written text and adopt the closest to modern pronunciation. Debussy's settings of the poetry of Charles d'Orléans and Villon should then be sung along these guidelines.

A list of IPA symbols (according to the Barbeau-Rhode method) and a brief review of the phonic characteristics of the contemporary French language opens this chapter; it is followed by a description of each vowel and consonant sound with its spelling representation. Finally, problems specific to the word-to-word transitions, such as linking and liaisons, are discussed. Explanations and suggestions are formulated with only one intention in mind: how best to guide the English-speaking singer in the diction and pronunciation of Debussy's texts.

# List of Symbols

## Conventional notation:

Italic type is used for French orthography: *chanson*.
Single quotes are used for English glosses: 'church'.
Parallel diagonal lines are used for phonetic representations according to usage in the newest manuals of French phonology: Example: /ɛ/.
Liaison occurs: robes à queue.
Liaison does not occur: nous/au.
~ placed over a vowel indicates nasalization: /lɔ̃ gə/: *longue.*
( ) indicates optional sounds: /pɑ̃ se(ə)/: *pensée.*
Capital C: Consonant.
A letter crossed out diagonally is not to be pronounced: *cloche$.*
Capital Z, T, R, N are liaison consonant sounds.

## Standard IPA for vowel sounds:

### A. Oral vowel sounds:

| Symbol | Example | | Near-equivalent |
|---|---|---|---|
| 1. /i/ | br*i*se | 'breeze' | 'me' |
| 2. /y/ | l*u*ne | 'moon' | German ü |
| 3. /u/ | am*ou*r | 'love' | 'doom' |
| 4. /e/ | beaut*é* | 'beauty' | 'chaos' |
| 5. /ɛ/ | p*ei*ne | 'pain' | 'head' |
| 6. /o/ | b*eau* | 'beautiful' | 'dough' |
| 7. /ɔ/ | s*o*nore | 'sonorous' | 'because' |
| 8. /ø/ | bl*eu* | 'blue' | ——— |
| 9. /œ/ | fl*eu*r | 'flower' | 'b*i*rd' |
| 10. /a/ | ch*a*rme | 'charm' | 'nap' |
| 11. /ɑ/ | *â*me | 'soul' | 'far' |
| 12. /ə/ | v*a*lse | 'waltz' | 'about' |

### B. Nasal vowel sounds:

| | | | |
|---|---|---|---|
| 1. /ɑ̃/ | v*en*t | 'wind' | ——— |
| 2. /ɔ̃/ | s*on* | 'sound' | ——— |

| 3. /ɛ̃/ | matin | 'morning' | ——— |
| 4. /œ̃/ | parfum | 'perfume' | ——— |

## Standard IPA for semivowel sounds (also called semiconsonant sounds):

| 1. /j/ | soleil | 'sun' | 'yet' |
| 2. /w/ | soir | 'evening' | 'west' |
| 3. /ɥ/ | pluie | 'rain' | ——— |

## Standard IPA for consonant sounds:

| 1. /p/ | paix | 'peace' | 'pond' |
| 2. /b/ | bois | 'wood' | 'bat' |
| 3. /t/ | triste | 'sad' | 'tide' |
| 4. /d/ | déesse | 'goddess' | 'dot' |
| 5. /f/ | flûte | 'flute' | 'flute' |
| 6. /v/ | vague | 'wave' | 'veil' |
| 7. /k/ | coeur | 'heart' | 'calm' |
| 8. /g/ | agonie | 'agony' | 'agony' |
| 9. /s/ | silence | 'silence' | 'silence' |
| 10. /z/ | gazon | 'grass' | 'haze' |
| 11. /m/ | mer | 'sea' | 'may' |
| 12. /n/ | neige | 'snow' | 'need' |
| 13. /l/ | luth | 'lute' | 'lute' |
| 14. /r/ | rosée | 'dew' | ——— |
| 15. /ʃ/ | chevelure | 'hair' | 'ship' |
| 16. /ʒ/ | jardin | 'garden' | 'azure' |
| 17. /ɲ/ | rossignol | 'nightingale' | 'sling' |

# Phonic Characteristics of French

Several major principles differentiate the production of the French and English languages:

1. *Muscular precision*, opposed to laxity in English, must be used to produce vocalic stability (no glide) and a clear release of the consonants.
2. The *articulation* and *resonance* of the sounds take place in the *front* of the mouth—as opposed to the back in English—and produce generally brighter and crisper sounds.

3. *Increasing voicing* of the sounds, opposed to decreasing in English, makes plosive starts impossible; see glottal stop, p.18.

4. *The syllabic division* in French is directed by the principle of open syllabification, which means that a syllable, and therefore a music note, has a vowel sound for its center,[2] preceded by from one to three consonant or semiconsonant sounds. This phonetic rule is all the more important since music scores, whether published in France or elsewhere, do not show a phonic division of syllables, but a division according to spelling rules.

> a. Word example:
> music notes:
> printed text:                 l'ex–ta–se
> phonic division:            l'e–xta–se
> IPA transcription:         /lɛ ksta zə/
> **("C'est l'extase langoureuse")**
> b. Phrase example:
> music notes:
> printed text:                 sur les balcons
> phonic division:            su–rleş ba–lconş
> IPA transcription:         /sy rlɛ ba lkɔ̃/
> **("Recueillement")**

*Exception:* When a melodic phrase ends with a consonant, followed by a punctuation, breathing, or rest sign, the final consonant is sounded at the end of the note:

> Example:
> music notes:
> printed text:                 ses mil–le fleurs, Que la . . .
> phonic division:            seş mi–ⱡle fleurş, Que la . . .
> IPA transcription:         /sɛ mi lə flœ r kə la/
> **("Le Jet d'eau")**

5. *Stress and rhythm:* French has no tonic accent comparable to English. English has prominent and nonprominent syllables that are affected by a change in pitch and duration. In French all syllables, except the ultimate and penultimate, are equally prominent; this evenness of rhythm contributes to achieving a legato effect, the vowel sounds being uniformly produced.

There is, however, a stress affecting the last syllable of a sense-group, that is, a group of words that has in itself a certain meaning, though not necessarily complete. This last syllable is marked by a lengthening in duration of the vowel sound. Should the last syllable contain a schwa, as is often the case in French, the penultimate vowel sound then bears the stress, i.e., is lengthened, in which case the final schwa should hardly be sounded. (See pronunciation of the schwa, p.9.)

# I. Vowel sounds:

French has twelve oral and four nasal vowel sounds. Their formation depends on the position of the tongue (low, mid, high) in the mouth cavity, on the front-back axis (front, central, back), of the lips (rounded, protruded, unrounded), and on the position of the velum (open, closed), as shown on the following diagram:

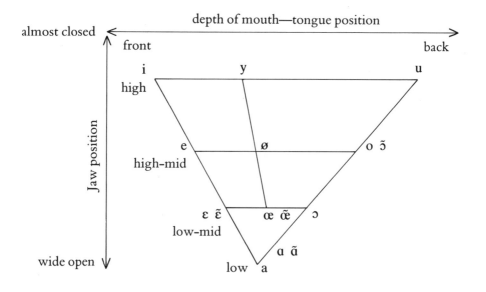

(The position of /ə/ is tentatively set between /œ/ and /ø/, because of its controversial quality.)[3]

## Guidelines for vowel sound production:

  a. The *muscles* of the lips, tongue, palate, and cheeks should remain firm but ready for fast changes of position.
  b. French vowel sounds are for the most part produced in the *front* area of the mouth; the tongue should be kept in a forward position, its tip resting gently against the lower ridge of the teeth.
  c. French vowel sounds show no change of quality in the course of their articulation. No diphthongization should alter their purity. It is important to maintain them throughout the duration of the corresponding music notes. This can be done by keeping the tongue and mouth musculature tense.[4]
  d. Initial vowel sounds, like all initial sounds in French, are to be voiced gently, then increased in intensity.

## Description of the individual vowel sounds:

Each vowel sound is presented with its IPA symbol, a description of tongue position, jaw aperture, and lip position (see diagram above), its various spellings, and corresponding examples.[5]

## A. Oral vowel sounds

| Symbol | Description | Spellings | Examples |
|---|---|---|---|
| 1. /i/ | Front, high, unrounded. | i<br>î (+ C)<br>ï<br>y | tige, pli*i*<br>île<br>haï<br>lyre |
| 2. /y/ | Central, high, rounded. | u + C<br>û + C<br>eu, eû (verb *avoir*)<br>ue(s) final | lune<br>flûte<br>eu, eût<br>vue |
| 3. /u/ | Back, high, rounded. | ou<br>où<br>oû<br>aoû | amour<br>où<br>soûle<br>août |

| | | | |
|---|---|---|---|
| 4. /e/ | Front, high-mid, unrounded. | é | étoiles |
| | | er, ez + final silent r, z | viviez, tournez |
| | | e + double C, except rr | essaim |
| | | isolated words | et, clef |
| | | -ai (future, past definite endings) | baissai |
| 5. /ɛ/ | Front, low-mid, unrounded. | è, ê, ë | mère, rêve, Noël |
| | | ai, aî | aimé, maîtresse |
| | | a + y | égayer |
| | | ei | neiger |
| | | e + double C | errer |
| | | eai | songeais |
| | | -et | coquet |
| | | -e + pronounced final C | mer |
| | | es, est (verb être) | tu es, il est |
| | | es (determiners) | les, ces |
| 6. /o/ | Back, low-mid, rounded. | o final | écho |
| | | ô | ô |
| | | ô + final silent C (except n) | tôt |
| | | o + s + vowel | rose |
| | | au, eau | au tombeau |
| | | o + final silent C | nos, flot |
| 7. /ɔ/ | Front, low-mid, rounded. | o + C | mort, robes |
| | | o + double C | comme, sonne |
| | | au + r | aurore |
| 8. /ø/ | Central, high-mid, rounded. | eu final | feu |
| | | eu + silent C | il pleut |
| | | eu + se | heureuse |
| | | eu + C in small number of words | meute |
| | | oeu final | voeu |

| | | | |
|---|---|---|---|
| 9. /œ/ | Central, low-mid, rounded. | eu + C<br>oeu + C<br>eu, oe + il, ill-<br>cu + e + il, ill- | fleur<br>coeur<br>deuil, oeil<br>cueille |
| 10. /a/ | Central, low, neutral. | a, à<br>e (exceptional) | parc, là<br>femme |
| 11. /ɑ/ | Back, low, neutral. | -as in certain words<br>â<br>-ase, -aze | hélas<br>âme<br>extase |
| 12. /ə/ | Central, high-mid, rounded. | C + e + C<br>-es, ent (verb endings)<br>-es (plural forms)<br>-e<br>-ai- (verb *faire*) | chevelure<br>échangent<br>cloches<br>murmure<br>faisait |

## The schwa:

The vowel sound /ə/ or schwa is represented in spelling by an *e*, also called "mute," "unstable," or "feminine"; in final position, it can also be spelled -*es* and -*ent* (but only in verb forms). The precise phonetic quality of the sound is one of the most disputed problems in French phonetics. (See note 3, p.306.)

Unlike the other vowel sounds, /ə/ is never found in tonic position; it is moreover the only vowel sound that may be post-tonic. It may also appear in pre-tonic position, but it cannot be initial in the syllable. Since the composer decides whether it should be sung or not, it is not, for the singer, a question of identifying it, but of sounding it correctly. Being atonic, it is somewhat more lax in articulation than the other French vowel sounds. At the end of a word in particular, it calls for a subdued sound quality; in some cases it becomes a mere expulsion of air, almost inaudible. Conversely, in central position and in monosyllabic words, it retains a full sound value though unstressed.

Final *e* (*es*, *ent*):

1. Final e (es, ent) must be pronounced if given a long note or a note that differs from the preceding note.

2. If given a short note, final e (es, ent) must be pronounced when it is preceded by a consonant.

3. If given a short tied note and followed by a rest or a breathing mark, final e (es, ent) preceded by a vowel is hardly sounded, sometimes even dropped. The choice also depends on the style of the piece.

# B. Nasal vowel sounds

## Guidelines:

The nasalization of a vowel sound is produced by the lowering of the soft palate, which allows the airstream to penetrate in the nasal cavities. It is recommended to practice lowering and raising the velum in order to build some flexibility and clearly differentiate the nasal sounds from their oral counterparts. A pinch test can be performed on either side of the upper nose ridge to verify the appropriate nasal or oral resonance. A nasal sound should produce a vibration of the cartilage. Conversely, excessive nasality must be avoided, particularly in the higher register.

Nasal sounds are found in initial, central, and final position. Nasalization occurs in:

1. a, e, i, o, u + final m or n.
   Examples:

   | enfant, | lamente, | jasmin, | gazon, | parfum |
   |---|---|---|---|---|
   | /ɑ̃ fɑ̃/ | /la mɑ̃ tə/ | /ʒa smɛ̃/ | /ga zɔ̃/ | /pa rfœ̃/ |

2. a, e, i, o, u + m, n + consonant other than m and n.
   Examples:

   | mandoline, | silence, | fringant, | nymphes, | onde, |
   |---|---|---|---|---|
   | /mɑ̃ dɔ li nə/ | /si lɑ̃ sə/ | /frɛ̃ gɑ̃/ | /nɛ̃ fə/ | /ɔ̃ də/ |

   défunts
   /de fœ̃/

3. Prefix en + any letter of the alphabet.
   Examples:

   | enlèvement, | enivrait |
   |---|---|
   | /ɑ̃ lɛ və mɑ̃/ | /ɑ̃ ni vrɛ/ |

Inserting a short /m/ or /n/ between the nasal vowel sound and the following consonant sound must be avoided:
Example:
onde /ɔ̃ də/, not /ɔ̃n də/

Nasalization does not occur in:

a, e, i, y, o, u + m(m), n(n) + vowel, in words without prefix.

Examples:

ramure*s*,    solennel,    *i*mage,    sommeil,    lune
/ra my rə/   /sɔ la nɛ l/  /i ma ʒə/   /sɔ mɛj/   /ly nə/

To prevent the diffusion of nasalization to the preceding vowel sound, it is advisable not to anticipate the consonant sound /m/ or /n/.

| Symbol | Description | Spellings | Examples |
|---|---|---|---|
| 1. /ɑ̃/ | Central, low, neutral. | an, en final | ourag*an*, *en* |
| | | am, an, em, en + final silent C | s*an*g, tem*ps* |
| | | am, an, em, en + C (except m, n) | l*an*gueur, tem*p*le |
| | | prefix em + C | *em*porte*r* |
| | | prefix en + any letter | *en*velop*p*ai*s* |
| 2. /ɛ̃/ | Front, low-mid, unrounded. | in, ain, aim, ein final | jard*in*, m*ain* |
| | | in, im, ain, yn, ym, ein + C (except m, n) | étr*ein*te, pr*in*ce |
| | | en, in diphthong -ien | r*ien*, rev*ient* |
| | | in, ain, ein + final silent C | p*ins*, t*eint* |
| | | in, in diphthongs oin, uin | lo*in*, ju*in* |
| 3. /ɔ̃/ | Central, low-mid, rounded. | om, on final | n*om*, ray*on* |
| | | on + final silent C | j*oncs* |
| | | om, on + C (except m, n) | tomb*er*, s*on*ge |
| 4. /œ̃/ | Central, low-mid, rounded. | um, un final | chac*un*, parf*um* |
| | | um, un + C (except m, n) | déf*unts*, h*um*ble |

## II. Semivowel sounds

Semivowels, also called semiconsonant sounds, share the articulatory characteristics of vowels but, like consonants, cannot constitute a syllable. They generally occur between a consonant and a vowel sound and are to be pronounced much faster than vowel sounds. They are very seldom given a music note. In spelling, they are often represented by diphthongs.

French has three semivowel sounds: /j/, /w/ and /ɥ/.

| Symbol | Description | Spellings | Examples |
|---|---|---|---|
| 1. /j/ or 'yod' | Short /i/ | i, y initial + vowel | ḥier, yeux |
|  |  | C + i + vowel in central position | lierres, violes |
|  |  | C + i + vowel in final position (except -ie) | extasiés |

Note:   /j/ can also serve as a consonant sound, occurring at the end and in the middle of words:

| | |
|---|---|
| –ill–[6] | fille |
| vowel + ill + vowel | feuille, abeille |
| vowel + final -il | soleil |
| vowel + y + vowel | noyé, égayer |
| vowel + ï + vowel | naïades |
| in certain words, | |
| –i + vowel :/ij/ | prier, riant |

When letter i + vowel is given a music note, it sounds like an /i/.

Example: chrétienne /kre ti ɛ nə/

| 2. /w/ | Short /u/ | oi, oî /wa/ | soir |
|---|---|---|---|
|  |  | oy /wa/ | joyeux |
|  |  | eoi /wa/ | asseoir |
|  |  | oin /wɛ̃/ | pourpoint |
|  |  | ou + vowel | fouet, pirouette |
|  |  | sometimes in -ua /wa/ | aquarelle |

Note: if *ou* is given a music note, it should be pronounced /u/.
Example: épanoui /e pa nu i/

| 3. | /ɥ/ | Short /y/ | C + ui, ué, ua | persuadeɏ, pluiȼ |
| | | | C cluster + i | fluide |

Note: a. In consonant cluster + /ɛ/, it is pronounced /y/.
Example: cruelle /kry e lə/
  b. If u + vowel is given a music note, it should be
  sounded /y/.
  Example: nuageȼ /ny a ʒə/

## III. Consonant sounds

A consonant sound is produced by the obstruction by various articulators of the channel in which the airstream travels. French has seventeen consonant sounds, classified in three ways, according to (a) the action of the vocal cords, (b) the manner in which the airstream circulates through the vocal tract, and (c) the area in the vocal tract where the airstream is obstructed.
A French consonant sound can therefore be described as:
  a. *voiced* or *voiceless* (with vibration of the cords, or without vibration).
  b. *stop* or *explosive*, if the vocal tract is completely closed.
  *fricative*, if the narrowed vocal tract is obstructed.
  *resonant*, if the tract is modified by organs of articulation.
  c. *bilabial* (upper and lower lips).
  *labiodental* (lower lip and upper teeth).
  *dental* (tip of tongue and upper teeth).
  *palatal* (back of tongue and back of palate).
  *velar* (back of tongue and soft palate).
  *alveolar* (tip of tongue and gum ridge).

## Guidelines for consonant sound production:

  a. *Articulation* must be precise and swift. The articulators must move firmly and rapidly to produce the necessary clarity and energy. Lack of articulatory tension gives the following vowel sound a heavy and pasty quality.

b. No *aspiration* (escape of air) must occur, particularly in initial position. (See increasing voicing, p.5).

c. *Final pronounced consonant letters* must be released distinctly and loudly.

d. *Two* consonant letters of the *same kind* are pronounced as one.

e. Letter *h* is not pronounced.

f. In order to produce /l/, contact must be very firm between the tip of the tongue and the upper teeth.

g. Pronunciation of letter *r*: In singing art songs, the French singer still and predominantly uses the flipped /r/ produced by the tip of the tongue against a point set between the hard palate and the upper gum ridge. Final *r* should be barely sounded. Flipped /r/ becomes a rolled /r/ to distinguish the imperfect from the future and conditional forms of certain verbs.

   Example: *mourait / mourra, mourrait*
   'died' / 'will die', 'would die'

h. /ɲ/ is a combination of /n/ and /j/. The tongue should touch the hard palate from the upper gums back to the beginning of the soft palate.

i. *Final consonant letters* are not always pronounced. Letter *s*, marking plural forms, is never pronounced except in liaisons. It is recommended to check word pronunciation in a better than average dictionary.

| Symbol | Description | Spellings | Examples |
|--------|-------------|-----------|----------|
| 1. /b/ | Voiced, stop, bilabial. | b, bb | bois, abbé |
| 2. /p/ | Voiceless, stop, bilabial. | p, pp<br>b + s, t | pirate, apparu<br>obstinées, subtil |
| 3. /d/ | Voiced, stop, dental. | d | doigts |

| | | | |
|---|---|---|---|
| 4. /t/ | Voiceless, stop, dental. | t, tt | plainte, flottantes |
| | | th | luth |
| | | d (in liaison) | m'apprend à |
| 5. /g/ | Voiced, stop, velar. | g + a, o, u | gare, figure |
| | | gu + e, i | langueur |
| 6. /k/ | Voiceless, stop, velar. | c + a, o, u | cueillaison |
| | | c final, in a certain number of words: | bouc, bec, estoc |
| | | ch, usually in words of Greek origin: | chrétienne, choeur |
| | | cc + a, o, u | accourez |
| | | qu | coquin |
| | | g, in liaison | long exil |
| 7. /v/ | Voiced, fricative, labiodental. | v | cheveux |
| 8. /f/ | Voiceless, fricative, labiodental. | f, ff | froids, souffrance |
| | | f final | furtif, soif |
| | | ph | séraphins |
| 9. /z/ | Voiced, fricative, alveolar. | s between vowels | rose, jase |
| | | s in liaison | jeunes yeux |
| | | x in liaison | aux amours |
| | | z | zéphyr, gazon |
| 10. /s/ | Voiceless, fricative, alveolar. | s, ss | soleil, impressions |
| | | t + i + vowel | insatiables |
| | | sc + e, i | sceptre |
| | | c + e, i | noces, encensoir |
| | | ç + a, o, u | glaçons |
| | | s final in a few words | lys, Damis |

| | | | |
|---|---|---|---|
| 11. /ʒ/ | Voiced, fricative, palatal. | g + e, i<br>ge + a, o, u<br>j | songer<br>pigeon<br>jeune |
| 12. /ʃ/ | Voiceless, fricative, palatal. | ch | chère, blanche |
| 13. /m/ | Voiced, resonant, bilabial | m, mm | âme, immensité |
| 14. /n/ | Voiced, resonant, dental. | n, nn<br><br>mn | nuit, échelonnement<br>automne |
| 15. /l/ | Voiced, resonant, palatal. | l, ll | lys, corolles |
| 16. /ɲ/ | Voiced, resonant, palatal. | gn | joignons, peigne |
| 17. r/ | Voiced, resonant, dental. | r, rr<br><br>r final, except in first conjugation infinitives and suffixes -er, -ier | tresse, errant<br>mer, sur |

## Word-to-word transitions

Each separate letter with its corresponding sound(s) has been identified and described, either by itself or in combination. The grouping of words into phrases and sentences follows the general phonetic rules of open syllabification and even stress that characterize French diction. Mastery of the word-to-word transitions contributes to the production of true legato; control of the consonant and vowel flow between words is therefore most important to acquire, since no perceptible interruption should occur between words and consequently between music notes, unless indicated by the notation.

Word transition can be best defined in terms of word-to-word linking (or *enchaînement*) and liaison:

I. *Word-to-word linking* (or *enchaînement*):

Linking is a natural transition occurring between two words, in which the final sound of the first word becomes the initial sound of the second word. Four situations arise, as follows:

    a.  Consonant + consonant

    b.  Consonant + vowel

    c.  Vowel + vowel

    d.  Final *e* + vowel

a.  Consonant + consonant:

The final consonant sound of the first word becomes the initial consonant sound of the second word, provided that no punctuation, breath, or rest breaks the continuity of the melody and the meaning of the text.

    Example:

    l'amour vainqueur

    /la mu rvɛ̃ kœ r/

    (**"Clair de lune"**)

    des lis divins

    /dɛ li sdi vɛ̃/

    (**"Romance"**)

b.  Consonant + vowel:

The final consonant sound of the first word becomes the initial consonant sound of the second word, provided that no punctuation, breath, or rest breaks the continuity of the melody and the meaning of the text.

    Example:

    soif affame

    /swa fa fa mə/

    (**"Chevaux de bois"**)

    pour un coeur

    /pu rœ̃ kœ r/

    (**"Il pleure dans mon coeur"**)

If the final consonant letter of the first word has no sound

value (is never pronounced in any position), it is dropped; a hiatus is then produced. (See Section c below.)
    Example:
il est fai~~t~~ à ton image
/i lɛ fɛ a tɔ̃ ni ma ʒə/
**("Fleur des blés")**

Some words end with two consonant letters that have no sound value; both consonants are dropped, producing a hiatus.
    Example:
le tem~~ps~~ a laiss~~s~~é
/lə tɑ̃ a lɛ se/
**("Rondel")**

c.  Vowel + vowel:
    The intervocalic transition, also called *hiatus*, is, for an English-speaking singer, a difficult technique to master. In English, the final vowel sound of a word dies away progressively and the initial vowel sound is produced with a glottal stop that interrupts the word-to-word transition. In French, the mechanism is reversed, so that a final vowel sound ends briefly and an initial vowel sound starts smoothly without any closing of the glottis; the transition from one vowel sound to another is therefore uninterrupted.
    Example:
tourn*oi~~t~~ au* son
/tu rnwa o sɔ̃/
**("Le Faune")**

*où e~~st~~ leur tombeau*
/u ɛ lœ rtɔ̃ bo/
**("Le Tombeau des Naïades")**

In order to avoid the glottal stop, it is recommended to exhale very slightly before sounding the initial vowel.

d.  Final *e* + vowel:
    In words ending in -*e*, elision occurs only if the next word starts with a vowel sound; in this case, the consonant sound or sounds preceding final -*e* are carried over the next syllable.

Example:
com̸m̸ il pleu̸
/kɔ mi lplø/
(**"Il pleure dans mon coeur"**)

votr̸ âm̸ e̸s̸t̸
/vɔ trɑ mɛ/
(**"Clair de lune"**)

If the next word starts with a consonant sound, final -*e* is not elided and has a note.
Example:
d'une lune ros̸ e̸t̸ grise
/dy nə ly nə ro ze gri zə/
(**"Mandoline"**)

II. *Liaison*
Liaison is the linking that occurs between a consonant letter that is silent by itself and the vowel sound of the next word, provided the two adjacent words are linked by some grammatical relationship. It is therefore necessary to know whether a word has or has no liaison (or latent) consonant sound and also what is its syntactic relation with the next word.
There are four liaison consonant sounds:[7]

1. /Z/ spelled s, z, or x.
   Example:
   le̸ vieux arbre̸
   /lɛ vjø Za rbrə/
   (**"De Rêve"**)
2. /T/ spelled t or d.
   Example:
   vient endormir
   /vjɛ̃ Tɑ̃ dɔ rmi r/
   (**"De Soir"**)
3. /R/ spelled r.
   Example:
   glacer à mon front̸
   /gla se Ra mɔ̃ frɔ̃/
   (**"Green"**)

4. /N/ spelled n.
   Example:
   lointain‿appel
   /lwɛ̃ tɛ Na pɛ l/
   **("Les Cloches")**

Words that have preserved a liaison are usually words occurring in close grammatical relationship such as adjectives, pronouns, or words for which liaison performs a special function such as expressing the plural. Liaison does not take place between words belonging to different sense-groups or words separated by punctuation, breath, or rest.
Liaisons are of three kinds:
   a. Compulsory liaisons
   b. Forbidden liaisons
   c. Optional liaisons

a. *Compulsory liaisons* are found in the following situations:
   1. Determiner or indefinite + noun.
      Example:
      mon‿âme,   des‿arbres
      /mɔ̃ Na mə/ /dɛ Za rbrə/
   2. Adjective (attributive, numeral, possessive, demonstrative) + noun.
      Example:
      grand‿Iris,   nos deux‿esprits
      /grã Zi ris/   /no dø Zɛ spri/
   3. Pronoun + verb, pronoun + pronoun.
      Example:
      nous nous‿en‿allons
      /nu nu Zã Na lõ/
      **("Romance")**
   4. Third person plural verb form + vowel in any word.
      Example:
      dirent‿alors
      /di rə Ta lɔ r/
      **("Les Ingénus")**

5.  Plural noun + adjective.
    Example:
    soirs i̯lluminés̯
    /swa r̄Zi ly mi ne/
    (**"Le Balcon"**)
6.  Monosyllabic words (adverbs and prepositions) + vowel.
    Example:
    sans̯espoir,   en̯or
    /sɑ̃ Zɛ spwa r/ /ɑ̃ N̄ɔ r/

b.  *Forbidden liaisons*: No liaison can occur in:
    1.  Singular noun + predicate.
        Example:
        La nui̯t / a
        /la nɥi    a/
        (**"De Rêve"**)
    2.  Inverted subject pronoun + vowel.
        Example:
        aimons̯-nous̯ / e̯t dormons̯
        /ɛ mɔ̃ nu        e dɔ rmɔ̃/
        (**"Aimons-nous et dormons"**)
    3.  Various types of words in accented position, such as past participle + vowel.
        Example:
        lavés̯ / au fon̯d
        /la ve    o   fɔ̃/
        (**"Le Balcon"**)
    4.  Conjunction *et* + vowel.
        Example:
        e̯t / il me regarda
        /e    i lmə rə ga rda/
        (**"La Chevelure"**)
    5.  . . . + h aspirate.
        Example:
        sans̯ /ḥaine
        /sɑ̃    ɛ nə/
        (**"Il pleure dans mon coeur"**)

c. *Optional liaisons* are more numerous in singing than in speaking French, since some of the poetic reading style of nineteenth-century diction is still observed by contemporary French singers in Debussy's songs. They can be formed with:

1. Plural noun + verb.
   Example:
   fleurs‿enlacent
   /flœ　rZɑ̃ la sə/
   **("De Fleurs")**

2. Verb + vowel.
   Example:
   vient‿endormir
   /vjɛ̃　Tɑ̃ dɔ rmi r/
   **("De Soir")**
   m'apprend‿à jouer
   /ma prɑ̃　Ta ʒu e/
   **("La Flûte de Pan")**

3. Polysyllabic adverbs and prepositions.
   Example:
   pour toujours‿ainsi
   /pu　rtu ʒu　rZɛ̃ si/
   **("La Chevelure")**

Of all problems of French pronunciation, the most difficult are the accurate production of vowel sounds and the distinction of where liaisons occur. Good ear-training practice and competent guidance in pronunciation, coupled with a sound theoretical knowledge of French phonetics, provide the singer with the excellent technical groundwork from which artistry can arise.

# Chapter II

## Debussy and His Time

During the last two decades of the nineteenth century, there were almost no dividing lines between the artistic disciplines. It was a time of cooperation in the search for new aesthetic guidelines and forms. Debussy became intimately associated with his contemporaries, and no artistic or intellectual development escaped his notice. His curiosity was boundless, and his creative energy responded eagerly to innovations. As the years passed he removed himself from the contemporary scene, either willingly or involuntarily. Because he had achieved a personal style that soared by itself, he had less need or desire to partake in the artistic trends of the early twentieth century. He chose a form of semireclusion and devoted himself to the creation of his major works.

Two-thirds of Debussy's vocal production was composed in the 1880's and 1890's. It naturally reflects the composer's association with his time: Each *mélodie* is linked to the artistic and literary climate of the period. Behind each of them, also, are events, travels, and people.

At the time of Debussy's earliest song settings (c. 1880), a feeling of unrest had become apparent in every class of French society. The carefree years of the Second Empire had ended in disaster and violence with the Franco-Prussian War and the Commune uprisings (1870). The Third Republic and its countless scandals inspired a sense of political degeneration. The Industrial Revolution and its ensuing frenzy for material satisfaction had spoilt the beauty of the countryside and the charm of the cities. The theories of Scientism, raised to a cult by the Positivists, frightened sensitive souls, aware that too many questions were left unanswered: God was forgotten at the expense of Progress. Against the deep spiritual disillusion that was taking over people's minds, outcries of revolt then rose from a cultural elite.

As was often the case in nineteenth-century France, the change came down from the North. England had already lived through industrialization, bourgeois conformism supremacy, and moral and artistic rebellions. English aesthetes had joined forces and advocated the search for beauty in an exquisite world. Translations of English poets such as Tennyson, Keats, and Swinburne became available. The Paris World Exhibition of 1867 introduced the Pre-Raphaelite painters to the Parisian public; works of Burne-Jones were shown in 1878, 1889, and 1893.

Germany's main contribution to the change was the operas of Wagner. Passionate French admirers flocked to Bayreuth and discovered ecstasy. The *Revue Wagnérienne* (Wagnerian Review), founded in Paris in 1885, proclaimed that Wagner, by blending Oriental mysticism and Celtic and Germanic myths in *Parsifal*, had given a concrete form to dream images. Gods and transcendence became the surest antidotes to Positivism and Rationalism: A disenchanted generation was escaping bleak reality into imaginary paradises.

The Paris World Exhibition of 1889 uncovered an entirely novel exotic world made up of Japanese prints, batik designs of Java, and Annamite and Javanese orchestras. The *gamelang* or Javanese orchestra featured the pentatonic scale, rich rhythms, percussion instruments, and stately dancers. During the same period, concerts of Russian music were given at the Trocadero, under the direction of Rimsky-Korsakov, and revealed vivid orchestral coloring.

The late nineteenth century saw a renewal of painting as well as a revival of interest in museums. Every eleven years art collections displayed treasures of classical and avant-garde painting: The highlights of the 1863 *Salon Officiel*, Courbet and Realism, were superseded in 1874 by the Impressionists, who were followed in 1885 by a school of poetic painting, the Symbolists. Both schools, in their separate ways, reacted against the story-telling techniques of Realism. The Impressionists transposed reality as it appealed to their sensorial imaginations at various times of the day; they reproduced immediate visual impressions of an object or an event. The Symbolists perceived a spiritual atmosphere beyond the reality of the senses and reinterpreted their impressions as symbols for the invisible world of the spirit. Art Nouveau, inspired by the arts and crafts movement of William Morris and the Pre-Raphaelites, stressed the importance of beauty in everyday surroundings and adorned everything with lines or arabesques, ascending in joy and descending in despair.

Symbol had indeed become the aesthetic keyword of the period, as an answer to stark reality and as a new way to communicate experience and awaken sensibility. The theories of the Swedish visionary philosopher Swedenborg (1688–1772), who had first claimed to see correspondences between the spiritual and natural worlds, traveled to Baudelaire through Edgar Allen Poe and appeared, in translation, on the Paris scene of 1875. Poets therefore became the first and foremost mediators between man and the enigmas of Nature in a world that disregarded spiritual life and social harmony; they would help mankind in rediscovering his lost unity with the world. The notion inherited from the Romantics that the language of art was a symbolic language reappeared under the Second Empire between 1860 and 1866, in the work of the Parnassian poets. This group of aesthetes, by protesting the artist's loss of independence in bourgeois patronage and by reacting against Zola's Naturalism, championed art for art's sake and demanded the cult of perfection in form; great emotions and profound thoughts could best be conveyed by purity of line and harmony. In 1866, four years after Debussy's birth, was published an anthology of poetry, *Le Parnasse Contemporain* (The Contemporary Parnassus), with contributions by Théophile Gautier, Théodore de Banville, Leconte de Lisle, Baudelaire, Hérédia, Verlaine, and Mallarmé among others—all names soon revered by the young Debussy.

Sensibilities revolted by naturalistic settings indulged in nostalgia. Banville and Verlaine looked back to an illusory eighteenth century and revived the evanescent silhouettes of Watteau's paintings in an atmosphere of *fêtes galantes*, where all was suggestion. Thanks to Verlaine, Mallarmé, who was unknown and little appreciated until then, soon rose to the heights of fame: His advocacy of poetry as a joyous experience derived from the slow discovery of hidden meanings, suggestions, and symbols won him the stature of oracle and magician. Young artists and aspiring writers convened at his Tuesday gatherings in respectful silence; they had found in Mallarmé a master. They also raved about the Flaubert of *St. Julien l'Hospitalier* (St. Julian the Hospitaller), Baudelaire, Poe, Verlaine, Wagner, the Pre-Raphaelites. Poets and art critics, painters and musicians, all spoke one language—the language of Symbolism.

When Debussy, aged twenty-four, returned to Paris after a two-year stay in Rome at the Villa Medici, he found an extraordinary atmosphere of artistic effervescence and literary ferment: New directions were sought and collaboration between the arts was urged. Although no school per se was actually formed and few of the Symbolist poets who appeared on the Parisian literary scene came near the original talent and creativity of Baudelaire and Verlaine—with the exception of Mallarmé—the poet Jean Moréas drew up the Manifesto of the Symbolists in 1886. Artists were grouping in cenacles, cafés, around reviews. Mythological, medieval, and Nordic legends were revived, symbolic associations reveled in, the mysteries of Nature probed beyond appearances, artistic forms transmuted into suggestion, incantation, musicality.

In painting, the Symbolist period flourished in the last decade of the century: 1891 was the year of the greatest acclaim for the movement. Puvis de Chavannes, Gustave Moreau, Maurice Denis, Redon pledged allegiance to the cult of imagination, turned to the past ages, and explored the tumultuous kingdom of dreams and nightmares. It was then that Debussy wrote his settings of Louÿs' *Chansons de Bilitis* (Songs of Bilitis), which were considered the peak of his achievement in the area of vocal music.

In retrospect, one cannot help but notice how much of an accelerating factor were Debussy's contemporaries—acquaintances, mentors, and friends—in his career and ensuing success. Debussy seldom found inspiration in the music circles of his time. His rebellion against academism and his scorn for tradition did not meet with the approval of most of his teachers at the *Conservatoire* nor find much encouragement among his colleagues at the Villa Medici or the musicians in vogue. His intellectual and artistic development came rather from his readings and his frequenting of the Paris Bohemia and of his friends. Throughout his last years at the *Conservatoire*, Debussy kept informed of the newest literary publications: Thanks to another pupil of Guiraud's, Raymond Bonheur, he became interested in one of the prominent Parnassian poets, Théodore de Banville. While in Rome (1885–87), he received—from his benefactor Vasnier and a bookseller friend, Baron—works by Verlaine,

Moréas, Shelley, Huysmans, and Charles Morice; he also read Shakespeare, Baudelaire, the Goncourts, Mallarmé, Laforgue, and avant-garde literary journals. A long correspondence was established with the notorious novelist Paul Bourget, who became one of his literary mentors.

Returning from Rome, Debussy began frequenting the Bohemian establishments of Paris, beginning with the *Chat Noir* (Black Cat), a Montmartre cabaret that was the favorite haunt of the Decadents. There he participated in musical activities, accompanied both an amateur group of singers and the Polish poet and singer Marie Krysinska[8]; rhymesters, chansonniers, and painters animated the pseudo-Gothic café, which was also visited by prominent writers such as Banville, Verlaine, Maupassant, and Paul Bourget. Among Debussy's friends was Adolphe Willette, illustrator of the first edition of "Mandoline," who drew charming Pierrots and Columbines. A journal was published in 1888 to narrate the joyous atmosphere of the cabaret, with cartoons by Forain, Steinlen, and Caran d'Ache.

Later Debussy came to dislike cabaret music and abandoned the *Chat Noir* for more sophisticated public places. One of them was the *Librairie de l'Art Indépendant* (Independent Art Bookstore), a small bookstore near the Opera, which became the meeting-place of the Symbolists from 1887 on; there Debussy must have seen Villiers de l'Isle-Adam, Henri de Régnier, Pierre Louÿs, Mallarmé, and Gide. The owner, Léon Bailly, was not only a publisher, dilettante writer, and art collector, but also patronized young and unknown artists. The young Symbolists held meetings in the *Librairie* to introduce and discuss recent literary productions. Other cafés familiar to Debussy were the *Vachette* in the Latin Quarter, headquarters of Moréas and Gide; *Chez Pousset* at the *Carrefour Châteaudun* (Châteaudun Circle), a gossip center for journalists; and the *Taverne Weber* on the *Rue Royale*. There came poets, novelists, pamphleteers, journalists, music critics, painters, caricaturists, and famous people such as Marcel Proust, Pierre Louÿs, Léon Daudet, Charles Maurras, Paul Robert the painter, and occasionally Whistler and Oscar Wilde. The clientele was of a higher standing than at the Montmartre cafés. Animated groups were formed around tables. Debussy would stand aside, listening and ordering Welsh rarebit and pale English ale; should the evening drag,

Debussy and his friend René Peter would move on to the adjacent bar, the Reynold's.

There the atmosphere was always gay and terribly noisy: Heavy drinking and occasional violent brawls went on among the clientele of jockeys, coachmen, stable lads, and trainers, most of them English, all lined up in a single row of tables while banjo and mandolin music was provided. Besides Toulouse-Lautrec, the local celebrities were Tom, the corpulent coachman of the Rothschilds; May Belfort, a singer from Ireland in a Kate Greenaway dress immortalized by Toulouse-Lautrec; and two famous clowns from the *Nouveau Cirque* (New Circus), Footitt and Chocolat, with whom Debussy would discuss clowning techniques, music, or even poetry and philosophy.

Debussy also became a frequent caller at more professional circles, either in the field of music or literature. In 1888 he went to Bayreuth for the first time; in 1889 he became a member of the *Société Nationale de Musique* (National Music Society). This association was the most important place in Paris for the production and performance of new music; its membership comprised open-minded musicians and enlightened amateurs. Debussy attended many of its concerts at which his works were performed; there also he became further acquainted with the leading musicians of his generation. The private circles at which he was a caller from 1887 to 1894 were salons associated with contemporary artistic and literary movements. He was a welcome guest at the home of René Peter, a writer of comedies, at the composer Chausson's, at art patron Lucien Fontaine's, and at Belgian painter Alfred Stevens'. Debussy found in Ernest Chausson a compassionate older brother; brilliant figures in the arts came to his salon, artists such as Renoir, Manet, Degas, Redon, Rodin, and Eugène Carrière, musicians such as César Franck, Vincent d'Indy, Duparc, Chabrier, Fauré, the violinist Eugène Ysaïe, and writers such as Henri de Régnier, Gide, Mallarmé, and Colette. Chausson also introduced Debussy to the aristocratic drawing rooms of the *Faubourg St. Germain* (St. Germain Quarter), where Debussy conducted an amateur choir, interpreted Wagner's music on the piano, and accompanied his own melodies.

Two literary salons hosted the Symbolists and gave Debussy the best opportunities for literary acquaintanceship. At Pierre

Louÿs' there were Wednesday receptions attended by poets such as Gustave Kahn, Hérédia, Régnier, Valéry, Tinan. Wagner was the usual topic of discussion. Seeming more absorbed in his reveries than in the discussions around him, Debussy sometimes sang parts of *Pelléas et Mélisande* and accompanied himself on Louÿs' harmonium. The famous Tuesday gatherings at Mallarmé's were the meeting-place of the new intelligentsia of the 1880's and 1890's. There came poets, Mallarmé's faithful followers, such as Stuart Merrill, Verlaine, Moréas, Villiers de l'Isle-Adam, then in 1885 Rodenbach, Charles Morice, H. de Régnier, Viélé-Griffin, Arthur Symons. In 1895 a group of very young writers, P. Louÿs, A. Gide, P. Valéry, Camille Mauclair, Claudel, Maeterlinck, joined painters such as Berthe Morisot, Renoir, Monet, Degas, Gauguin, Redon; there were also essayists, critics, novelists, editors. Mallarmé entertained in his dining room around a jar of tobacco, leaning against the mantel, eight visitors seated around the table; all listened reverently to the endlessly brilliant monologues of their host. It is not known how Debussy met Mallarmé, but it has been assumed that he had known him since 1890. To be admitted to the inner circle was in itself a sure sign of intellectual superiority.

To narrow the field of influence on Debussy to the individuals is to mention those who knew him closely—his teachers, mentors, acquaintances, and friends. Of humble birth, Debussy could never have acquired careful training without help; furthermore, his well-known financial difficulties prompted many a generous offer. Names stand out such as Albert Lavignac and Ernest Guiraud, his teachers at the *Conservatoire*; Mme. von Meck, the Russian patroness who employed him as an artist in residence during three summers and introduced him to the works of the new Russian composers; Mme. Blanche Vasnier, the amateur singer for whom he wrote many of his early songs and whose husband befriended him, guiding his readings and hosting him daily; Robert Godet, a Swiss journalist and musicologist, and a man of ideals with whom Debussy went to Bayreuth; René Peter, who had planned to collaborate on projects with Debussy; Pierre Louÿs, who for ten years was his intimate friend and gave him constant and considerable support; Gabriel Mourey, a poet, novelist, playwright, critic, and translator of Poe and Swinburne, who became a lifelong friend; and

of course Debussy's second wife, Emma Bardac, for whom he
wrote some of his later songs. Looking after Debussy's career
were sympathetic and generous publishers, for example Jacques
Durand, who became his friend, or Georges Hartmann, who
supplied him with a yearly income and additional financial aid
when necessary.

Befriended, patronized, encouraged, Debussy strangely let
most of his relationships come to abrupt endings. One major
event in his life, which alienated many of his friends, was the
tragic termination of his marriage to Rosalie Texier and his
elopement with Emma Bardac in June 1904. His marriage to
Mme. Bardac and the birth of his daughter came at a time of
professional success. At last his long and often difficult search
for certainty, material and aesthetic, was over. Now that he was
holding up his own style of writing, that his personal life was
settling down, he no longer needed the stimulation of intellectual encounters in cafés and circles, nor was the comforting
presence of friends so imperative. That is not to say that he
excluded himself completely from the outside world; he always
remained receptive to new aesthetic ventures.

During the early years of the twentieth century, Paris was
becoming the center of attraction for artists from all over
Europe, particularly in the music field. Although Wagner was
still enjoying popularity with the French public, other German
composers such as Richard Strauss and Gustav Mahler were also
highly praised. The fusion of arts that had been advocated by
Wagner and the Symbolists found a talented adept in Diaghilev,
the Russian ballet director who invited great composers,
choreographers, dancers, and artists to collaborate on ballets.
The first Paris performance of his *Ballets Russes* (Russian Ballets) took place in 1909, followed by more revolutionary productions such as the *Prélude à l'après-midi d'un faune* (Prelude
to the Afternoon of a Faun) in 1912, with the collaboration of
Debussy and Nijinsky, and in 1913 the *Rite of Spring*, with
music by Stravinsky and choreography by Nijinsky.

New trends also developed in painting, for Symbolism offi-
cially was no more. A sudden reevaluation of Impressionism
arose from the feeling that this was, at last, a genuine French
style of painting, all gracefulness, simplicity, and happiness. In

1905 the Paris Autumn Salon featured a new group of painters called the Fauves, among whom were Matisse, Derain, Van Dongen, and Rouault. Intense colors and bold brushstrokes characterized their works and expressed in a style devoid of pretense the purely visual impact of nature. The movement was of short duration (1903–1907) and was superseded by Cubism. Analytical Cubism (1910–1912) with names like Picasso and Braque concentrated on exploring shapes and using sober colors. What differentiated, indeed, the aesthetic values of the pre-World War I era from the last decades of the nineteenth century was an emphasis on sincerity, as opposed to what was considered an unsparing display of emotion. It explains the attempt, at all levels of artistic endeavors, to simplify styles, which was leading into the neoclassical styles of the postwar era.

As Lockspeiser explains in his biography of Debussy, Debussy was certainly not indifferent to these changes, since he had always welcomed experiments. Yet he was a little put off by some of the new directions, and he avoided certain events on the Paris music scene. Although he collaborated with Stravinsky, he was soon bewildered by the mightiness of Stravinsky's works. He considered the Parisian enthusiasm for Mahler and Strauss mere snobbery, and the music of Schoenberg shocked him. What he called "artistic bluff"[9] was something he could not condone. He therefore took refuge within himself and spurned any imitation of what could be best said in another language. Accordingly he considered himself a French musician, both in aesthetics and feelings, and cultivated a greater simplicity and sincerity of style.

Although years now elapsed between the composition of new melodies, poetry never lost hold of his imagination. Verlaine and Mallarmé were now dead; nevertheless they remained his favorite poets and inspired some of his later songs. No new poetic school was looming in the early part of the twentieth century. Mallarmé's promising young friend Valéry was waiting for a propitious time to speak out. Yet many poets of this period were turning to a more concrete view of the world and a more straightforward means of expression. In keeping with the development of his sensitivity and the simplification of his style of writing, Debussy turned for inspiration to older forms of poetry. French poets of the late Middle Ages and the Baroque era influenced the production of new melodies, characterized by subtlety, restraint, and suggestive qualities.

One last event darkened the latter years of his life and inspired his last vocal work: the Franco–German conflict of 1914. "Noël" was the only *mélodie* in which Debussy associated artistry and humanitarian thoughts. Which brings forth the final remark that, even though Debussy's musical development was closely linked with the currents of his day, it was only in the area of aesthetics. Debussy remained an outsider to every field of human endeavor but those of the arts, literature in particular.

# Chapter III

## Debussy and the Poets

The art song went through a period of renewal during the latter part of the nineteenth century. Composers such as Massenet, Duparc, and Fauré borrowed from the intimacy of the German Romantic *lied* and introduced new flowing harmonies into the French language. Claude Debussy played an essential and inventive part in this renewal by relieving the *mélodie* (art song) of the Germanic influence and by creating original impressions of the poems he chose to set to music; not only did he have sensitivity and taste, but also and above all a remarkable sense of and respect for the French language. Paul Dukas was of the opinion that, of all musicians, Debussy possessed the finest ability to explore the mood of a poem and render it to perfection. The artistry of his songs, therefore, came equally from his innovative musical thought and from his most intimate association with poetry. It has been said of Debussy, in broader terms and repeatedly, that it was poets and not musicians who influenced his art at every stage of his career.

The list of his published songs shows that he set texts from fifteen French poets; of these, twelve were nineteenth-century writers, ten of whom were his contemporaries. The fifty-nine songs presently published can be grouped as follows:

19 settings of Verlaine[10]
5 settings of Baudelaire
5 settings of Paul Bourget
5 settings of Debussy's own poems
4 settings of Théodore de Banville
4 settings of Mallarmé
3 settings of Pierre Louÿs
3 settings of Tristan L'Hermite[11]
3 settings of Villon
2 settings of Charles d'Orléans
1 setting of André Girod[12]
1 setting of Paul Gravollet
1 setting of Vincent Hyspa
1 setting of Leconte de Lisle

1 setting of Grégoire Le Roy
1 setting of Musset

Contemporaries of Debussy were Banville, Bourget, Girod, Gravollet, Hyspa, Leconte de Lisle, Le Roy, Louÿs, Mallarmé, and Verlaine. Baudelaire had died shortly after Debussy's birth. Musset was a Romantic; Charles d'Orléans and Villon were fifteenth-century poets, and Tristan L'Hermite was an early seventeenth-century poet. Some have been considered major poets: Villon, Charles d'Orléans, Musset, Leconte de Lisle, Baudelaire, Verlaine, and Mallarmé; some minor: Tristan L'Hermite, Banville, Bourget, Louÿs, Le Roy; others are virtually unknown. The chronology of the songs shows that two of these poets inspired Debussy at various times of his life: Mallarmé and Verlaine.

Although it is somewhat unsatisfactory to categorize an artist's life and works into periods—overlapping often takes place—successive stages can be observed in Debussy's output of songs in relation to his affinities and the times. Three main divisions broadly reveal an early period mainly influenced by the Parnassian poetic movement, then a period of development under the banner of Symbolism, and finally a period of maturity when Debussy achieved the restrained refinement of a more classic style.

## I. Early songs (1880–1887)

Debussy began to compose songs when he was at the *Conservatoire*; he was wavering between the lyrical style of Massenet, then in vogue, and his own poetic instinct and aspirations. Soon the wish to please the beautiful amateur singer Madame Blanche Vasnier was instrumental in increasing his production of songs. Indeed, of the forty songs (published and unpublished) written between 1880 and January 1885 when he left for the Villa Medici in Rome, twenty-five were dedicated to Madame Vasnier (nine published). Eleven were settings of Banville poems (four published), of which five were dedicated to Madame Vasnier. Seven were settings of Bourget poems (five published), of which six were also dedicated to Madame Vasnier.[13] Debussy seemingly found in the lyrical effusions of these poets a propitious ground for conveying his passionate feelings to Madame Vasnier. Yet, even so, it would be an oversimplification of Debussy's talent to see in these songs only poetic transparency and lovely Massenet-like harmonies.

## 1. *Alfred de Musset* (1810–1857)

Debussy's earliest songs were settings of Musset's poems, one of them the famous "Ballade à la lune," Musset's masterpiece of gracefulness and fantasy. Of the four settings he composed, only "Rondeau" was published at a later date (1932). The individuality of Musset as a Romantic poet[14] was to give emotion priority over feeling and sensibility over passion; at the time he wrote "Rondeau" (1842), Musset claimed that a poet should be able to feel for nature or a woman a sudden irrational wave of emotion, be it ecstasy or suffering, and express it in a sweeping, rhythmic form with simple and natural eloquence. Musset's poetry was meant to touch a vast audience and convey an all-powerful, direct emotion: Here intimations of Baudelaire can already be found. Unconventional and sincerely touching, his poetry kept some of its intensity within limits, coloring it with painful irony; this restrained expression of emotion could not but appeal to the passionately reserved lyricism of young Debussy.

## 2. *Théodore de Banville* (1823–1891)

Théodore de Banville, a Parnassian poet, was known for the virtuosity of his poetic technique. His early works, *Les Cariatides* (Caryatides, 1842) and *Les Stalactites* (Stalactites, 1846), were inspired by the beauty of Greek art and consisted of short and minutely chiseled pieces that owed more to formal brilliancy than to any original inspiration. Yet, if on the one hand Banville's search for perfection of form made him a Parnassian, on the other hand his charm, his subtle combination of irony and melancholy, and above all his call for music in poetry inspired the Symbolists. "Pierrot," "Zéphyr," and "La Dernière Pensée de Weber,"[15] set to music by Debussy, were early lyrical poems that contained no passionate torments or desperate invocations. Their poetic appeal remained impersonal yet showed concern for musical effect, owing to the inserted refrains and the use of uneven meters. The themes of death and the loss of love appeared, but that of remembrance prevailed. This was no great poetry, yet poetry harmonious and nostalgic enough to inspire young Debussy's developing poetic instinct. What was important for Debussy about this poetry was that it foreshadowed the Verlaine of *Fêtes galantes*, whose attraction for Debussy was all the more immediate and suggestive because it was prepared by Banville.

### 3. *Paul Bourget* (1852–1935)

Bourget was adulated by the bourgeoisie of his time for his prolific production of psychological novels. Poetry had been his earliest literary effort; at one point he had been considered a promising poet, although not outstanding. His third volume of verse, *Les Aveux* (Confessions), appeared in 1882 when Debussy, still at the *Conservatoire*, was working as an accompanist at the singing class of Madame Moreau-Sainti. Debussy must have met Bourget, already a well-known writer, at the *Chat Noir* cabaret. Although their friendship was of short duration, a good many letters were exchanged and Bourget probably introduced Debussy to the poetry of Jules Laforgue.[16] Bourget did not belong to any literary school. If any school influenced him, it was Naturalism;[17] the feverish avant-garde experiments in poetry never affected him. His poetry remains somewhat conventional, but clear and rational in the French tradition of classic simplicity. Strangely, Debussy's settings of Bourget's poems came after his first settings of Verlaine's *Fêtes galantes*, thereby suggesting that his choice of Bourget's poems had been prompted in part by the Vasniers, and most likely by Madame Vasnier's predilection for them. Bourget's lyricism was in perfect tune with the sentimental atmosphere popular in the early '80's; the *carpe diem* (seize the day) theme and mildly erotic undertones were more or less demanded of young poets of the time. His delicacy of feeling, however, and the musicality of his verse inspired Debussy with harmonious melodic lines and a charm that transcended the sentimentality of the poetry and revealed Debussy's genuine expression of love for Madame Vasnier.

### 4. *Charles Leconte de Lisle* (1818–1894)

Also a Parnassian poet, Leconte de Lisle inspired Debussy to three settings, of which only one, "Jane," was published, as recently as 1982. A commanding figure in the group, he dominated his disciples by his poetic achievements and his lofty nature. The Symbolists, who acknowledged Banville as one of their elders, did not feel so indulgent toward Leconte de Lisle's poetry, in which they saw only rigidity and monotony. Even today the true originality of Leconte de Lisle has been slighted, his sincerity of emotion hidden behind formal purity. "Jane" is the first Scottish song of the *Poèmes antiques* (Ancient Poems), dated 1850 and written in the style of Robert Burns. Although conventional in the feelings expressed and the surroundings described, it discloses behind the adventure of a love affair in an exotic country the poet's longing for his own enchanted land.

## II. The years of growth (1887–1904)

On his return from Rome, Debussy began exploring and absorbing what was said, thought, and created in Parisian artistic circles. He was now ready to experiment with new musical forms, and he drew inspiration from the most stimulating and innovative poems of his time. The first and most influential poet was Verlaine.

1. *Paul Verlaine* (1844–1896)

Debussy began setting Verlaine's poems as early as 1882, alternating with settings of Banville's poetry. Both poets shared a liking for a musical language and in some of their poems evoked the same eighteenth-century atmosphere. Banville indeed had encouraged Verlaine to pursue his musical experiments in poetry. Debussy, as a musician, was naturally attracted to poets who wrote in symbiosis with music. He had read Verlaine's *Fêtes galantes* in the Vasnier library: So began an association that would last more than twenty years. Strangely, no direct and close acquaintance was ever established between the poet and the composer, despite the fact that one of Debussy's first piano teachers, Madame Mauté, was Verlaine's mother-in-law. They might have seen each other at Madame Mauté's or, even later, in the cafés frequented by the literary Bohemia or at Mallarmé's Tuesday gatherings, but they never formed any long-lasting ties. Yet Verlaine stands out as one of the foremost and durable influences on Debussy's vocal works.

Verlaine at first followed the Parnassian poetic rules: Leconte de Lisle and Baudelaire were his masters. Then his friendship with the revolutionary poet Rimbaud encouraged him to break with Parnassian constraint and evolve his own style. His poetic production was at its peak between 1865 and 1875, then died away as the circumstances of his life became increasingly difficult. Of the seventeen poems of Verlaine set to music by Debussy, eight came from *Fêtes galantes*, five from *Romances sans paroles* (Romances without Words), and four from *Sagesse* (Wisdom).[18]

*Fêtes galantes*, Verlaine's second published volume of verse (1869), was written when the poet was twenty-five, before he met his wife, Mathilde Mauté; charming works of art, they sounded at first like some of Banville's *Cariatides*. A *fête galante* was an eighteenth-century version of a garden party like those that Boucher, Lancret, and Watteau had painted with such elegance. The world of Watteau, in particular, was revived in the Parisian exhibitions of the 1860's; Banville fell under its spell, and Théophile Gautier and the Goncourt brothers wrote about it. In this world were found no orgies or bacchanals, but an operatic Arcadia of velvet lawns, bluish trees, and fountains where strolled carefree groups of young people in a timeless festival. Yet a secret melancholy, some languor was hiding behind the brilliance of this evanescent world and the delicate refinement of its atmosphere. What Verlaine borrowed was its mood of elegant playfulness and the subdued sensuality of the Commedia dell'arte; what he added was his own sadness at the sophisticated libertinage of the elegant amusements and a sense of love's transient futility. Similarly the buffoonery of the Commedia dell'arte characters inspired Verlaine with an amused comment on the folly of man. The *Fêtes galantes* are masterpieces of concision, mockery, and melancholy, in which an ambiguous moon—absent from Watteau's paintings—casts an indirect reflection and dubious gleam on the world below.

Verlaine's next volume, *Romances sans paroles*[19] (1872–73), was dedicated to Rimbaud and contains some of Verlaine's most beautiful poems bearing no traces of particular influences. It is divided into four sections: *Ariettes oubliées* (Forgotten Airs), *Paysages belges* (Belgian Landscapes), *Birds in the night* (sic), and *Aquarelles* (Watercolors). The richest intimations permeate *Ariettes oubliées*: Verlaine was at this time torn by his ambivalent emotions, on the one hand his tumultuous passion for the young poetic genius Arthur Rimbaud, on the other by the remorse he felt toward his wife; a similar ambiguity appears in the tone of the poems, in which, beneath the seemingly exquisite surface, the voice remains restless and constrained. *Paysages belges* are recollections of his travels with Rimbaud: new and colorful sights and sounds, happy memories of vagabondage on Flemish roads and through Flemish cities. Then comes the autumnal season of the English *Aquarelles*, beautiful and serene in the disconcerting city of London, but so close to winter gloom. Circumstances were not too favorable; not only was young Rimbaud tracked by the police on his mother's orders, but Verlaine's adolescent wife was filing for separation. Threats became ominous, pleading was necessary, the lovers' intimacy precarious. The fragile landscapes of Verlaine's soul, dangling between dream and reality, happiness and despair, ecstasy and guilt, are recaptured in a virtuosity of meters, rhymes, resonances, and in a vertiginous ballet of poetic innovations, fluidity of rhythms—music again and always.

The turbulent adventures of the lovers ended dramatically. One hot day of July 1873, Rimbaud informed Verlaine of his wish to break off; Verlaine shot twice at Rimbaud and wounded him. He spent two years in prison, legally separated from his wife and converted to religious fervor. Then he went to teach French in an English boarding school in Lincolnshire (1875). His volume of verse *Sagesse* is for the most part of religious inspiration. Yet the three poems selected by Debussy recall some of the *Aquarelles* in that they are impressionistic renditions of the English landscape, with the difference that a sort of peaceful agreement can now be felt between Verlaine's soul and the countryside. The rhythmic arrangement and uneven meter of two of these poems and the suggestive quality of their word combinations were to be Verlaine's best attempts at musicality in his poetry.

Debussy indeed found in Verlaine a kindred spirit, an echo of his conception of poetry as music, the same distaste for eloquence, an equal preference for variations in shading and flexibility of rhythms. Both men were whimsical, sensitive, and attentive to the voices of their inner landscape. A turning point had been reached in Debussy's career, and he could now experiment freely without feeling bound by tradition and the prevailing styles of writing.

## 2.  *Charles Baudelaire* (1821–1867)

After winning the Prix de Rome, Debussy spent two years at the Villa Medici in Rome, from 1875 to 1877. It was then that he came under the spell of Baudelaire. Returning from Rome, he broke with the Vasniers, traveled twice to Bayreuth, and set five poems from *Les Fleurs du Mal* (The Flowers of Evil): This was another decisive stage in his aesthetic development. Baudelaire, translator of Edgar Allen Poe, herald of Richard Wagner in France, precursor of Verlaine, Mallarmé, and the Symbolists, was *the* poet in the pantheon of all French poets. An extremely conscious artist, he combined critical intelligence and poetic proficiency to perfection. His poetry contained neither narrative, nor philosophical message, nor political issues: It was all music and sensuousness contained within a controlled, structured form. For Baudelaire, words alone could convey the mystery of life and poetic truth was reached only in the spontaneous flow of poetic images. In an article on Wagner,[20] Baudelaire had stressed the power of music to suggest ideas, feelings, and images; the musicality of his poems did not come from the logical arrangement of the language, but from the recreated tone and atmosphere, in which scents, colors, and sounds answered one another, creating mysterious correspondences between the poet and nature. This secret alchemy of the senses demanded of the poetic soul a total renunciation of the reasoning self so that an intuitive apprehension of the Invisible could emerge from the Visible.[21] The ecstatic journey of the poet then led to a glimpse of the Beyond, thereby proclaiming the immortality of the soul.

Baudelaire's spiritual quest found an echo in Debussy's preference for a wide range of inner feelings over dramatic action in music. Both wanted flexible rhythms to better suit the movements of the dreaming soul; music, like poetry, should be human, true to life, so that it reaches a deeper expressive power; sensuousness is the gate to spiritual ecstasy; nature and its symbols are the only sources of learning about the Infinite. Music and poetry are therefore inseparable in the soul's communion with the Invisible. Debussy's five settings from *Les Fleurs du Mal* were composed in homage to Baudelaire and, initially, under Wagner's influence. Yet, as was pointed by Jarocinski, Debussy managed to separate himself from Wagner during the sixteen months that elapsed between the composition of the first and the last song. Debussy finally cast off all influences and, by giving "free rein to his real creative powers," put in place "his own musical idiom."[22]

### 3. *Vincent Hyspa* (1865–1938)

Two minor poets inspired Debussy's next songs, in 1890 and 1891. The first one, Hyspa, was best known as a chansonnier; Debussy must have met him at the *Chat Noir* with Erik Satie. Hyspa not only wrote humorous songs, but indulged in writing lyrical poetry.

### 4. *Grégoire Le Roy* (1862–1941)

Le Roy belonged to the Belgian Symbolist school; he was a friend of Maeterlinck's and must have met Debussy at the *Brasserie Pousset.* His poetry was for the most part lyrical and showed fine sensibility and a precise conception of the simplicity of life and daily realities. The actual circumstances behind Debussy's choice of these two poets have not been ascertained.

### 5. *Pierre Louÿs* (1870–1935)

It was shortly before the composition of *Proses Lyriques* that the poet Pierre Louÿs is said to have discovered Claude Debussy, possibly at the *Auberge du Clou* (the Nail Inn) or at the *Librairie de l'art indépendant* (Independent Art Bookstore) or at one of Mallarmé's gatherings. There has been disagreement on the part Louÿs played in Debussy's career, precisely on his influence on Debussy's aesthetic development. Certainly he provided Debussy with both moral and financial support, as their correspondence shows: Debussy was forever impecunious and Louÿs generous. Whatever the case, friendship struck with them and lasted a good many years.

Pierre Louÿs was above all an aesthete, a great admirer of Wagner and the Pre-Raphaelite movement. Intimately acquainted with Oscar Wilde and André Gide, he was also an assiduous caller at Mallarmé's and Hérédia's literary salons. He knew all the young avant-garde writers and artists of Paris and entertained them in his own drawing room; there, on several occasions, Debussy presented parts of *Pelléas et Mélisande*, which he was then composing. Louÿs' enthusiasm for Greek literature inspired his *Chansons de Bilitis* (Songs of Bilitis,

1894), a collection of translated poems by Bilitis, an imaginary hedonist in ancient Greece and a contemporary of Sappho. Although it was a hoax that took in many readers, the work was written in poetic prose of beautiful simplicity and great rhythmic musicality, for Louÿs regarded music as the perfect vehicle for artistic expression. It was with these songs of Louÿs that Debussy's power of poetic insight reached its zenith; the intimacy of the aesthetic communion between the two artists brought forth what was recognized by music critics as the most accomplished of Debussy's songs.

Afterwards, Debussy went through some intense experiences in both his private and public life; a great amount of his time, energy, and expectations was devoted to *Pelléas et Mélisande*, which was not formally accepted for production until May 1901. Debussy also composed piano arrangements, published orchestral and instrumental pieces, performed in public, and worked on artistic projects with friends. There were depressing moments such as the end of his relationship with Gabrielle Dupont or the rejection of *Pelléas*, and happier times with his marriage to Rosalie Texier in 1899. Symbolism had had its most ebullient spokesmen. Verlaine, the great fallen voice, was consecrated prince of the poets just before dying in utmost wretchedness. Mallarmé had retired to Fontainebleau, four years before his death in 1898. The nineteenth century was over.

## III. The years of maturity (1904–1918)

Six years elapsed before Debussy returned to song writing. His poetic inclination had not altogether abandoned him, and literature was at the source of more undertakings: Maeterlinck, for example, inspired *Pelléas et Mélisande*; Dante Gabriel Rossetti, *La Saulaie* (Willowwood Sonnets); Poe, *Le Diable dans le beffroi* (The Devil in the Belfry) and *La Chute de la maison Usher* (The Fall of the House of Usher); Shakespeare, *King Lear*; and d'Annunzio, *Le Martyre de Saint-Sébastien* (The Martyrdom of Saint Sebastian). His last period of song settings paid an ultimate and moving tribute to Verlaine but was dominated by older poets, Charles d'Orléans, Villon, and Tristan L'Hermite; it culminated with three settings of Mallarmé. What characterized this period of maturity was the classic perfection of the songs: The composer's voice turned increasingly inward, shunning high lyricism, achieving simpler harmonies. Chronologically included in this period are "Dans le Jardin" (In the Garden) after Paul Gravollet in 1903 and Debussy's own "Noël des enfants qui n'ont plus de maisons" (Christmas Carol of the Homeless Children) in 1915.

## 1. *Paul Gravollet* (1863–?)

Gravollet was the pseudonym of Jeulin,[23] who was known in the theatrical circles of the *Comédie Française* as a teacher of diction and declamation, author of a diction textbook, and co-author of a light opera and a comedy. He also contributed two volumes of verse: The first one, entitled *Les Frissons* (Shivers), contains twenty-two poems that were set to music by various composers of the time, among them Debussy, André Caplet, Vincent d'Indy, Ravel, Paul Vidal, and Widor.

## 2. *Charles d'Orléans* (1391–1465)

Nostalgia for earlier times had pervaded most of the nineteenth-century artistic and literary movements, with the exception perhaps of Naturalism. The Romantics and the Symbolists had revived the Middle Ages, the Parnassians, ancient Greece; the so-called *école romane* (Romanesque school) founded by the former Symbolist Jean Moréas in 1891 was inspired by the Pleiad poets of the sixteenth century and the seventeenth-century poets. Therefore it was not mere chance that Debussy drew inspiration from poets of the past.

Charles d'Orléans was a gallant man, nephew and cousin of kings, a lyrical poet who represented the epitome of chivalrous breeding and emotional restraint. A sincere poet but a lordly one, he wrote ballads and rondels with dignity verging on aloofness; his artistry was compared to a miniaturist's, but his tone was simple and true, his choice of words sound and natural. When he expressed disenchantment or despair, he did so in a measured language with ease and detachment.

## 3. *François Villon* (1431–1465?)

Of other vintage was Villon, younger contemporary of Charles d'Orléans. Charles d'Orléans has been known as a perfect artist, but Villon has been acclaimed as the first great

French poet. Charles d'Orléans was a miniaturist, Villon painted frescoes. He was a man from the masses, who spoke of himself, of others, of his time, and of love and death with a touching simplicity. Never did the eyes of a woman or the gracefulness of the first day of spring inspire him the way they inspired Charles d'Orléans; his poetry probed into the adventure of living and the lives of the departed. He never cried, moaned, or indulged in his own torments: Tears were choked back under sarcasm, emotion was suppressed, yet a charitable tone that was never moralistic or maudlin always prevailed. From the common people he borrowed a language ironical, passionate, and straightforward; the strong urgency of his voice in his *Grand Testament* has been and still is felt as the genuine expression of a people's brutal judgment on its time. Three of Villon's ballads undoubtedly inspired Debussy to his most convincing and directly expressive melodies.

### 4.   *Tristan L'Hermite* (1601–1655)

In 1904 Debussy combined two rondels of Charles d'Orléans and two stanzas from Tristan L'Hermite's *Le Promenoir des deux amants* (The Walk of the Two Lovers), which he entitled "La Grotte" (The Grotto), into his *Trois Chansons de France* (Three Songs of France). The title in itself is an indication of Debussy's growing involvement in the definition of French aesthetics; it must not be forgotten that his reputation was now reaching international dimensions and that with every performance of *Pelléas* the cult of Debussy was growing as opposed to the cult of Wagner. In any event, Debussy again took up "La Grotte" in 1910, added two more groups of stanzas, and published them under their original title.

Tristan L'Hermite was a courtier and the author of tragedies, novels, and poems, a minor poet but one of the most original of the Baroque period. Caught between Renaissance and Classical poetry, he never captivated the attention of his contemporaries, who saw in him an anachronistic remnant of dying-out lyricism; today he has been rehabilitated and is considered a precursor of Symbolism. The *Promenoir* is a long elegiac poem that seduces by its musicality, the touching quality of the poet's amorous complaints, and the suggestive correspondence between the lovely landscape and the dreaming soul. Quite characteristic of

Baroque aesthetics is the preciosity of the language of the seventeenth-century courtier poet; but the game that Tristan L'Hermite played was to be played in earnest: There was nothing that the poet was more aware of or disliked more intensely than the artificiality of court society.

This fulgent game of love had been Debussy's destiny when, in June 1904, breaking all conventions, he left his wife Lilly for Madame Sigismond Bardac. The *Trois Chansons de France* was dedicated to Madame Bardac, as was the second series of Verlaine's *Fêtes galantes*, composed in remembrance of the beautiful month of June and as a last and melancholy tribute to Debussy's favorite poet.

### 5. *Stéphane Mallarmé* (1842–1898)

During the 1910's Debussy was pursuing a feverish schedule of writing, publishing, performing, accompanying, and conducting, in the face of failing health. In the summer of 1913 he set three poems by Mallarmé, which were to be his last poetic songs.

Mallarmé was one of the most distinguished ornaments of the last decades of the nineteenth century. His distinction came from a deceptively simple life-style and personality and the exquisite refinement of his poetic mind. Hailed by Verlaine as a *poète maudit* (damned poet), elected Prince of the Poets after Hugo, Leconte de Lisle, and Verlaine, this humble English teacher became not only the leader of avant-garde poetry but the high priest of poetry, serving it with total devotion and disinterestedness. Obsessed all his life by an ideal of perfection, he saw in poetry the complete synthesis of image and sound. His originality consisted in making poetry with words and not ideas; a poem was neither a description nor a symbol, but a mood. His quiet innovations originated from his awareness that the language of contemporary western civilization was no longer a poetic language. His courtship of language overindulged in the sound of words and the sensuous importance of imagery: No nineteenth-century poet was closer to Baroque preciosity than Mallarmé when he unleashed the verbal ornateness of his imagination in a deluge of elaborate thoughts or feelings.

Respect and fervor were the keynote of Mallarmé's Tuesday gatherings: Lovers of literature assembled there to hear sentences disarticulated, words recreated and grouped according to musical affinities. It was poetry for the initiated few, inevitably hermetic; but no deliriums, no complacencies, no prophetic inspiration, no display were to be found in it. The man was honest, lucid, and hospitable, the artist conscientious and talented, the intellectual brilliant and whimsical. When he died he was genuinely regretted by his friends, among whom were Debussy and Pierre Louÿs. Fifteen years after his death, his memory was not forgotten: Debussy set three of Mallarmé's poems and dedicated them to the poet and to the poet's daughter. Almost thirty years earlier, he had set for Madame Vasnier one of Mallarmé's very early poems, "Apparition" (1884). Mallarmé's influence extended to one of Debussy's most innovative pieces, *Prélude à l'après-midi d'un faune* (Prelude to the Afternoon of a Faun), inspired by Mallarmé's eclogue. The poems that Debussy chose to set were none of the hermetic poems that shut Mallarmé off from many readers, as if Debussy had hesitated or been discouraged. The transparent suggestiveness of the early poems, their rich imagery and traditional form, and Mallarmé's art of illusion found a perfect transposition in the delicately shaded harmonies of Debussy, beautifully balanced between the real and the unreal.

A glance through a list of Debussy's compositions based on literary texts confirms his impregnation, so to speak, with literature of French and foreign origin. What sets Debussy's songs apart is that they are all settings of French poems; this fact alone emphasizes his unusual sensitivity to the word arrangement, the music, the rhythms and nuances of the French language. As the contemporary French composer Henri Sauguet pointed out: "With Debussy, music does not travel along its own path, alongside, below or even above the poem, it is entirely moved by the poem itself."[24]

# Chapter IV

## Songs

## "Nuit d'étoiles"
### (Starry Night)

**Date of composition:** *c. 1880.*[25]
**Date of publication:** *1882.*
**Publisher:** *Société artistique d'édition d'estampes et de musique, Paris.*
**Dedicated to Madame Moreau-Sainti.**
**Source:** *Théodore de Banville, "La Dernière Pensée de Weber." In* Les Stalactites, *1846.*

Banville's inspiration for the poem was a popular waltz purportedly composed by Carl Maria von Weber, in reality by Weber's friend, Reissiger. On a starry night, the poet is walking in a fragrant garden, lulled by a soft harmonious melody; he thinks of his bygone love and recalls, dreamily, images of his beloved. The mildly melancholy tone and the musicality of the poem are conveyed by the alternation of isometric stanzas and a heterometric refrain; within the refrain recur even and uneven short lines of three and four syllables and a repetition of words and sounds.

"Nuit d'étoiles," the earliest of Debussy's published works, was written when he was studying at the *Conservatoire.* It was dedicated to Madame Moreau-Sainti, who was holding classes for amateur singers from the bourgeoisie. Debussy became her accompanist in 1881 and met there Blanche Vasnier, one of the pupils. In his setting of the poem Debussy omitted the second quatrain and its accompanying refrain and changed the title to the first line of the poem.[25a] The quatrains stand out in a more animated rhythm, whereas the refrain repeats its melody, slowing down as the poet dreams of his bygone love. The melodic line is very much in the style of Massenet, but the first four chords of the accompaniment anticipate some of Debussy's later compositions.

# nųi de twa l
# **Nuit d'étoiles**
# Night of stars

nųi    de twa lə
**Nuit   d'étoiles**
Night of stars

su    tɛ    vwa lə
**Sous   tes   voiles**
Under   your   veils

su   ta   bri   ze   tɛ   pa rfœ̃
**Sous   ta   brise   et   tes   parfums,**
Under   your   breeze   and   your   perfumes,

tri stə   li rə
**Triste   lyre**
Sad    lyre

Ki    su pi rə
**Qui   soupire,**
That sighs,

ʒə rɛ    vo   za mu   rde fœ̃
**Je rêve   aux amours défunts.**
I   dream of   loves    defunct.

ʒə rɛ    vo   za mu   rde fœ̃
**Je rêve   aux amours défunts.**
I   dream of   loves    defunct.

la   sə rɛ nə   me lɑ̃ kɔ li ə
**La   sereine   mélancolie**
The serene    melancholy

Nuit d'étoiles
Sous tes voiles
Sous ta brise et tes parfums,
   Triste lyre
   Qui soupire,
Je rêve aux amours défunts.
Je rêve aux amours défunts.

La sereine mélancolie
Vient éclore au fond de mon coeur,
Et j'entends l'âme de ma mie
Tressaillir dans le bois rêveur.

Nuit d'étoiles,
   Sous tes voiles,
Sous ta brise et tes parfums,
   Triste lyre
   Qui soupire,
Je rêve aux amours défunts.
Je rêve aux amours défunts.

Je revois à notre fontaine
Tes regards bleus comme les cieux,
Cette rose, C'est ton haleine,
Et ces étoiles sont tes yeux.

Nuit d'étoiles
   Sous tes voiles,
Sous ta brise et tes parfums,
   Triste lyre
   Qui soupire,
Je rêve aux amours défunts.
Je rêve aux amours défunts.

vjɛ̃    te klɔ    ro    fɔ̃    də mɔ̃ kœ r
**Vient éclore    au    fond    de mon coeur,**
Comes to bloom in the depths of my    heart,

(*Forty-three Songs for Voice and Piano*. New York: International, pp. 1–4.)

e    ʒɑ̃ tɑ̃    lɑ mə    də ma mi ə
**Et    j'entends l'âme    de ma mie**
And I hear    the soul of my love

trɛ sa ji    rdɑ̃    lə    bwa²⁶ rɛ vœ r
**Tressaillir dans le    bois    rêveur.**
Quiver    in    the wood dreaming.

nɥi    de twa lə
**Nuit    d'étoiles,**
Night of stars,

su    tɛ    vwa lə
**Sous    tes    voiles,**
Under your veils,

su    ta    bri    ze    tɛ    pa rfœ̃
**Sous    ta    brise et    tes    parfums,**
Under your breeze and your perfumes,

tri stə    li rə
**Triste lyre**
Sad    lyre

ki    su pi rə
**Qui    soupire,**
That sighs,

ʒə rɛ    vo    za mu    rde fœ̃
**Je rêve    aux amours défunts,**
I    dream of    loves    defunct,

Starry night,
  Beneath your veils,
Beneath your breeze and your scents,
  Sad lyre
  That sighs,
I dream of bygone loves.
I dream of bygone loves.

Serene melancholy
Comes along to bloom in the depths of my heart,
And I hear the soul of my love
Quiver in the dreaming woods.

Starry night,
  Beneath your veils,
Beneath your breeze and your scents,
  Sad lyre
  That sighs,
I dream of bygone loves.
I dream of bygone loves.

I see again at our fountain
Your glances blue as the skies;
This rose is your breath,
And these stars are your eyes.

Starry night,
  Beneath your veils,
Beneath your breeze and your scents,
  Sad lyre
  That sighs,
I dream of bygone loves.
I dream of bygone loves.

ʒə rɛ      vo   za mu   rde fœ̃
**Je rêve   aux amours défunts.**
I  dream of   loves    defunct.


ʒə rə vwa   za nɔ trə fɔ̃ tɛ nə
**Je revois   à   notre fontaine**
I   see again at our    fountain


tɛ    rə ga   rblø  kɔ mə   le   sjø
**Tes   regards bleus comme les cieux,**
Your glances blue   as       the skies,


sɛ tə   ro zə  sɛ    tɔ̃    na lɛ nə
**Cette rose, C'est ton   haleine,**
This   rose,  it is   your breath,


e    sɛ    ze twa lə sɔ̃   tɛ    zjø
**Et   ces   étoiles  sont tes   yeux.**
And these stars       are   your eyes.


        nɥi     de twa lə
        **Nuit   d'étoiles**
        Night of stars


        su    tɛ    vwa lə
        **Sous   tes   voiles,**
        Under your veils,


su    ta    bri   ze tɛ    pa rfœ̃
**Sous ta    brise et tes   parfums,**
Under your breeze and your perfumes,


        tri stə   li rə
        **Triste lyre**
        Sad     lyre

ki    su pi rə
**Qui  soupire,**
That sighs,

ʒə  rɛ      vo    za mu    rde fœ̃
**Je  rêve    aux  amours  défunts.**
I    dream  of    loves    defunct.

ʒə  rɛ      vo    za mu    rde fœ̃
**Je  rêve    aux  amours  défunts.**
I    dream  of    loves    defunct.

# "Fleur des Blés"
## (Flower of Wheat)

**Date of composition:** *c. 1880.*
**Date of publication:** *1891.*
**Publisher:** *Vve E. Girod, Paris.*
**Dedicated to Madame E. Deguingand.**
**Source:** *André Girod.*

A favorite French poetic device consists in portraying a young
and beautiful woman as a flower. This convention appears, in
particular, in sentimental verse and cabaret songs. The flower in
Girod's poem is a pretty and innocent country lass.

A young lover tells his beloved how, as he was walking along
a wheatfield, he felt impelled to gather a bouquet for her. He
urges her to fasten his bouquet on her bodice, because the ears of
wheat remind him of her wavy golden hair, the poppies of her
red lips, and the cornflowers of the blue of her pure eyes.

Both a narrative and a pledge of love, the poem is evenly
divided into two sections. Its setting, similes, and tone are rather
conventional, yet express the straightforward fervor and youthfulness of an ingenuous loving soul.

Debussy dedicated his song to Mme. Emile Deguingand, the
young wife of a lawyer, who was also a pupil at Mme. Moreau-
Sainti's singing class. He was then studying at the *Conservatoire.* Like the poem, the song is built around two melodic
sections successively repeated. Its vocal part narrates the story
and details the beloved's beauty, while its alert rhythm expresses
the amorous happiness of the young man; the accompaniment
depicts the breeze ruffling the ocean of wheat. The pentatonic
scale conveys the rusticity of the scene and the simplicity of
feelings. Like the poem, the song ends quite abruptly—a simple
love needs no words.

# flœ rde ble
# **Fleur des blés**
## Flower of wheat

| lə | lɔ̃ | dɛ ble | | kə | la | bri zə |
|---|---|---|---|---|---|---|
| **Le** | **long des blés** | | | **que la** | | **brise** |
| Along | | the | wheatfield | that | the | breeze |

| fɛ | tɔ̃ dy le | pɥi | de fri zə |
|---|---|---|---|
| **Fait** | **onduler puis** | | **défrise** |
| Causes to wave | | then | uncurls |

| ã | nœ̃ | de zɔ rdrə | kɔ kɛ |
|---|---|---|---|
| **En un** | | **désordre** | **coquet,** |
| In a | | disarray | coquettish, |

| ʒe | tru ve | də bɔ nə | pri zə |
|---|---|---|---|
| **J'ai** | **trouvé de bonne** | | **prise** |
| I have | found | of fair | catch |

| də ti | | kœ ji | rœ̃ | bu kɛ |
|---|---|---|---|---|
| **De t'y** | | **cueillir un** | | **bouquet** |
| To you there | gather | a | | bouquet |

| mɛ | lə vi | ta tɔ̃ | kɔ rsa ʒ(ə) |
|---|---|---|---|
| **Mets-le vite** | | **à ton** | **corsage;** |
| Put it | quickly | on your | bodice; |

| i | lɛ | fɛ | a tɔ̃ | ni ma ʒə |
|---|---|---|---|---|
| **Il** | **est** | **fait** | **à ton** | **image** |
| It is | | made | in your | likeness |

| ã | mɛ mə tã | kə | pu | rtwa |
|---|---|---|---|---|
| **En** | **même temps** | **que** | **pour** | **toi. . .** |
| At the same | time | as | for | you. . . |

Le long des blés que la brise
Fait onduler puis défrise
En un désordre coquet,
J'ai trouvé de bonne prise
De t'y cueillir un bouquet.

Mets-le vite à ton corsage;
Il est fait à ton image
En même temps que pour toi. . .
Ton petit doigt, je le gage,
T'a déjà soufflé pourquoi:

Ces épis dorés, c'est l'onde
De ta chevelure blonde
Toute d'or et de soleil;
Ce coquelicot qui fronde
C'est ta bouche au sang vermeil.

Et ces bluets, beau mystère!
Points d'azur que rien n'altère,
Ces bluets ce sont tes yeux
Si bleus qu'on dirait, sur terre,
Deux éclats tombés des cieux.

(*Forty-three Songs for Voice and Piano.* New York: International, pp. 8–10.)

Along the wheatfield that the breeze
Waves and then uncurls
In stylish disarray,
I thought it right
To gather a bouquet for you.

tɔ̃   pə ti   dwa    ʒə lə   ga ʒə
**Ton petit doigt, je le gage,**
Your little finger, I it wager,

ta       de ʒa   su fle      pu rkwa
**T'a     déjà    soufflé    pourquoi:**
You has already whispered why:

sɛ    ze pi dɔ re    sɛ    lɔ̃ də
**Ces    épis dorés, c'est l'onde**
These ears golden, it is the wave

də ta     ʃə və ly rə    blɔ̃ d(ə)
**De ta     chevelure blonde**
Of your hair       blonde

tu tə    dɔ     re   də sɔ lɛ j
**Toute d'or    et   de soleil;**
All      of gold and of sunshine;

sə    kɔ kə li ko   ki     frɔ̃ də
**Ce   coquelicot qui    fronde**
This poppy      which scoffs

sɛ    ta    bu    ʃo     sɑ̃    vɛ rmɛ j
**C'est ta    bouche au     sang vermeil.**
It is your mouth with the blood ruby.

e    sɛ    bly ɛ       bo      mi stɛ r(ə)
**Et   ces   bluets,      beau    mystère!**
And these cornflowers, beautiful mystery!

pwɛ̃    da zy    rkə rjɛ̃     na ltɛ r(ə)
**Points d'azur   que rien    n'altère,**
Specks of azure that nothing changes,

Fasten it quickly to your bodice;
It was made up in your likeness
As it was made for you. . .
A little bird, I wager,
Has already whispered to you
why:

These golden ears are the waves
Of your blonde hair,
All gold and sunlit;
This rebellious poppy
Is your blood-red mouth.

And these cornflowers, lovely
mystery!
Azure specks that nothing can
change,
These cornflowers are your eyes,
So blue that they seem to be, on
earth,
Two fallen fragments from
heaven.

| sɛ | blyɛ | sə | sɔ̃ | tɛ | zjø |
|----|------|-----|-----|-----|-----|
| **Ces** | **bluets** | **ce** | **sont** | **tes** | **yeux** |
| These | cornflowers | they | are | your | eyes |

| si | blø | kɔ̃ | di rɛ | sy | rtɛ rə |
|----|-----|-----|-------|-----|--------|
| **Si** | **bleus** | **qu'on** | **dirait,** | **sur** | **terre,** |
| So | blue | that one | would say, | on | earth, |

| dø | ze kla | tɔ̃ be | dɛ | sjø |
|----|--------|--------|-----|-----|
| **Deux** | **éclats** | **tombés** | **des** | **cieux.** |
| Two | fragments | fallen | from the | heavens. |

# "Zéphyr"
## (Zephyr)

**Date of composition:** *November 1881.*
**Date of publication:** *1932.*
**Publisher:** *B. Schott's Söhne, Mainz.*
**Source:** *Théodore de Banville, "Triolet, à Philis." In* **Les Cariatides, Livre Troisième—En habit zinzolon—n° II, 1842.**

Banville wrote this anacreontic epigram between the ages of sixteen and eighteen. It is a fairly conventional piece, in the tradition of Renaissance gallant poetry: The poet fancies the intimacy he could enjoy, were he a winged breeze. The mood is wistfully erotic and the rhythm airy.

Debussy set this poem most likely during the course of one of his journeys with the von Mecks. The song was part of Alexander von Meck's collection, along with "Rondeau" and the *Danse bohémienne* (Bohemian Dance) for piano, and it follows closely the structure and the tone of the poem; the title of the poem, "Triolet, à Philis," was changed to "Zéphyr" by the publisher.

# ze fi r
# **Zéphyr**
# Zephyr

| si | ʒe tɛ | lə | ze fi | rɛ le |
|----|-------|-----|-------|-------|
| **Si** | **j'étais** | **le** | **Zéphyr** | **ailé,** |
| If | I were | the | Zephyr | winged, |

| ʒi rɛ | mu ri | rsy | rvɔ trə bu ʃə |
|-------|-------|-----|----------------|
| **J'irais** | **mourir sur** | **votre** | **bouche.** |
| I would go | to die | on your | mouth. |

| sɛ | vwa lə | ʒã | nɔ rɛ | la | kle |
|----|--------|-----|-------|-----|-----|
| **Ces** | **voiles,** | **j'en** | **aurais** | **la** | **clé,** |
| These | veils, | I of them | would have | the | key, |

| si | ʒe tɛ | lə | ze fi | rɛ le |
|----|-------|-----|-------|-------|
| **Si** | **j'étais** | **le** | **Zéphyr** | **ailé.** |
| If | I were | the | Zephyr | winged. |

| prɛ | de | sɛ̃ | pu | rki | ʒə bry lɛ |
|-----|-----|-----|-----|-----|------------|
| **Près** | **des** | **seins,** | **pour** | **qui** | **je brûlais,** |
| Next to | the | breasts, | for | which I | yearned, |

| ʒə mə | gli sə rɛ | dã | la | ku ʃə |
|-------|-----------|-----|-----|-------|
| **Je** | **me** | **glisserais** | **dans la** | **couche.** |
| I | myself | would creep | into the | bed. |

| si | ʒe tɛ | lə | ze fi | rɛ le |
|----|-------|-----|-------|-------|
| **Si** | **j'étais** | **le** | **Zéphyr** | **ailé,** |
| If | I were | the | Zephyr | winged, |

| ʒi rɛ | mu ri | rsy | rvɔ trə bu ʃə |
|-------|-------|-----|----------------|
| **J'irais** | **mourir sur** | **votre** | **bouche.** |
| I would go | to die | on your | mouth. |

Si j'étais le Zéphyr ailé,
J'irais mourir sur votre bouche.
Ces voiles, j'en aurais la clé,
Si j'étais le Zéphyr ailé.
Près des seins, pour qui je brûlais,
Je me glisserais dans la couche.
Si j'étais le Zéphyr ailé,
J'irais mourir sur votre bouche.

(Mainz: Schott & Eschig, 1932)

———————————•———————————

Were I the winged Zephyr,
I would go to expire on your mouth.
I would own the key to these veils,
Were I the winged Zephyr.
Next to those breasts for which I yearned,
I would glide into bed.
If I were the winged Zephyr,
I would go to expire on your mouth.

# ————————"Pierrot"————————
## *(Pierrot)*

**Date of composition: *c. 1881.***
**Date of publication: *1 May 1926.***
**Publisher: La Revue musicale, *Paris.***
**Dedicated to Madame Vasnier.**
**Source: *Théodore de Banville, "Les Caprices, en dizains à la manière de Clément Marot", III, 6. In* Les Cariatides, *1848.***

Pierrot was a pantomime character, created and immortalized by the French mime Jean-Gaspard Debureau (1796–1848). The amusing story recounts how, after performing at Harlequin's wedding, Pierrot is strolling in deep thought along the boulevard. A pretty girl ogles him, but he walks by indifferently. High above, calm and mysterious, the horned white moon is watching and, suddenly amused, recognizes her friend Debureau.

The title page of Debussy's setting bears the first four bars of a popular eighteenth-century tune: "Au clair de la lune" (In the Moonlight), which theme recurs throughout the accompaniment of the song and provides a basis for subtle humor. Debussy cleverly harmonizes and transforms the tune with parallel sevenths; he thus creates a piquant version of the popular tune that enlivens this charming anecdote. The song ends in a melisma[26a] characteristic of Debussy's vocal works written for the high tessitura of Madame Vasnier's soprano voice.

# pjɛ ro
# **Pierrot**
## Pierrot

| lə | bɔ̃ | pjɛ ro | kə | la | fu lə | kɔ̃ tɑ̃ plə |
|---|---|---|---|---|---|---|
| **Le** | **bon** | **pierrot** | **que** | **la** | **foule** | **contemple** |
| The | good | Pierrot | whom | the | crowd | gazes at |

| ɛ jɑ̃ | fi ni | lɛ | nɔ sə | da rlə kɛ̃ |
|---|---|---|---|---|
| **Ayant** | **fini** | **les** | **noces** | **d'Arlequin** |
| Having | finished | the | wedding | of Harlequin |

| sɥi | tɑ̃ | sɔ̃ ʒɑ̃ | lə | bu lə va | rdy |
|---|---|---|---|---|---|
| **Suit** | **en** | **songeant** | **le** | **boulevard** | **du** |
| Follows | while | dreaming | the | boulevard | of the |

| tɑ̃ plə |
|---|
| **temple.** |
| temple. |

| y nə | fi jɛ | to | su plə | ka za kɛ̃ |
|---|---|---|---|---|
| **Une** | **fillette** | **au** | **souple** | **casaquin.** |
| A | girl | with a | soft | blouse. |

| ɑ̃ | vɛ̃ | la ga sə | də | sɔ̃ | nœ | jkɔ kɛ̃ |
|---|---|---|---|---|---|---|
| **En** | **vain** | **l'agace** | **de** | **son** | **oeil** | **coquin** |
| In | vain | him provokes | with | her | eye | roguish |

| e | sə pɑ̃ dɑ̃ | mi ste ri jø | ze | li sə |
|---|---|---|---|---|
| **Et** | **cependant** | **mystérieuse** | **et** | **lisse** |
| And | meanwhile | mysterious | and | calm |

| fə zɑ̃ | də lɥi | sa | ply | ʃɛ rə | de li sə |
|---|---|---|---|---|---|
| **Faisant** | **de lui** | **sa** | **plus** | **chère** | **délice** |
| Making | of him | her | most | dear | delight |

Le bon pierrot que la foule contemple
Ayant fini les noces d'Arlequin
Suit en songeant le boulevard du temple.
Une fillette au souple casaquin
En vain l'agace de son oeil coquin
Et cependant mystérieuse et lisse
Faisant de lui sa plus chère délice
La blanche lune aux cornes de taureau
Jette un regard de son oeil en coulisse
A son ami Jean Gaspard Debureau.
Ah. Ah.

(*Quatre chansons de jeunesse.*
Paris: Jobert, 1969)

| la | blɑ̃ ʃə | ly | no | kɔ rnə | də | tɔ ro |
|----|---------|-----|-----|--------|-----|-------|
| **La** | **blanche** | **lune** | **aux** | **cornes** | **de** | **taureau** |
| The | white | moon | with | horns | of | bull |

Good Pierrot, gazed at by the crowd,

Being done with Harlequin's wedding,

Walks dreamily along the Boulevard du Temple.

| ʒɛ | tœ̃ | rə ga | rdə | sɔ̃ | nœ | jɑ̃ | ku li sə |
|----|-----|-------|-----|-----|-----|-----|----------|
| **Jette** | **un** | **regard** | **de** | **son** | **oeil** | **en** | **coulisse** |
| Casts | a | glance | with | her | eye | | sidelong |

A young girl in a soft blouse

Vainly teases him with her roguish eye;

And meanwhile, mysterious and calm,

| a | sɔ̃ | na mi | ʒɑ̃ | ga spa | rdə by ro |
|----|-----|-------|-----|--------|-----------|
| **A** | **son** | **ami** | **Jean** | **Gaspard** | **Debureau.** |
| To | her | friend | Jean | Gaspard | Debureau. |

Taking in him greatest delight,

The white moon with horns like a bull

| ɑ | ɑ |
|----|----|
| **Ah.** | **Ah.** |
| Ah. | Ah. |

Cast a sidelong glance

At her friend Jean Gaspard Debureau.

Ah. Ah.

# _ "**Aimons-nous et dormons**" _
## *(Let us love and sleep)*

**Date of composition:** *c. 1881.*
**Date of publication:** *1933.*
**Publisher:** *Theodore Presser, Bryn Mawr, Pennsylvania.*
**Dedicated to Paul Vidal.**
**Source:** *Théodore de Banville,* Les Exilés, Odelettes, Améthystes, Rimes dorées, Rondels, Les Princesses, 36 ballades joyeuses, *1862.*

In this lyrical piece the poet beckons his beloved to love and sleep, enjoining her to disregard the adverse elements of nature. Love prevails over nature, death, and God. The even rhythms of the three stanzas convey a mood of calm confidence in the power of love.

Debussy dedicated this setting to Paul Vidal, his fellow student and friend at the *Conservatoire.* The melody flows harmoniously and repeats itself with variants throughout the piece, providing some pleasant sound effects.[26b]

ɛ mɔ̃ nu e dɔ rmɔ̃
# Aimons-nous et dormons
## Let us love and sleep

ɛ mɔ̃     nu     e     dɔ rmɔ̃
**Aimons-nous et     dormons**
Let us     love     and sleep

sɑ̃     sɔ̃ ʒe     ro     rɛ stə dy
**Sans     songer     au     reste     du**
Without thinking of the rest     of the
mɔ̃ də
**monde;**
world;

ni     lə     flo     də la     mɛ r     ni
**Ni     le     flot     de la     mer, ni**
Neither the waves of the sea,     nor
lu ra gɑ̃     dɛ     mɔ̃
**l'ouragan des     monts,**
the storm     of the mountains,

tɑ̃     kə     nu     nu
**Tant     que nous nous**
As long as     we     each other
zɛ mɔ̃
**aimons.**
love.

ne flœ rə ra     ta     tɛ tə     blɔ̃ də
**N'effleurera ta     tête     blonde,**
Shall touch     your head blonde,

ka     rla mu     rɛ     ply     fɔ r
**Car l'amour est     plus fort**
For     love     is     more strong

Aimons-nous et dormons
Sans songer au reste du monde;
Ni le flot de la mer, ni l'ouragan
des monts,
Tant que nous nous aimons.
N'effleurera ta tête blonde,
Car l'amour est plus fort
Que les Dieux et la mort.

Le soleil s'éteindrait
Pour laisser ta blancheur plus
pure;
Le vent qui jusqu'à terre incline la
forêt,
En passant n'oserait
Jouer avec ta chevelure,
Tant que tu cacheras
Ta tête entre mes bras.

Et lorsque nos coeurs
S'en iront aux sphères
heureuses
Où les célestes lys écloront sous
nos pleurs,
Alors, comme deux fleurs,
Joignons nos lèvres
amoureuses,
Et tâchons d'épuiser
La mort dans un baiser!

(Bryn Mawr: Presser, 1933)

kə  lɛ  djø  e  la  mɔ r
**Que  les  Dieux  et  la  mort.**
Than  the  Gods  and the  death.

lə  sɔ lɛ  jse tɛ̃ drɛ
**Le  soleil  s'éteindrait**
The  sun  would fade

pu  rle se  ta  blɑ̃ ʃœ  rply
**Pour  laisser  ta  blancheur plus**
To  let  your pallor  more
py rə
**pure;**
pure;

lə  vɑ̃  ki  ʒy ska  tɛ  rɛ̃ kli nə la
**Le  vent, qui  jusqu'à  terre  incline  la**
The  wind, which to the  ground bends  the
fɔ rɛ
**forêt**
forest,

ɑ̃  pɑ sɑ̃  no zə rɛ
**En  passant  n'oserait**
In  passing  would not  dare

ʒu e  ra vɛ  kta  ʃə və ly rə
**Jouer  avec  ta  chevelure,**
Play  with  your  hair,

tɑ̃  kə  ty  ka ʃə ra
**Tant  que tu  cacheras**
As long  as  you will hide

Let us love and sleep
Without thinking about the
rest of the world;
Neither the waves of the sea nor
the storms in the mountains,
As long as we love each
other,
Shall touch your blonde head,
For love is stronger
Than the Gods and death!

The sun rays would fade
To let your pallor be more
pure.
The wind, which bends the forest
to the ground,
Would not dare, as it passes
by,
To play with your hair,
As long as you hide
Your head between my
arms!

And when both our hearts
Depart for the joyful spheres
Where the celestial lilies will
bloom with our tears,
Then, like two flowers,
Let us join our loving lips,
And let us attempt to wear
Death out with a kiss!

ta      tɛ      tɑ̃ trə    mɛ    bra
**Ta      tête    entre    mes bras.**
Your    head    between    my    arms.


e       lɔ rskə    no    dø    kœ r
**Et      lorsque   nos   deux  coeurs**
And     when      our    two    hearts


sɑ̃     ni rɔ̃    to     sfɛ rə     zœ rø zə
**S'en   iront    aux    sphères   heureuses**
Shall   leave    for the  spheres   happy


u       lɛ  se lɛ stə li    se klɔ rɔ̃    su     no
**Où     les  célestes lys   écloront    sous   nos**
Where   the  celestial lilies  will bloom  under  our
plœ r
**pleurs,**
tears,


a lɔ     rkɔ mə    dø    flœ r
**Alors,   comme    deux  fleurs,**
Then,    like      two    flowers,


ʒwa ɲɔ̃    no    lɛ vrə    za mu rø zə
**Joignons  nos   lèvres   amoureuses,**
Let us join our   lips     loving,


e       ta ʃɔ̃     de pɥi ze
**et      tâchons   d'épuiser**
And     let us try  to wear out


la      mɔ     rdɑ̃    zœ̃ be ze
**La     mort    dans   un baiser!**
The     death   in      a kiss!

# "Jane"
## (Jane)

**Date of composition:** *c. 1881.*
**Date of publication:** *1982.*
**Publisher:** *Theodore Presser, Bryn Mawr, Pennsylvania.*
**Dedicated to Madame Vasnier.**
**Source:** *Leconte de Lisle, "Chansons écossaises" n° 1. In* **Poèmes antiques,** *1852.*

Three octosyllabic stanzas, each followed by the same refrain, make up this short lyrical piece written in the style of Robert Burns. Leconte de Lisle intended it to be natural and simple. Indeed the freshness of its theme brings to mind the shepherds' amorous complaints of the seventeenth- and eighteenth-century *pastourelles* (pastorals): A broken-hearted young man yearns for the blue eyes of a pretty maiden; should she spurn his love, he would die, for her eyes have captured his heart forever.

The conventional language of the poem does not alter its charm. On the contrary, one feels almost reassured in knowing that the pains of love can be the same for all; as such they lose some of their poignancy.

Debussy wrote a delightful setting on a sweet melody that lingers on "J'irai puiser ma mort prochaine" with striking simplicity and sincerity of feeling.[26c]

# ʒa n
# **Jane**
Jane

ʒə pɑ li    e    tɔ̃    bɑ̃    lɑ̃ gœ r
**Je  pâlis  et  tombe  en  langueur:**
I   pale  and  fall  into  languor:

də    bo    zjø    mɔ̃    ble se    lə
**Deux  beaux  yeux  m'ont  blessé  le**
Two   lovely  eyes   me have  wounded  the

kœ r
**coeur.**
heart.

ro zə    pu rpre    e    tu    ty mi də
**Rose  pourprée  et  tout  humide,**
Rose  crimson  and  all  watery,

sə  ne tɛ    pɑ  sa    lɛ    vrɑ̃  fø
**Ce  n'était  pas  sa  lèvre  en  feu;**
It   was   not  her  lip   in  fire;

se tɛ    sɛ  zjø    dœ̃  si    bo    blø
**C'étaient  ses  yeux  d'un  si  beau  bleu**
It was   her  eyes  of a  such  fine  blue

su    lɔ    rdə  sa    trɛ sə    fly i də
**Sous  l'or  de  sa  tresse  fluide.**
Below  the gold  of  her  braid  flowing.

ʒə pɑ li    e    tɔ̃    bɑ̃    lɑ̃ gœr
**Je  pâlis  et  tombe  en  langueur:**
I   pale  and  fall  into  languor:

Je pâlis et tombe en langueur:
Deux beaux yeux m'ont blessé le
coeur.

Rose pourprée et tout humide
Ce n'était pas sa lèvre en feu;
C'étaient ses yeux d'un si beau
bleu
Sous l'or de sa tresse fluide.

Je pâlis et tombe en langueur:
Deux beaux yeux m'ont brisé le
coeur.

Toute mon âme fut ravie,
Doux étaient son rire et sa voix;
Mais ses deux yeux bleus, je le
vois
Ont pris mes forces et ma vie.

Je pâlis et tombe en langueur:
Deux beaux yeux m'ont brisé le
coeur.

Hélas, la chose est bien certaine:
Si Jane repousse mon voeu,
Dans ses deux yeux d'un si beau
bleu
J'irai puiser ma mort prochaine.

Je pâlis et tombe en langueur:
Deux beaux yeux m'ont brisé le
coeur.

(Bryn Mawr: Presser, 1982)

dø    bo    zjø   mɔ̃    bri ze  lə   kœ r
**Deux beaux yeux m'ont brisé le coeur.**
Two   lovely eyes  me have broken the heart.

tu tə   mɔ̃   nɑ mə fy    ra vi ə
**Toute mon âme  fut   ravie,**
All     my    soul  was   enraptured,

du    ze tɛ    sɔ̃   ri    re   sa   vwa
**Doux étaient son rire  et   sa   voix;**
Sweet were     her  laugh and  her  voice;

mɛ    sɛ    dø    zjø   blø    ʒə  lə   vwa
**Mais ses   deux yeux bleus,  je  le   vois**
But   her   two   eyes  blue,  I   it   see

ɔ̃    pri   mɛ    fɔ rsə   ze    ma   vi ə
**Ont  pris  mes  forces  et    ma   vie.**
Have taken my   strength and   my   life.

ʒə pɑ li   e    tɔ̃    bɑ̃   lɑ̃ gœ r
**Je pâlis et   tombe en   langueur:**
I   pale  and  fall   into languor:

dø    bo    zjø   mɔ̃    bri ze  lə   kœ r
**Deux beaux yeux m'ont brisé le coeur.**
Two   lovely eyes  me have broken the heart.

e lɑ s   la   ʃo    zɛ   bjɛ̃   sɛ rte nə
**Hélas,  la   chose est  bien  certaine:**
Alas,   the  thing is   most  certain:

I grow pale and languid:
Two lovely eyes have wounded my heart.

This watery crimson rose,
It was not her fiery lip;
It was her eyes of such fine blue
Below her golden flowing braid.

I grow pale and languid:
Two lovely eyes have broken my heart.

My entire soul was enraptured,
So sweet were her laugh and her voice;
But her two blue eyes, I see,
Have taken my strength and my life.

I grow pale and languid:
Two lovely eyes have broken my heart.

Alas, it is most certain:
If Jane rejects my suit,
In her two eyes of such fine blue,
I will soon meet my death.

I grow pale and languid:
Two lovely eyes have broken my heart.

si  ʒanə  rəpusə  mɔ̃  vø
**Si Jane  repousse mon voeu,**
If  Jane  rejects  my  suit,

dɑ̃  sɛ  dø  zjø  dœ̃  si  bo  blø
**Dans ses deux yeux d'un si  beau bleu**
In  her two  eyes  of a  such fine  blue

ʒire  pɥize  ma  mɔ  rprɔʃɛnə
**J'irai  puiser  ma  mort  prochaine.**
I will go  to find  my  death  immediate.

ʒə  pɑli  e  tɔ̃  bɑ̃  lɑ̃gœr
**Je  pâlis  et  tombe en  langueur:**
I  pale  and fall  into  languor:

dø  bo  zjø  mɔ̃  brize  lə  kœr
**Deux beaux yeux m'ont  brisé  le  coeur.**
Two  lovely  eyes  me have  broken  the  heart.

# ——"En sourdine" (Muted)—— first version
## *"Calmes dans le demi-jour"*
## *(Calm in the half-light)*

**Date and place of composition:** *16 September 1882, Vienna.*
**Date of publication:** *1944.*
**Publisher:** *Elkan-Vogel, Philadelphia.*
**Dedicated to Madame Vasnier.**
**Source:** *Paul Verlaine, Fêtes galantes, 1869.*

"Calmes dans le demi-jour" is Debussy's first version of Verlaine's poem "En sourdine"; this is the only poem of *Fêtes galantes* that is not inspired by the eighteenth century.

In the silence of a late summer's day, two lovers lie under the shade of some branches after the ecstasy of love. One implores the other to let no thoughts, memories, or schemes break the suspended moment of bliss. Dusk is falling, though; autumn is close, and soon the nightingale will sing its desperate song. In this muted dreamlike atmosphere where reality is transposed into suggestion, the poet's soul dangles precariously between happiness and premonitions. Nature may respond and surrender to the languor of the soul, yet it may also forebode anguish.

"En sourdine" was the first Verlainian poem to inspire Debussy.[26d] He set it to music during his second journey with the von Mecks, for Madame Vasnier's high voice range. (See second version in *Fêtes galantes*, 1st series, p.177).

ka lmə dã lə də mi ʒu r
# Calmes dans le demi-jour
## Calm in the half-light

| ka lmə | dã | lə | də mi ʒu r |
|--------|-----|------|------------|
| **Calmes** | **dans** | **le** | **demi-jour** |
| Calm | in | the | half-light |

| kə | lɛ | brã ʃə | o tə | fõ |
|-----|-----|---------|-------|-----|
| **Que** | **les** | **branches** | **hautes** | **font,** |
| That | the | branches | high | make, |

| pe ne trõ | bjɛ̃ | nɔ | tra mur |
|-----------|------|-----|---------|
| **Pénétrons** | **bien** | **notre** | **amour** |
| Let us permeate | well | our | love |

| rdə | sə | si lã sə | prɔ fõ |
|------|-----|----------|---------|
| **De** | **ce** | **silence** | **profond.** |
| With | this | silence | deep. |

| fõ dõ | no | zɑ m(ə) | no | kœ |
|-------|-----|----------|-----|-----|
| **Fondons** | **nos** | **âmes,** | **nos** | **coeurs** |
| Let us join | our | souls, | our | hearts |

| rʒe | no | sã | sɛ kstɑ zje |
|------|-----|-----|-------------|
| **Et** | **nos** | **sens** | **extasiés,** |
| And | our | senses | raptured, |

| pa rmi | lɛ | va gə | lã gœ r |
|--------|-----|--------|----------|
| **Parmi** | **les** | **vagues** | **langueurs** |
| Amid | the | vague | languors |

| dɛ | pɛ̃ | (z)e | dɛ | zɑ rbu zje |
|-----|------|-------|-----|-------------|
| **Des** | **pins** | **et** | **des** | **arbousiers.** |
| Of the | pines | and | the | arbutus. |

Calmes dans le demi-jour
Que les branches hautes font,
Pénétrons bien notre amour
De ce silence profond.

Fondons nos âmes, nos coeurs
Et nos sens extasiés,
Parmi les vagues langueurs
Des pins et des arbousiers.

Ferme tes yeux à demi,
Croise tes bras sur ton sein,
Et de ton coeur endormi
Chasse à jamais tout dessein.

Laissons-nous persuader
Au souffle berceur et doux,
Qui vient à tes pieds rider
Les ondes de gazon roux.

Et quand, solennel, le soir
Des chênes tombera,
Voix de notre désespoir,
Le rossignol chantera.
Voix de notre désespoir,
Le rossignol chantera.

(From a dated manuscript at the
Bibliothèque Nationale, Paris.
Manuscript presented by
Gustave Samazevilh.)

———————•———————

Calm in the half-light
Made by the high branches,
Let us permeate our love
With this deep silence.

fɛrmə tɛ zjø (z)a də mi
**Ferme tes yeux à demi,**
Close your eyes halfway,

krwa zə tɛ bra sy rtɔ̃ sɛ̃
**Croise tes bras sur ton sein,**
Cross your arms on your breast,

e də tɔ̃ kœ rɑ̃ dɔ rmi
**Et de ton coeur endormi**
And from your heart sleeping

ʃa sa ʒa mɛ tu de sɛ̃
**Chasse à jamais tout dessein.**
Banish for ever all scheme.

lɛ sɔ̃ nu pɛ rsya de
**Laissons-nous persuader**
Let ourselves be persuaded

(r)o su flə bɛ rsœ re du
**Au souffle berceur et doux,**
By the wind lulling and soft,

ki vjɛ̃ (t)a tɛ pje ri de
**Qui vient à tes pieds rider**
Which comes at your feet to ripple

lɛ zɔ̃ də də gɑ zɔ̃ ru
**Les ondes de gazon roux.**
The waves of grass russet.

e kɑ̃ sɔ la nɛl lə swa
**Et quand, solennel, le soir**
And when, solemn, the evening

Let us join our souls, our hearts
And our raptured senses,
Amid the vague languors
Of the pines and arbutus.

Close your eyes half-way,
Cross your arms on your breast,
And from your drowsy heart,
Forever chase all scheme.

Let ourselves be persuaded
By the lulling soft wind
That comes, rippling at your feet
The waves of russet grass.

And when the evening solemnly
Falls from the oaks,
Like the voice of our despair,
The nightingale will sing.
Like the voice of our despair,
The nightingale will sing.

rdɛ     ʃɛ nə    tɔ̃ bə ra
**Des     chênes tombera,**
From the oaks    will fall,

vwa   də   nɔ trə   de zɛ spwar
**Voix de notre désespoir,**
Voice of our     despair,

lə    rɔ si ɲɔ     lʃɑ̃ tə ra
**Le rossignol chantera.**
The nightingale will sing.

vwa   də   nɔ trə   de zɛ spwa
**Voix de notre désespoir,**
Voice of our     despair,

rlə   rɔ si ɲɔ     lʃɑ̃ tə ra
**Le rossignol chantera.**
The nightingale will sing.

# "Mandoline"
## *(Mandolin)*

**Date and place of composition:** *25 November 1882, Vienna.*
**Date of publication:** *1 September 1890.*
**Publisher:** *Durand and Schoenewerk, Paris. In* La Revue illustrée, *with illustrations by Willette.*
**Dedicated to Madame Vasnier.**
**Source:** *Paul Verlaine,* Fêtes galantes, *1869.*

This graceful poem recalls a pastoral Watteau-like scene where, in an enchanting rural setting, elegant shepherds and characters from the Commedia dell'arte serenade lovely ladies. This joyful and refined universe is recreated with sensuous rapture and a secret nostalgia on the part of the poet: What a supreme ecstasy it would be to partake in the final frenzy! Yet, when seen and heard more closely, these revelers play a cruel and frivolous game, and their vertiginous dance fades away in a futile dream.

"Mandoline" is by far the most popular of Debussy's early songs and represents his first attempt at transposing irony. It was written when Debussy was staying in Vienna with the von Mecks: Elated memories of pleasant times can be traced in the happy mood of the setting. The lively rhythms capture the irony of the poem, whereas chords of open fifths echo the strumming of the mandolin. A long and joyous melisma ends the piece.[27]

# mã dɔ li n
# **Mandoline**
# Mandolin

lɛ    dɔ nœ    rdə se re na də
**Les  donneurs de  sérénades**
The  givers    of    serenades

e    lɛ  bɛ lə  ze ku tø zə
**Et   les  belles  écouteuses**
And  the  lovely  listeners

e ʃã ʒə    dɛ    prɔ po  fa də
**Echangent des    propos  fades**
Exchange   some remarks  dull

su    lɛ  ra my rə  ʃã tø zə
**Sous  les  ramures  chanteuses**
Under  the  branches  singing

sɛ    ti rsi  se  sɛ    ta mɛ̃ tə
**C'est   Tircis  et   c'est   Aminte**
There is Tircis  and there is Aminte

e   sɛ   le tɛ rnɛ  lkli tã drə
**Et   c'est   l'éternel  Clitandre,**
And  there is  the eternal  Clitandre,

e   sɛ   da mi  ski  pu  rmɛ̃ tə
**Et   c'est   Damis qui  pour mainte**
And  there is  Damis who for    many

kry ɛ lə  fɛ    mɛ̃    vɛ    rtã drə
**Cruelle fait    maint  vers  tendre.**
Cruel    makes many  verse  tender.

Les donneurs de sérénades
Et les belles écouteuses
Echangent des propos fades
Sous les ramures chanteuses

C'est Tircis et c'est Aminte
Et c'est l'éternel Clitandre,
Et c'est Damis qui pour mainte
Cruelle fait maint vers tendre.

Leurs courtes vestes de soie,
Leurs longues robes à queues,
Leur élégance, Leur joie
Et leurs molles ombres bleues,

Tourbillonnent dans l'extase
D'une lune rose et grise,
Et la mandoline jase
parmi les frissons de brise.
La, la, la,. . .

*(Claude Debussy Songs 1880–
1904.* New York: Dover, 1981)

The serenaders
And the lovely listeners
Exchange dull remarks
Under the singing branches.

There is Tircis and Aminte
And eternal Clitandre
And Damis[27a] who for many
A cruel one makes many tender
verses.

| lœ | rku rtə | vɛ stə | də | swa |
|---|---|---|---|---|
| **Leurs** | **courtes** | **vestes** | **de** | **soie,** |
| Their | short | jackets | of | silk, |

| lœ | rlɔ̃ gə | rɔ bə | za | kø |
|---|---|---|---|---|
| **Leurs** | **longues** | **robes** | **à** | **queues,** |
| Their | long | dresses | with | trains, |

| lœ | re le gɑ̃ sə | lœ | rʒ wa |
|---|---|---|---|
| **Leur** | **élégance,** | **Leur** | **joie** |
| Their | elegance, | their | joy |

| e | lœ | rmɔ lə | zɔ̃ brə | blø |
|---|---|---|---|---|
| **Et** | **leurs** | **molles** | **ombres** | **bleues,** |
| And | their | soft | shadows | blue, |

| tu rbi jɔ nə | dɑ̃ | lɛ kstɑ zə |
|---|---|---|
| **Tourbillonnent** | **dans** | **l'extase** |
| Whirl | in | the ecstasy |

| dy nə | ly nə | ro | ze | gri zə |
|---|---|---|---|---|
| **D'une** | **lune** | **rose** | **et** | **grise,** |
| Of a | moon | pink | and | gray, |

| e | la | mɑ̃ dɔ li nə | ʒɑ zə |
|---|---|---|---|
| **Et** | **la** | **mandoline** | **jase** |
| And | the | mandolin | chatters |

| pa rmi | lɛ | fri sɔ̃ | də | bri zə |
|---|---|---|---|---|
| **parmi** | **les** | **frissons** | **de** | **brise.** |
| Amid | the | shivers | of the | breeze. |

| la | la |
|---|---|
| **La,** | **la. . .** |
| La, | la. . . |

Their short silk jackets,
Their long dresses with trains,
Their elegance, their joy
And their soft blue shadows

Whirl in the ecstasy
Of a pink and gray moon,
And the mandolin chatters
Amid the trembling breezes.

La, la . . .

# "Rondeau"

## (Rondeau)

**Date of composition:** *1882.*
**Date of publication:** *1932.*
**Publisher:** *B. Schott's Söhne, Mainz.*
**Dedicated to Alexander von Meck.**
**Source:** *Alfred de Musset,* **Poésies nouvelles,** *1852.*

Musset's thoughts on love were firmly rooted in the belief not only that love is a central force in the world, but also that lovemaking without genuine feeling is blasphemy. For the poet, nothing was more true than the beautiful. Yes, women could be vain, deceptive, and ignorant, but they did have beauty. Beauty meant pleasure, and pleasure and beauty were sources of poetry.

"Rondeau" is a lyrical poem about love and beauty. The poet watches and lulls pretty Manon to sleep in his arms. He is tenderly moved by her unadorned beauty, and, as she dreams, he discovers with increased emotion the secret impulses of her heart: Never was there a sweeter task than to attend to the sleep of innocence and beauty.

Alas! morning is pitiless: The virgin dawn becomes crude daylight, the pretty girl hastily decks herself out for further conquests. The lover, disenchanted and wistful, comments on the transience of love.

A *rondeau* is a traditional poetic form of three stanzas and thirteen lines with only two rhymes throughout; the opening words are used two times for refrain. The anecdote in Musset's poem is told in two successive moments: The sweet scene of the night and the disappointment of the following morning. The middle stanza deals with the lover's poetic flight in which, with sincere lyricism, he exploits and transforms the conventional imagery of Renaissance poetry: Now the rose is a wild rose, more intimate and fragile. There is no bitterness, no resentment, no heartbreaking Romantic grief, no sarcasm at the end of the poem. The pain remains light, the feelings are restrained beneath a sad smile, and their expression is full of charm.

Debussy composed his setting of "Rondeau" during or after his second journey with the von Mecks. The young composer altered the lyrics in three areas;[27b] the change of *bouquet printanier* to *printemps virginal* unhappily breaks the vocalic harmony of the original rhymes. The piano prelude sets a swaying rhythm, whereas the fluid mobility of the melodic line conveys the lover's happiness. A dramatic mood interrupts the tender evocation in the last stanza, when the rhythm increases its speed and announces an unhappy ending. The song concludes sadly with the lover's disenchanted remarks on love.

rɔ̃ do
# Rondeau
Rondeau

| fy | ti | lʒa mɛ | du sœ | rdə kœ | rpa rɛ jə |
|---|---|---|---|---|---|
| **Fut-il** | | **jamais** | **douceur** | **de** | **coeur** **pareille** |
| Was there | ever | sweetness | of | heart | as such |

| a | vwa | rma nɔ̃ | dɑ̃ | mɛ | bra |
|---|---|---|---|---|---|
| **A** | **voir** | **Manon** | **dans** | **mes** | **bras,** |
| To | see | Manon | in | my | arms, |

sɔ me je
**sommeiller.**
slumber.

| sɔ̃ | frɔ̃ | kɔ kɛ | pa rfy mə | lɔ re je |
|---|---|---|---|---|
| **Son** | **front** | **coquet** | **parfume** | **l'oreiller,** |
| Her | brow | coquettish | perfumes | the pillow, |

| dɑ̃ | sɔ̃ | bo | sɛ̃ | ʒɑ̃ tɑ̃ | sɔ̃ | kœ |
|---|---|---|---|---|---|---|
| **Dans** | **son** | **beau** | **sein,** | **j'entends** | **son** | **coeur** |
| In | her | fair | bosom, I hear | | her | heart |

rki vɛ jə
**qui veille.**
which is awake.

Fut-il jamais douceur de coeur pareille
A voir Manon dans mes bras, sommeiller.
Son front coquet parfume l'oreiller,
Dans son beau sein, j'entends son coeur qui veille.
Un songe passe et s'en vient l'égayer.

Ainsi s'endort la fleur d'églantier
Dans son calice enfermant une abeille.
Moi, je la berce, un plus charmant métier,
    Fut-il jamais?

œ̃  sɔ̃ʒə  pɑsə  e  sɑ̃  vjɛ̃
**Un songe  passe  et  s'en  vient**
A  dream  goes by  and  comes
lе ɡe je
**l'égayer.**
her enliven.


ɛ̃ si  sɑ̃ dɔ  rla flœ  rde ɡlɑ̃ ti e
**Ainsi  s'endort  la fleur  d'églantier**
Thus  falls asleep  the blossom  of sweetbrier

dɑ̃  sɔ̃  ka li  sɑ̃ fɛ rmɑ̃  ty  na bɛ jə
**Dans  son  calice  enfermant  une  abeille.**
In  its  calyx  imprisoning  a  bee.


mwa  ʒə  la  bɛ rsə  œ̃  ply  ʃa rmɑ̃
**Moi,  je  la  berce, un  plus  charmant**
I,  I  her rock,  a  more pleasant
me tje
**métier,**
occupation,


fy  ti  lʒa mɛ
**Fut-il  jamais?**
Was there  ever?


mɛ  lə  ʒu  rvjɛ̃  e  lɔ rɔ rə
**Mais  le  jour  vient, et  l'aurore**
But  the  daylight  comes,  and  the dawn
vɛ rmɛ jə
**vermeille**
rosy

Mais le jour vient, et l'aurore
vermeille
Effeuille au vent son printemps
virginal,
Le peigne en main et la perle à
l'oreille
A son miroir, Manon va
m'oublier.
Hélas! l'amour sans lendemain ni
veille
  Fut-il jamais?

*(Debussy et ses mélodies.*
Oeuvres complètes I, Zen-on,
1982)

———————•———————

Was there ever such sweet sight
in one's heart
As the sight of Manon
slumbering in my arms.
Her coquettish brow perfumes
the pillow,
In her fair bosom, I hear her heart
awake.
A dream slips by and comes
along to brighten her face.

Thus does the sweetbrier
blossom fall asleep
Enclosing a bee in its calyx.
As for me, I lull her, a more
delightful occupation,
  Was there ever?

e fœ jo vɑ̃ sɔ̃ prɛ̃ tɑ̃ vi rʒi nal
**Effeuille au vent son printemps virginal,**
Sheds to the wind its springtime virginal,

lə pɛ ɲɑ̃ mɛ̃ e la pɛ rla
**Le peigne en main et la perle à**
The comb in hand and the pearl in

lɔ rɛ jə
**l'oreille**
the ear

a sɔ̃ mi rwa r ma nɔ̃ va mu bli je
**A son miroir, Manon va m'oublier.**
At her mirror, Manon will me forget.

e lɑ s la mu rsɑ̃ lɑ̃ də mɛ̃ ni
**Hélas! l'amour sans lendemain ni**
Alas! the love without morrow or

vɛ jə
**veille**
yesterday

fy ti lʒa mɛ
**Fut-il jamais?**
Was there ever?

But daylight comes and rosy dawn
Sheds to the wind its spring-like virginity.
Comb in hand and a pearl in her ear,
Manon will forget me at her mirror.
Alas! Love without morrow or yesterday,
    Was there ever?

# "Pantomime"
## *(Pantomime)*

**Date of composition:** *1882.*
**Date of publication:** *1 May 1926.*
**Publisher: La Revue musicale,** *Paris.*
**Dedicated to Madame Vasnier.**
**Source:** *Paul Verlaine,* **Fêtes galantes,** *1869.*

The characters of the French pantomime, the *pastorale*, and the Commedia dell'arte appear together in this second poem of Verlaine's *Fêtes galantes.* Four little tableaux show first Pierrot (previously encountered in Banville's "Pierrot"), then Clitandre the lover (as in "Mandoline"), Cassandre the old fool and Harlequin the incorrigible jester from Bergamo, and finally nimble young Columbine. The first stanza, in particular, recalls the scene from Deburau's *Histoire du théâtre à quatre sous* (History of the Halfpenny Theater) in which Pierrot, seated on the ground, holds a bottle in his hand and eats a pâté. The farcical universe of the comedy turns abruptly sour in the second stanza with the unnoticed tear of the old dupe and becomes dream in the last stanza: Columbine, the sharp-witted soubrette, discovers in her heart the sweet taste of love.

In these simply structured vignettes, the double world of onstage and offstage, fantasy and reality, is deceptively evoked. Its ambiguity lies in the uncertainty as to when the stock character stops and the human being begins. Truly Cassandre sheds a tear, Columbine dreams, and Pierrot eats unabashedly, but Harlequin pirouettes and does so four times!

Only one year separated the composition of "Pantomime" from "Pierrot." Debussy took liberties with the text as he did in some of his other early settings of Verlaine; here he repeated entire lines and added a long ornamented melisma favorably suited to Madame Vasnier's voice.[27c] The vivacious treatment of the first three stanzas allows no insight into the true emotions of the actors portraying the characters. They are treated by Debussy as puppets; therefore they lose Verlaine's depth of dimension and in some respects remain grotesque. Only Columbine escapes this lot: Then the tempo slows into flowing arpeggios. Yet the minor mode of the last vignette is not final, and the melody reverts to the brilliancy of its beginning, thus ignoring Verlaine's compassionate depiction of the pantomime world.

# pɑ̃ to mi m
# **Pantomime**
## Pantomime

| pjɛ ro | ki | na | rjɛ̃ | dœ̃ | kli tɑ̃ drə |
|---|---|---|---|---|---|
| **Pierrot** | **qui** | **n'a** | **rien** | **d'un** | **Clitandre** |
| Pierrot | who | has | nothing | of a | Clitandre |

| vi | dœ̃ | fla kɔ̃ | sɑ̃ | ply | za tɑ̃ drə |
|---|---|---|---|---|---|
| **Vide** | **un** | **flacon** | **sans** | **plus** | **attendre** |
| Empties | a | flask | without | more | waiting |

| e | pra ti | kɑ̃ ta | mœ̃ pɑ te |
|---|---|---|---|
| **Et,** | **pratique,** | **entame un** | **pâté** |
| And, | practical, | cuts into a | pâté |

| pjɛ ro | ki | na | rjɛ̃ | dœ̃ | kli tɑ̃ drə |
|---|---|---|---|---|---|
| **Pierrot** | **qui** | **n'a** | **rien** | **d'un** | **Clitandre** |
| Pierrot | who | has | nothing | of a | Clitandre |

| vi | dœ̃ | fla kɔ̃ | sɑ̃ | ply | za tɑ̃ drə |
|---|---|---|---|---|---|
| **Vide** | **un** | **flacon** | **sans** | **plus** | **attendre** |
| Empties | a | flask | without | more | waiting |

| ka sɑ̃ | dro | fɔ̃ | də | la və ny |
|---|---|---|---|---|
| **Cassandre,** | **au** | **fond** | **de** | **l'avenue,** |
| Cassandre, | at the | end | of | the avenue, |

| vɛ | rsy nə | la rmə | me kɔ ny |
|---|---|---|---|
| **Verse** | **une** | **larme** | **méconnue** |
| Sheds | a | tear | solitary |

| sy | rsɔ̃ | nə vø | de ze ri te |
|---|---|---|---|
| **Sur** | **son** | **neveu** | **déshérité** |
| For | his | nephew | disinherited |

Pierrot qui n'a rien d'un
Clitandre
Vide un flacon sans plus attendre
Et, pratique, entame un pâté
Pierrot qui n'a rien d'un
Clitandre
Vide un flacon sans plus attendre

Cassandre, au fond de l'avenue,
Verse une larme méconnue
Sur son neveu déshérité

Ce faquin d'Arlequin combine
L'enlèvement de Colombine
Et pirouette quatre fois
Et pirouette quatre fois

Colombine rêve, surprise
De sentir un coeur dans la brise
Et d'entendre en son coeur des
voix
Et d'entendre en son coeur des
voix
Ah—

(*Quatre Chansons de jeunesse.*
Paris: Jobert, 1969)

———————•———————

Pierrot who has nothing of
Clitandre about him
Empties a flask without delay,
And, practical, cuts into a pâté.
Pierrot who has nothing of
Clitandre about him
Empties a flask without delay.

sə      fa kɛ̃       da rlə kɛ̃      kɔ̃ bi nə          Cassandre, at the end of the
**Ce**     **faquin**    **d'Arlequin**    **combine**     avenue,
This    scoundrel   of Harlequin   plots            Sheds a solitary tear
                                                     For his disinherited nephew.

lɑ̃ lɛ və mɑ̃      də    kɔ lɔ̃ bi nə              Harlequin, that scoundrel, plots
**L'enlèvement**  **de**   **Colombine**           The abduction of Columbine
The abduction   of    Columbine               And pirouettes four times,
                                                     And pirouettes four times.

e      pi ru ɛ tə    ka trə    fwa           Columbine dreams, surprised
**Et**     **pirouette**   **quatre**   **fois**      To feel a heart in the breeze
And    pirouettes   four      times          And to hear voices in her heart,
                                                     And to hear voices in her heart.
                                                     Ah—
e      pi ru ɛ tə    ka trə    fwa
**Et**     **pirouette**   **quatre**   **fois**
And    pirouettes   four      times


kɔ lɔ̃ bi nə     rɛ və       sy rpri zə
**Colombine**   **rêve,**     **surprise**
Columbine    dreams,     surprised

də    sɑ̃ ti     rœ̃ kœ      rdɑ̃    la    bri zə
**De**   **sentir**  **un coeur dans**  **la**   **brise**
To    feel     a   heart  in     the  breeze

e      dɑ̃ tɑ̃      drɑ̃ sɔ̃    kœ      rdɛ    vwa
**Et**    **d'entendre**  **en**  **son**   **coeur**   **des**   **voix**
And    to hear      in    her    heart   some   voices

e      dɑ̃ tɑ̃      drɑ̃ sɔ̃    kœ      rdɛ    vwa
**Et**    **d'entendre**  **en**  **son**   **coeur**   **des**   **voix**
And    to hear      in    her    heart   some   voices

ɑ
**Ah—**
Ah—

# ———— "Clair de lune" ————
## *(first version) (Moonlight)*

**Date of composition:** *1882.*
**Date of publication:** *1 May 1926.*
**Publisher: La Revue musicale,** *Paris.*
**Dedicated to Madame Vasnier.**
**Source:** *Paul Verlaine,* **Fêtes galantes,** *1869.*

The atmosphere of this poem is inspired by the *fêtes galantes* of eighteenth-century paintings. A masked musical interlude takes place in the moonlight, in a rococo setting of trees, fountains, and marble statues. The scene seems a perfect occasion for merriment; but this is no ordinary *fête galante.* The first line of the poem tells us that this is Verlaine's selected vision of the gathering, which, in turns, reflects the poet's mood and outlook on life. For beneath the rich and happy game of masks and disguise there is sadness: The songs and lute ring false and melancholy, and the moonlight, birds, and fountains also suggest disquietude. Nothing is said explicitly; everything is ambiguously implied. A cleverly contrived crescendo leads to the unmistakable discord of the last stanza when sobs blend with ecstasy.

Debussy's first setting of "Clair de lune" was composed at about the same time as "Mandoline." In order to match the poem's classic restraint of composition, Debussy wrote an elegant and concise melody. This setting shows few of the melancholy undertones of the poem; its melodic line, supported by the predominantly major mode of the accompaniment, expresses the peaceful overtones of Verlaine's poem.[28]

# klɛ rdə ly n
# **Clair de lune**
## Light of moon

| vɔ | trɑ | mɛ | tœ̃ | pe i za ʒə | ʃwa zi |
|---|---|---|---|---|---|
| **Votre** | **âme** | **est** | **un** | **paysage** | **choisi** |
| Your | soul | is | a | landscape | chosen |

| kə | vɔ̃ | ʃa rmɑ̃ | ɪna skə | ze |
|---|---|---|---|---|
| **Que** | **vont** | **charmant** | **masques** | **et** |
| Which | go | charming | masquers | and |

| bɛ rga ma skə |
|---|
| **bergamasques** |
| bergamasquers |

| ʒu ɑ̃ | dy | ly | te | dɑ̃ sɑ̃ | e | ka zi |
|---|---|---|---|---|---|---|
| **Jouant** | **du** | **luth** | **et** | **dansant** | **et** | **quasi** |
| Playing | the | lute | and | dancing | and | almost |

| tri stə | su | lœ | rde gi zə mɑ̃ |
|---|---|---|---|
| **Tristes** | **sous** | **leurs** | **déguisements** |
| Sad | beneath | their | disguises |

| fɑ̃ ta skə |
|---|
| **fantasques** |
| fantastic |

| tu | tɑ̃ | ʃɑ̃ tɑ̃ | sy | rlə | mɔ də | mi nœ r |
|---|---|---|---|---|---|---|
| **Tout** | **en** | **chantant** | **sur** | **le** | **mode** | **mineur** |
| While | in | singing | in | the | mode | minor |

| la mu | rvɛ̃ kœ | re | la | vi | ɔ pɔ rty nə |
|---|---|---|---|---|---|
| **L'amour** | **vainqueur** | **et** | **la** | **vie** | **opportune,** |
| The love | victorious | and | the | life | opportune, |

Votre âme est un paysage choisi
Que vont charmant masques et
bergamasques
Jouant du luth et dansant et quasi
Tristes sous leurs déguisements
fantasques

Tout en chantant sur le mode
mineur
L'amour vainqueur et la vie
opportune
Ils n'ont pas l'air de croire à leur
bonheur
Et leur chanson se mêle au clair de
lune
Et leur chanson se mêle au clair de
lune

Au calme clair de lune triste et
beau
Qui fait rêver les oiseaux dans les
arbres
Et sangloter d'extase les jets d'eau
Les grands jets d'eau sveltes
parmi les marbres.
Les grands jets d'eau sveltes
parmi les marbres.
Ah—
Au calme clair de lune triste et
beau

(*Quatre Chansons de jeunesse.*
Paris: Jobert, 1969)

| i | lnɔ̃ | pɑ | lɛ | rdə | krwa | ra | lœ |
|---|---|---|---|---|---|---|---|
| **Ils** | **n'ont** | **pas** | **l'air** | **de** | **croire** | **à** | **leur** |
| They | do | not | seem | to | believe | in | their |

rbɔ nœ r
**bonheur**
happiness

| e | lœ | rʃɑ̃ sɔ̃ | sə mɛ | lo |
|---|---|---|---|---|
| **Et** | **leur** | **chanson** | **se mêle** | **au** |
| And | their | song | mingles | with the |

klɛ rdə ly nə
**clair de lune**
moonlight

| e | lœ | rʃɑ̃ sɔ̃ | sə mɛ | lo |
|---|---|---|---|---|
| **Et** | **leur** | **chanson** | **se mêle** | **au** |
| And | their | song | mingles | with the |

klɛ rdə ly nə
**clair de lune**
moonlight

| o | ka lmə klɛ | rdə ly nə tri |
|---|---|---|
| **Au** | **calme clair** | **de lune triste** |
| With the | calm moonlight | sad |

ste bo
**et beau**
and beautiful

| ki | fɛ | rɛ ve | lɛ | zwa zo | dɑ̃ | lɛ |
|---|---|---|---|---|---|---|
| **Qui** | **fait** | **rêver** | **les** | **oiseaux** | **dans** | **les** |
| That | makes | dream | the | birds | in | the |

za rbrə
**arbres**
trees

Your soul is a chosen landscape
Charmed by masquers and
bergamasquers,[28a]
Playing the lute and dancing and
half
Sad beneath their fantastic
disguises.

Even while they sing in the minor
mode
Of love triumphant and life
opportune,
They do not seem to believe in
their felicity
And their songs blend with the
moonlight,
And their songs blend with the
moonlight,

With the calm moonlight, sad
and beautiful,
That makes the birds dream in
the trees
And sob with ecstasy the
fountains,
The tall slender fountains among
the marbles,
The tall slender fountains among
the marbles,
Ah—
In the calm moonlight, sad and
beautiful.

e    sɑ̃ glɔ te   dɛ ksta zə   lɛ   ʒɛ   do
**Et    sangloter  d'extase    les  jets  d'eau**
And  sob         with ecstasy the jets of water

lɛ   grɑ̃   ʒɛ   do    svɛ ltə   pa rmi   lɛ
**Les  grands  jets  d'eau   sveltes   parmi   les**
The  tall       jets  of water slender  among  the
ma rbrə
**marbres.**
marbles.

lɛ   grɑ̃   ʒɛ   do    svɛ ltə   pa rmi   lɛ
**Les  grands  jets  d'eau   sveltes   parmi   les**
The  tall       jets  of water slender  among  the
ma rbrə
**marbres.**
marbles.

ɑ
**Ah**
Ah

o        ka lmə  klɛ     rdə ly nə  tri   ste
**Au       calme   clair   de  lune   triste et**
With the calm    moonlight        sad   and
bo
**beau.**
beautiful.

# ——————"Beau soir"——————
## *(Beautiful evening)*

**Date of composition:** *1883.*
**Date of publication:** *1891.*
**Publisher:** *Vve E. Girod, Paris.*
**Source:** *Paul Bourget, "En voyage" n° VII. In* Dilettantisme.
*In* Les Aveux II, *1882.*

It is the time of day when nature becomes utterly beautiful before sinking into the oblivion of darkness. Now the poet's soul is stirred by the existential questions of youth and age, life and death. The beauty of the landscape inspires the hedonist message to enjoy life as it lasts.

Bourget wrote this lyrical piece on the occasion of a trip to Ireland and Scotland in 1881. It is by no means original in content, for the Horatian "Seize the day" theme has been well exploited by the Renaissance and Romantic poets. The poem is given weight, on one hand, by the unpretentious treatment of the theme and, on the other, by the broad sweeping motion of the verse that captures the overwhelming immensity and beauty of the world.

Debussy's setting is among the most lyrical of his early songs. The broad phrasing of the melodic line renders the poet's sense of beauty and surge of happiness. The expressive slowing down at the end conveys the intimation of death, with enough restraint to avoid sentimental effusion.

# bo swa r
## Beau soir
## Beautiful evening

| lɔ rsko | sɔ lɛ | jku ʃɑ̃ | lɛ ri vjɛ rə |
|---------|-------|--------|--------------|
| **Lorsqu'au** | **soleil** | **couchant les** | **rivières** |
| When in the sun | setting | the rivers | |

| sɔ̃ | ro zə |
|-----|-------|
| **sont** | **roses,** |
| are | rose, |

| e | kœ̃ | tjɛ də | fri sɔ̃ | ku | rsy | rlɛ |
|---|-----|--------|---------|----|----|-----|
| **Et** | **qu'un** | **tiède** | **frisson** | **court** | **sur** | **les** |
| And | when a | mild | shiver | runs | over | the |

| ʃɑ̃ | də | ble |
|-----|----|----|
| **champs** | **de** | **blé,** |
| fields | of | wheat, |

| œ̃ | kɔ̃ sɛ | jdɛ | trœ rø | sɑ̃ blə | sɔ rti |
|----|--------|-----|--------|---------|--------|
| **Un** | **conseil** | **d'être** | **heureux** | **semble** | **sortir** |
| A | counsel | to be | happy | seems | to emanate |

| rdɛ | ʃo zə |
|-----|-------|
| **des** | **choses** |
| from | things |

| e | mɔ̃ te | vɛ | rlə | kœ | rtru ble |
|---|--------|----|-----|----|----------|
| **Et** | **monter** | **vers** | **le** | **coeur** | **troublé** |
| And | rise | to | the | heart | troubled |

| œ̃ | kɔ̃ sɛ | jdə | gu te | lə | ʃa rmə | dɛ |
|----|--------|-----|-------|----|--------|----|
| **Un** | **conseil** | **de** | **goûter** | **le** | **charme** | **d'être** |
| A | counsel | to | enjoy | the | charm | of being |

| tro | mɔ̃ də |
|-----|--------|
| **au** | **monde** |
| in the | world |

Lorsqu'au soleil couchant les rivières sont roses,
Et qu'un tiède frisson court sur les champs de blé,
Un conseil d'être heureux semble sortir des choses
    Et monter vers le coeur troublé;

Un conseil de goûter le charme d'être au monde
Cependant qu'on est jeune et que le soir est beau,
Car nous nous en allons, comme s'en va cette onde
    Elle à la mer, Nous au tombeau.

(*Claude Debussy Songs 1880–1904.*
New York: Dover, 1981)

———————•———————

When, in the setting sun, rivers are rose
And a mild tremor runs over the wheatfields,
Some advice to be happy seems to emanate from things
    And rise toward the troubled heart.

sə pɑ̃ dɑ̃    kɔ̃    nɛ   ʒœ   ne   kə    lə
**Cependant qu'on est jeune et que le**
While      one    is    young and while   the

swa     rɛ   bo
**soir      est beau,**
evening   is    beautiful,

| | | | | | | |
|---|---|---|---|---|---|---|
| Some advice to enjoy the delight in being alive, | | | | | | |

ka   rnu   nu   zɑ̃   na lɔ̃   kɔ mə   sɑ̃
**Car   nous   nous   en   allons,   comme   s'en**
For   we          go   away,    as       goes

va   sɛ   tɔ̃ də
**va   cette   onde**
away   this   water

ɛl   a   la   mɛr   nu   o
**Elle   à   la   mer,   nous   au**
It    to   the   sea,    we    to the

tɔ̃ bo
**tombeau.**
tomb.

Some advice to enjoy the delight in being alive,
While one is young and the evening beautiful,
For we go away as the water goes away:
    It to the sea, we to the tomb.

# ——"Paysage sentimental"——
## (Sentimental Landscape)

**Date of composition:** *1883.*
**Date of publication:** *15 April 1891.*
**Publisher: La Revue illustrée,** *Société nouvelle d'Editions musicales, Paris.*
**Dedicated to Madame Vasnier.**
**Source:** *Paul Bourget, "Amour." In* Les Aveux I, *1882.*

In the shifting pallor of a mild winter afternoon, two lovers kiss tenderly under the branches. Their melancholy happiness resembles the soft gloom of the winter sky. Briefly, in the stillness of the woods, they kiss more desperately as they see the passing away of the season. Everything around them—leaves, branches, sun rays, valley—is fatefully telling of the end of the year. Even though death surrounds them, their happiness is very much alive and peaceful.

The title of the poem recalls Verlaine's first line of "Mandoline." In Bourget's poem the analogy between the outer and inner landscapes is stated without ambiguity in the first and third stanzas. The second stanza narrows the angle of description of the scene and underlines the closeness of the link between emotions and landscape. The languid atmosphere of the poem is conveyed by a choice of muffled vocalic sounds in the rhymes. The general feeling is reassuring, made up of tender love and peaceful happiness.

In his setting,[29] Debussy stresses more the inner landscape than the outer, although he does attempt some scenery impressionism. The melody flows melancholy and repetitive in the first and last stanzas. The second stanza interrupts the quiescent description of love and landscape, and sets a slightly more dramatic pace to emphasize the desperate exchange of kisses.[29a]

# pe i za ʒ   sã ti mã ta l
## Paysage sentimental
### Landscape sentimental

| | | | | | | | |
|---|---|---|---|---|---|---|---|
| lə | sjɛ | ldi vɛ | rsi | du | si | tri stə | si |
| **Le** | **ciel** | **d'hiver,** | **si** | **doux,** | **si** | **triste,** | **si** |
| The | sky | of winter, | so | soft, | so | sad, | so |

| | |
|---|---|
| dɔ rmã | |
| **dormant,** | |
| dormant, | |

| | | | | | |
|---|---|---|---|---|---|
| u | lə | sɔ lɛ | jɛ rɛ | pa rmi | dɛ |
| **Où** | **le** | **soleil** | **errait** | **parmi** | **des** |
| Where | the | sun | wandered | amidst | some |

| | |
|---|---|
| va pœ | rblã ʃə |
| **vapeurs** | **blanches,** |
| mists | white, |

| | | | | | | |
|---|---|---|---|---|---|---|
| e tɛ | pa rɛ | jo | du | o | prɔ fɔ̃ | sã ti mã |
| **Etait** | **pareil** | **au** | **doux,** | **au** | **profond** | **sentiment** |
| Was | like | the | soft, | the | deep | feeling |

| | | | |
|---|---|---|---|
| ki | nu | rã de | tœ rø |
| **Qui** | **nous** | **rendait** | **heureux** |
| That | us | made | happy |

| | |
|---|---|
| me lã kɔ li kə mã | |
| **mélancoliquement** | |
| melancholically | |

| | | | | | | |
|---|---|---|---|---|---|---|
| pa | rsɛ | ta prɛ mi di | də | be ze | su | lɛ |
| **Par** | **cet** | **après-midi** | **de** | **baisers** | **sous** | **les** |
| On | that | afternoon | of | kisses | under | the |

| | |
|---|---|
| brã ʃə | |
| **branches** | |
| branches | |

Le ciel d'hiver, si doux, si triste, si dormant,

Où le soleil errait parmi des vapeurs blanches,

Etait pareil au doux, au profond sentiment

Qui nous rendait heureux mélancoliquement

Par cet après midi de baisers sous les branches

Branches mortes qu'aucun souffle ne remuait

Branches noires avec quelque feuille fanée

Ah! que ta bouche s'est à ma bouche donnée

Plus tendrement encore Dans ce grand bois muet

Et dans cette langueur de la mort de l'année

La mort de tout sinon de toi que j'aime tant

Et sinon du bonheur dont mon âme est comblée

Bonheur qui dort au fond de cette âme isolée

Mystérieux, paisible et frais comme l'étang

Qui pâlissait au fond de la pâle vallée.

(*Forty-three Songs for Voice and Piano*. New York: International, 1961)

brã ʃə      mɔ rtə   ko kɛ̃      su flə      nə
**Branches  mortes  qu'aucun  souffle    ne**
Branches   dead    that no   breath     not

rə my ɛ
**remuait,**
stirred,

brã ʃə      nwa rə   (z)a vɛ   kɛ lkə      fœ jə
**Branches  noires  avec     quelque    feuille**
Branches   black   with     some       leaf

fa ne ə
**fanée,**
withered,

a      kə     ta     bu ʃə     sɛ       ta    ma
**Ah!   que   ta     bouche   s'est    à     ma**
Ah!   how   your   mouth    itself has to   my

bu ʃə      dɔ ne ə
**bouche   donnée**
mouth     given

ply    tã drə mã    tã kɔ r    dã     sə    grã
**Plus  tendrement encore   Dans  ce    grand**
More  tenderly    still     in     that  vast

bwa    my ɛ
**bois   muet**
wood  silent

e      dã     sɛ tə   lã gœ   rdə    la    mɔ    rdə
**Et    dans  cette   langueur de    la    mort  de**
And   in     that    languor  of     the   death of

la ne ə
**l'année**
the year

The winter sky, so soft, so sad
and so still,
In which the sun wandered amid
white mist,
Was like the soft and deep feeling
That filled us with happy
melancholy,
On that afternoon of kisses under
the branches.

Dead branches stirred by no
breath,
Black branches with a few
withered leaves,
Ah! how your mouth gave itself
to mine
More tenderly still in the vast,
silent wood,
And in the languor of the year's
end.

The end of everything, but you
whom I love so much,
And but happiness which fills my
soul,
This happiness that lies dormant
in the depth of my lonely soul,
Mysterious, peaceful and cool
like the pale pond
Down in the pale valley!

la    mɔ    rdə tu         si nɔ̃   də twa
**La    mort de    tout,        sinon   de toi**
The    death of    everything, except   of you

kə        ʒɛ mə    tɑ̃
**que    j'aime    tant,**
whom    I love    so much,


e      si nɔ̃  dy bɔ nœ    rdɔ̃       mɔ̃   na
**Et    sinon du bonheur dont        mon   âme**
And    except the happiness of which my    soul

mɛ   kɔ̃ ble ə
**est    comblée**
is    filled


bɔ nœ    rki    dɔ    ro    fɔ̃    də sɛ
**Bonheur qui    dort    au    fond de cette**
Happiness which sleeps in the depth of this

tɑ    mi zɔ le ə
**âme    isolée**
soul    lonely


mi ste ri jø    pɛ zi blə e    frɛ    kɔ mə
**Mystérieux, paisible et    frais    comme**
Mysterious,    peaceful and    cool    like

le tɑ̃
**l'étang**
the pond


ki    pɑ li sɛ    to    fɔ̃    də la    pɑ lə
**Qui    pâlissait    au    fond    de la    pâle**
That    grew pale in the    bottom    of the    pale

va le ə
**vallée.**
valley.

# ——"Voici que le printemps"—
## *(Here Comes Spring)*

**Date of composition: *1884.***
**Date of publication: *1907.***
**Publisher: *Société nouvelle d'Editions musicales, Paris.***
**Dedicated to Madame Vasnier.**
**Source: *Paul Bourget, "Romance," in* Dilettantisme. *In* Les Aveux II, *1882.***

This descriptive celebration of spring in the style of Renaissance poetry portrays spring as an agile young page in traditional garb, dashing down the road with two birds on his shoulders. On his way, nature tenderly acclaims him, flowers and birds salute him. The whole gamut of comparisons and descriptions culminates with the theme of love. The nightingale sings of love and the blackbird, its antitype, of the absence of love. The poem has sincerity, charm, good composition, and clarity of expression, but it lacks nuances and power of suggestion, not to mention depth of feeling and thought.

Again Russian influences have been found in this setting. One should notice the discrepancy between the dates of composition and publication: Debussy may have been in financial difficulty and released this early song for publication. The opening bars of the accompaniment set a fairly brisk and light pace to illustrate the coming of spring. The rhythm slows in two areas, once to describe the miraculous blossoming of the flowers and again, quite expectedly, to emphasize the nightingale's languorous love song.

# vwa si kə lə prɛ̃ tã
# **Voici que le printemps**
# Here is that the spring

| vwa si | kə | lə | prɛ̃ tã | sə | fi | sle ʒe |
|---|---|---|---|---|---|---|
| **Voici** | **que** | **le** | **printemps,** | **ce** | **fils** | **léger** |
| Here is | that | the | spring, | this | son | nimble |

| da vril |
|---|
| **d'Avril** |
| of April |

Voici que le printemps, ce fils léger d'Avril
Beau page en pourpoint vert brodé de roses blanches
Paraît leste, fringant et les poings sur les hanches
Comme un prince acclamé revient d'un long exil

| bo | pa | ʒã | pu rpwɛ̃ | vɛ r |
|---|---|---|---|---|
| **Beau** | **page** | **en** | **pourpoint** | **vert** |
| Handsome | page | in | doublet | green |

| brɔ de | də | ro zə | blã ʃə |
|---|---|---|---|
| **brodé** | **de** | **roses** | **blanches** |
| embroidered | with | roses | white |

Les branches des buissons verdis rendent étroite
La route qu'il poursuit en dansant comme un fol;
Sur son épaule gauche il porte un rossignol
Un merle s'est posé sur son épaule droite.

| pa rɛ | lɛ stə | frɛ̃ gã | e | lɛ | pwɛ̃ | sy |
|---|---|---|---|---|---|---|
| **Paraît** | **leste,** | **fringant** | **et** | **les** | **poings** | **sur** |
| Appears | light, | dashing | and | the | fists | on |

| rlɛ | ã ʃə |
|---|---|
| **les** | **hanches** |
| the | hips |

Et les fleurs qui dormaient sous les mousses des bois
Ouvrent leurs yeux où flotte une ombre vague et tendre
Et sur leurs petits pieds se dressent pour entendre
Les deux oiseaux siffler et chanter à la fois

| kɔ | mœ̃ prɛ̃ | sa kla me | rə vjɛ̃ | dœ̃ |
|---|---|---|---|---|
| **Comme** | **un** | **prince** | **acclamé** | **revient** | **d'un** |
| Like | a | prince | hailed | returns | from a |

| lɔ̃ | (k)ɛ gzi l[30] |
|---|---|
| **long** | **exil** |
| long | exile |

lɛ brɑ̃ ʃə də bɥi sɔ̃ vɛ rdi
**Les branches des buissons verdis**
The branches of the bushes turned green
rɑ̃ də (t)e trwa tə
**rendent étroite**
make narrow

la ru tə ki lpu rsɥi ɑ̃ dɑ̃ sɑ̃
**La route qu'il poursuit en dansant**
The road that he follows while dancing
kɔ mœ̃ fɔl
**comme un fol;**
like a fool;

sy rsɔ̃ ne po lə go ʃi lpɔ rtœ̃
**Sur son épaule gauche il porte un**
On his shoulder left he carries a
rɔ si ɲɔ l[31]
**rossignol**
nightingale

œ̃ mɛ rlə sɛ po ze sy rsɔ̃ ne po lə
**Un merle s'est posé sur son épaule**
A blackbird has alighted on his shoulder
drwa tə
**droite.**
right.

e lɛ flœ rki do rmɛ su lɛ
**Et les fleurs qui dormaient sous les**
And the flowers which slept under the
mu sə de bwa
**mousses des bois**
moss of the woods

Car le merle sifflote et le
rossignol chante
Le merle siffle ceux qui ne sont
pas aimés
Et pour les amoureux
languissants et charmés
Le rossignol prolonge une
chanson touchante.

*(Forty-three Songs for Voice*
*and Piano.* New York:
International, 1961)

———————— • ————————

Here comes spring, April's light-
footed son,
A fair page in green doublet
embroidered with white roses,
See him come, nimble, dashing,
with his hands on his hips,
Like a prince acclaimed,
returning from long exile.

The twigs of the greening bushes
narrow
The road along which he dances
and frolics;
On his left shoulder he holds a
nightingale,
On his right one a blackbird has
alighted.

And the flowers asleep under the
moss of the woods
Open their eyes in which drifts a
dim and tender shadow;
They rise on their little feet to
hear
The two birds whistle and sing
together.

u vrə    lœ    rsjø  u          flɔ   ty
**Ouvrent leurs yeux où         flotte une**
Open     their  eyes  in which floats a

nɔ̃ brə   va          ge    tɑ̃ drə
**ombre  vague       et     tendre**
shadow  indefinite  and   tender

e    sy   rlœ   rpə ti  pje   sə   drɛ sə
**Et  sur  leurs petits pieds se   dressent**
And  on   their  tiny    feet  stand up

pu        rɑ̃ tɑ̃ drə
**pour     entendre**
in order  to hear

lɛ   dø    zwa zo  si fle    (r)e  ʃɑ̃ te
**Les deux oiseaux siffler  et    chanter**
The  two   birds    whistle and   sing

(r)a la fwa
**à la fois**
together

ka    rlə  mɛ rlə    si flɔ tə  e    lə
**Car  le   merle     sifflote   et   le**
For   the  blackbird whistles  and  the

rɔ si ɲɔ    lʃɑ̃ tə
**rossignol  chante**
nightingale sings

lə   mɛ rlə    si flə    sø    ki    nə  sɔ̃   pɑ
**Le   merle     siffle    ceux  qui   ne  sont  pas**
The  blackbird whistles  those who   are        not

ze me
**aimés**
loved

For the blackbird is whistling and the nightingale singing;
The blackbird whistles of those who are not loved,
And for the languishing and spellbound lovers
The nightingale prolongs his touching song.

e       pu     rlɛ  za mu rø      lɑ̃ gi sɑ̃        ze
**Et    pour  les  amoureux  languissants et**
And   for     the  lovers         languishing  and
ʃa rme
**charmés**
enchanted


lə      rɔ si ɲɔ      lprɔ lɔ̃      ʒy nə  ʃɑ̃ sɔ̃
**Le    rossignol    prolonge une    chanson**
The   nightingale  prolongs a        song
tu ʃɑ̃ tə[32]
**touchante.**
touching.

# ———— "Apparition" ————
## (Apparition)

Date of composition: *1884.*
Date of publication: *1 May 1926.*
Publisher: La Revue musicale, *("La Jeunesse de Debussy"),*
   Paris.
Dedicated to Madame Vasnier.
Source: *Stéphane Mallarmé, "Apparition." First published by
   Verlaine in* Lutèce, *November–December 1883.*

Although he was twenty years old when he wrote "Apparition," Mallarmé was still disconsolate over his mother's death,
which had occurred when he was five. In 1863 he was about to
marry (or was already married to) Maria Gerhart. The poem is
one of the rare examples of commissioned work in Mallarmé's
life: It was written on behalf of his best friend Henri Cazalis for
Cazalis' fiancée, a beautiful blonde named Ettie Yapp. It is
considered one of the least obscure of Mallarmé's poems, yet
every word is allusion and symbol.

   The imagery and atmosphere of the madrigal is very much
influenced by Pre-Raphaelite paintings. The four opening lines
of the two-part poem recall the day of the lovers' first kiss,
against a background of moonlight, seraphim, viols, and flowers. Yet what should be an entrancing moment has left behind a
note of disappointment: The moon gloomy, the seraphim in
tears, the viols sobbing, the blue corollas fading, the poet's heart
sad, as if the kiss had been a sacrilege. Suddenly, the poet's
somber reverie is interrupted by a flashback—the glorious vision of a young woman. This brief illuminating apparition in the
style of Burne-Jones, all smile and flaming hair, evokes Ettie
Yapp and also recalls Mallarmé's first vision of his wife-to-be in
the streets of Sens. But the hair, a symbol of love and beauty,
suddenly loses its voluptuousness, as if the poet would not share
the experience of passion. The young woman, alive and terrestrial, fades into a more ethereal figure that now resembles the
fairylike mother-image of the poet's childhood dreams. Contrasts are then established: The flame becomes snow, the sun
changes to stars, present dissolves into past, ardor into nostalgia.
Time raises a barrier which, while it shields the poet's heart, yet
paralyzes his vital impulses: The memory of the mother transforms the violence of his desire into an appeasing outpouring of

tenderness. The poem subtly underlines the division of the poet's soul, torn between several absolutes.

Debussy's setting of "Apparition" belongs to the Vasnier cycle of songs. The choice of a Mallarmé poem at such an early stage in Debussy's musical career, when Mallarmé was still unknown and unappreciated, shows Debussy's keen feeling for experiment in the musical language and his vivid intellectual curiosity. Not only did he have to deal with the music of the word associations, but with symbols, sensorial correspondences, and the confrontation of an inner world torn apart. The vocal part covers a wide range, going from a recitative effect to great note intervals. The harmonies chosen depict the fallen paradise of the opening lines. Appropriate dynamics enhance the opposition between the two visions, and the fading away of the ending that repeats *d'étoiles parfumées* accentuates the illusion of the mother apparition.[32a]

# a pa ri sjɔ̃
# Apparition
## Apparition

| la | ly nə | sa tri stɛ | dɛ | se ra fɛ̃ | zɑ̃ |
|----|-------|-----------|-----|-----------|-----|
| **La** | **lune** | **s'attristait.** | **Des** | **séraphins** | **en** |
| The | moon | was saddening. | Some | seraphim | in |

| plœ r |
|-------|
| **pleurs** |
| tears |

| rɛ vɑ̃ | la rʃɛ | o | dwa | dɑ̃ | lə |
|--------|--------|---|-----|-----|-----|
| **Rêvant,** | **l'archet** | **aux** | **doigts,** | **dans** | **le** |
| Dreaming, | the bow | in the | fingers, | in | the |

| ka lmə | dɛ | flœ |
|--------|-----|-----|
| **calme** | **des** | **fleurs** |
| calm | of the | flowers |

La lune s'attristait. Des séraphins en pleurs
Rêvant, l'archet aux doigts, dans le calme des fleurs
Vaporeuses, tiraient de mourantes violes
De blancs sanglots glissant sur l'azur des corolles.
C'était le jour béni de ton premier baiser.
Ma songerie aimant à me martyriser
S'enivrait savamment du parfum de tristesse
Que même sans regret et sans déboire laisse
La cueillaison d'un Rêve au coeur qui l'a cueilli.

rva pɔ rø zə    ti rɛ    də    mu rɑ̃ tə    vi ɔ lə
**Vaporeuses, tiraient de mourantes violes**
Vaporous,    drew    from    dying    viols

də    blɑ̃    sɑ̃ glo    gli sɑ̃    sy    rla zy
**De blancs sanglots glissant sur l'azur**
Some    white    sobs    gliding    over    the azure

rdɛ    kɔ rɔ lə
**des corolles.**
of the    corollas.

se tɛ    lə    ʒu    rbe ni    də tɔ̃    prə mje
**—C'était le jour béni de ton premier**
—It was    the day    blessed    of your    first

be ze
**baiser.**
kiss.

ma sɔ̃ ʒə ri    ɛ mɑ̃    ta    mə    ma rti ri ze
**Ma songerie aimant à me martyriser**
My dreaming    fond    of me    martyrizing

sɑ̃ ni vrɛ    sa va mɑ̃    dy    pa rfœ̃    də
**S'enivrait savamment du parfum de**
Was reveling    knowingly    in the    scent    of

tri stɛ sə
**tristesse**
sadness

kə    mɛ mə    sɑ̃    rə grɛ    e    sɑ̃
**Que même sans regret et sans**
Which    even    without    regret    and    without

de bwa rə    lɛ sə
**déboire laisse**
disappointment leaves

J'errais donc, l'oeil rivé sur le pavé vieilli
Quand avec du soleil aux cheveux, dans la rue
Et dans le soir, Tu m'es en riant apparue apparue
Et j'ai cru voir la fée au chapeau de clarté
Qui jadis sur mes beaux sommeils d'enfant gâté
Passait, laissant toujours de ses mains mal fermées.
Neiger de blancs bouquets d'étoiles parfumées, d'étoiles parfumées.

(*Quatre Chansons de jeunesse.*
Paris: Jobert, 1969)

●

The moon was saddening.
Seraphim in tears,
Dreaming, bow in hand, in the calm of vaporous flowers
Were drawing from dying viols
White sobs that glided over the blue corollas.
—It was the blessed day of your first kiss.
My fantasy that loves to torment me
Knowingly reveled in the scent of sadness
Which, even without regret and disappointment,
The gathering of a Dream leaves in the heart that has gathered it.
Thus I wandered, my eyes fixed on the worn pavement,
When with sun in your hair, in the street

la    kœ jɛ zɔ̃  dœ̃  rɛ   vo   kœ
**La   cueillaison d'un Rêve   au   coeur**
The   gathering  of a  Dream to the heart

rki  la   kœ ji
**qui  l'a   cueilli.**
that  it has  gathered.

ʒɛ rɛ       dɔ̃   lœ    jri ve sy   rlə
**J'errais    donc, l'oeil  rivé  sur  le**
I wandered thus,  the eye fixed on  the

pa ve    vjɛ ji
**pavé     vieilli**
pavement worn

kɑ̃     a vɛ  kdy  sɔ lɛ   jo    ʃə vø
**Quand avec du    soleil aux   cheveux,**
When  with some sun   in the  hair,

dɑ̃   la   ry
**dans la   rue**
in    the  street

e   dɑ̃   lə   swa r   ty   mɛ    zɑ̃
**Et  dans le   soir,   Tu   m'es   en**
And in   the  evening, you me has while

ri jɑ̃   ta pa ryə  a pa ryə
**riant   apparue   apparue,**
laughing appeared appeared,

e   ʒe   kry   vwa   rla fe ə   o
**Et  j'ai  cru   voir  la  fée  au**
And I have thought to see the fairy in the

ʃa po   də kla rte
**chapeau de clarté**
cap     of brightness

And in the evening, laughing, you appeared to me, appeared to me
And I thought I saw the fairy with her luminous cap
Who once through the lovely sleeps of my spoilt childhood
Would pass, letting her half-closed hands always
Snow white bouquets of perfumed stars, of perfumed stars.

ki ʒa di s sy rmɛ bo sɔ mɛ
**Qui jadis sur mes beaux sommeils**
Who once on my lovely sleeps

jdɑ̃ fɑ̃ gɑ te
**d'enfant gâté**
of child spoilt

pɑ sɛ lɛ sɑ̃ tu ʒu rdə sɛ mɛ̃
**Passait, laissant toujours de ses mains**
Would pass, letting always from her hands

ma lfɛ rme
**mal fermées.**
half-closed.

ne ʒe də blɑ̃ bu kɛ de twa lə
**Neiger de blancs bouquets d'étoiles**
Snow some white bouquets of stars

pɑ rfy me ə de twa lə pɑ rfy me ə
**parfumées, d'étoiles parfumées.**
perfumed, of stars perfumed.

# ————— "Ariettes oubliées" —————
## *(Forgotten Airs)*

Date of composition: *January 1885–March 1887; rearranged:*
   *1903.*
Date of publication: *a) separately: 1888. b) in a series: 1903.*
Publisher: *a) Vve E. Girod. b) E. Fromont, Paris.*
Dedicated to Mary Garden (1903 edition only).
Source: *Paul Verlaine,* Romances sans paroles, *1874;* Sagesse,
   *1881.*

   I.   "C'est l'extase" (It Is Ecstasy)
   II.  "Il pleure dans mon coeur" (It Weeps in My Heart)
   III. "L'ombre des arbres" (The Shadow of the Trees)
   IV.  Chevaux de bois (Wooden Horses)
   V.   Green—Aquarelle (Green—Watercolor)
   VI.  Spleen (Spleen)

*Ariettes oubliées* is the title of the first part of *Romances sans
paroles,* the other parts being *Paysages belges, Birds in the
Night,* and *Aquarelles* (Belgian Landscapes; Birds in the Night;
Watercolors). The words *Romances* and *Ariettes* reveal Verlaine's musical intentions in these poems. The title *Ariettes* was
inspired by Rimbaud: In 1872, during their first separation,
Rimbaud discovered a volume of Favart's[33] light operas in his
hometown library; he copied and sent to Verlaine one air of his
liking. *Oubliées* (forgotten) was added by Verlaine and lends
itself to a variety of interpretations: forgotten by the music
critics, by the general public, or by Rimbaud, by the time
Verlaine reviewed and collected his verse for publication in
1874.
   For his own series of *Ariettes oubliées,* Debussy selected three
of Verlaine's *Ariettes,* one poem from *Paysages belges* and
*Sagesse*[33a] and two from *Aquarelles.* At first he entitled them
*Ariettes* and had them published individually; fifteen years later
he reviewed them for a second publication and dedicated them
to Mary Garden, the creator of Mélisande. Debussy had started
working on them before he left for the Villa Medici and finished
them when he returned to Paris. They are considered very
important in his vocal production. Although still influenced by
Massenet, they strike an original note by their sensuousness and
expressive chromaticism; above all, they establish subtle correspondences with Verlaine's poems.

# I. "C'est l'extase"

**Date of composition: *March 1887*.**
**Source: Ariettes oubliées *I*. *In* Romances sans paroles.**

*Romances sans paroles* was prompted by Verlaine's fear of losing Rimbaud's love: After a few weeks of intense and happy relationship, both spiritual and sensual, Verlaine became aware of the ineluctable waning of passion. At least, if he could not retain Rimbaud's love, he could keep Rimbaud's respect for his poetry. He therefore created an exquisitely new poetic language, immaterial and fluid, all whispers, suggestions, and dreams, for someone who appreciated poetic innovations more than the feelings behind them.

The first *ariette* is a beautiful rendering of some early moments of passion. Verlaine wrote and published it after he asked Rimbaud to leave him for fear of legal reprisals from his wife; Rimbaud resented this forced separation. The first two verses of the poem tell of the ecstasy of passion, on a warm languorous evening, and the miraculous fusion of soul and nature. But was communion between the lovers truly achieved? Verlaine's incorrigible pessimism stands out in the last verse; he interrupts the ecstatic mood after love and begs of his beloved some reassuring answers: Are we one and the same soul? do we share the same ecstasy, however painful and nostalgic it may be? or will the dullness of reality destroy the dream of passion?

The fragile melody of the poet's soul is expressed in a variety of musical means: uneven meter of seven syllables conveying lightness and dreaminess, rich rhyming, assonances, and word repetitions. The poet's lament is suggested by a choice of muted sounds and colors for the natural setting: subdued grays, whispers of tiny voices, soft cries, and the muffled sound of rolling pebbles.

Debussy's setting is dominated by a mood of caressing reverie. The blissful state of soul and senses is, however, interrupted by flashes of doubt: In the third verse, a change of rhythm takes place that dramatizes the poet's entreaties. But the melody soon returns to the whispering overtones of the beginning. The sensuous languor of the vocal part offers an excellent opportunity for a perfect legato.

a rjɛ t   zu bli je
# Ariettes oubliées
Forgotten airs

sɛ   lɛ  ksta z
## I.  "C'est l'extase"
It is ecstasy

| lə | vɑ̃ | dɑ̃ | la | plɛ n |
|----|----|----|----|----|
| **Le** | **vent** | **dans** | **la** | **plaine** |
| The | wind | in | | the plain |

Le vent dans la plaine
Suspend son haleine.
(Favart)

| sy spɑ̃ | sɔ̃ | na lɛ n |
|----|----|----|
| **Suspend** | **son** | **haleine.** |
| Holds | its | breath. |

(Favart)

C'est l'extase langoureuse
C'est la fatigue amoureuse
C'est tous les frissons des bois
Parmi l'étreinte des brises
C'est, vers les ramures grises,
Le chœur des petites voix

| sɛ | lɛ ksta zə | lɑ̃ gu rø zə |
|----|----|----|
| **C'est** | **l'extase** | **languoureuse** |
| It | is the ecstasy | languorous |

O le frêle et frais murmure
Cela gazouille et susurre
Cela ressemble au cri doux
Que l'herbe agitée expire
Tu dirais, sous l'eau qui vire
Le roulis sourd des cailloux

| sɛ | la | fa ti | ga mu rø zə |
|----|----|----|----|
| **C'est** | **la** | **fatigue** | **amoureuse** |
| It is | the | fatigue | amorous |

| sɛ | tu | lɛ | fri sɔ̃ | dɛ | bwa |
|----|----|----|----|----|----|
| **C'est** | **tous** | **les** | **frissons** | **des** | **bois** |
| It is | all | the | tremors | of the | woods |

Cette âme qui se lamente
En cette plainte dormante
C'est la nôtre, n'est-ce pas?
La mienne, dis, et la tienne
Dont s'exhale l'humble antienne
Par ce tiède soir tout bas.

| pa rmi | le trɛ̃ tə | dɛ | bri zə |
|----|----|----|----|
| **Parmi** | **l'étreinte** | **des** | **brises** |
| Amid | the embrace | of the | breezes |

(*Claude Debussy Songs 1880–1904*. New York: Dover, 1981)

sɛ   vɛ   rlɛ ra my rə   gri zə
**C'est, vers   les ramures   grises,**
It is,   toward   the boughs   gray,

lə   kœ   rdɛ   pə ti tə   vwa
**Le   choeur   des   petites   voix**
The   choir   of the   little   voices

o   lə   frɛ   le   frɛ   my rmy rə
**O le   frêle   et   frais   murmure**
O the   frail   and   cool   murmuring

sə la   ga zu   je   sy sy rə
**Cela   gazouille et   susurre**
It   twitters   and   whispers

sə la   rə sã   blo   kri   du
**Cela   ressemble au   cri   doux**
It   resembles   the   cry   soft

kə   lɛ   rba ʒi te   ɛ kspi rə
**Que   l'herbe   agitée   expire**
Which   the grass   ruffled   expires

ty   di rɛ   su   lo   ki   vi rə
**Tu   dirais,   sous   l'eau   qui   vire**
You   would say,   under   the water   which   swirls

lə   ru li   su   rdɛ   ka ju
**Le   roulis   sourd   des   cailloux**
The   rolling   muffled   of the   pebbles

sɛ   tɑ mə ki   sə   la mã tə
**Cette   âme   qui   se   lamente**
This   soul   which   itself   laments

It is the languorous ecstasy,
It is the amorous fatigue,
It is all the tremors of the woods
As the breezes embrace them,
It is in the gray branches
The choir of tiny voices.

O the frail and fresh murmur,
How it twitters and whispers!
It resembles the soft cry
Breathed out by the ruffled grass. . .
You would say it is, under swirling waters,
The muffled rumbling of the pebbles.

This soul that mourns
With such subdued lament
Is ours, is it not?
It is my soul, say, and yours,
Exhaling the humble anthem
Very softly, on this warm evening?

ã       sɛ tə   plɛ̃ tə   dɔ rmã tə
**En    cette   plainte   dormante**
With this    plaint    dormant

sɛ      la      no trə   nɛ      sə pa
**C'est   la      nôtre,   n'est-ce pas?**
It is     the     ours,    is      it not?

la      mjɛ nə   di   e      la   tjɛ n(ə)[33b]
**La     mienne, dis, et    la   tienne**
The     mine,       say, and the yours

dɔ̃             sɛ gza lə    lœ̃          blã tjɛ nə
**Dont          s'exhale     l'humble    antienne**
From which  breathes out  the humble anthem

pa      rsə   tjɛ də  swa r   tu      bɑ
**Par   ce    tiède   soir    tout bas.**
On     this   warm   evening, very   softly.

## II. "Il pleure dans mon coeur"
### (It Weeps in My Heart)

**Date of composition:** *1885–1887.*
**Source:** *Paul Verlaine,* Ariettes oubliées *III. In* Romances sans paroles.

An epigraph by Rimbaud introduces this third *Ariette,* and it might have stood for a password or some magic phrase used between Rimbaud and Verlaine in special moments or to recall particular moods. The date of the poem has not been specified, but it was presumably the London rain that inspired the poem. Verlaine and Rimbaud spent several months together in London, from September 1872 until April 1873. There, a precarious situation seemed to prevail, so much so that Rimbaud kept finding excuses to leave Verlaine. Verlaine became sick with pain and longing.

His mood was reflected in this poem, which tells of the poet's tears and heart's discomfort. And yet he could find no reason for this languor, for, so far, there had been no betrayal (whose betrayal anyway? his wife's or Rimbaud's). There was no stifling passion or crushing hatred to blame for it. What then? The poet's mourning mood, his inexplicable sorrow, the relentless monotony of the rain patter, all brought about a tenacious and hopeless state of prostration.

Again Verlaine used fresh prosodic techniques to underline the tediousness of the day and the longing of his heart: rhymes irregularly placed and repeated, vocalic sounds chosen carefully to convey the dullness of feelings, numerous alliterations and assonances lulling the mind into painful lethargy.

In his version of "Il pleure dans mon coeur," Debussy stressed the boredom and melancholy of the poet watching the rain fall: He recommended a slow and monotonous tone quality, gave a steady rain pattern to the accompaniment and a recurrent melodic theme to the song. Six bars only interrupt the continuity, in a different tempo and key signature, in order to convey the poet's dismay at his inexplicable languor.[34]

# i lplœ r dɑ̃ mɔ̃ kœ r
## II. "Il pleure dans mon coeur"
### It weeps in my heart

i    lplø     du smɑ̃       sy    rla  vi l
**Il  pleut   doucement  sur  la   ville**
It   rains   gently       on   the  town
(A. Rimbaud)

i   lplœ rə dɑ̃    mɔ̃     kœ
**Il  pleure dans  mon    coeur**
It  weeps  in     my      heart

rkɔ        mi  lplø   sy    rla  vi lə
**Comme il    pleut sur   la   ville**
As         it  rains on    the  town

kɛ      lɛ    sɛ tə   lɑ̃ gœ(r)
**Quelle est   cette  langueur**
What    is    this   languor

(r)ki  pe nɛ trə  mɔ̃    kœ r
**Qui   pénètre  mon    coeur**
That   pervades my     heart

o  brɥi   du      də la   plɥi(ə)
**O  bruit  doux  de la   pluie**
O  sound soft    of the  rain

pa      rtɛ       re   sy    rlɛ  twa
**Par    terre     et   sur  les   toits!**
On the  ground  and  on    the   roofs!

pu      rɛ̃  kœ     rki   sɑ̃ nɥi(ə)
**Pour  un  coeur qui    s'ennuie**
For     a   heart that  languishes

Il pleut doucement sur la ville
(A. Rimbaud)

Il pleure dans mon coeur
Comme il pleut sur la ville
Quelle est cette langueur
Qui pénètre mon coeur

O bruit doux de la pluie
Par terre et sur les toits!
Pour un coeur qui s'ennuie
O le bruit de la pluie!

Il pleure sans raison
Dans ce coeur qui s'écoeure
Quoi! nulle trahison?
Ce deuil est sans raison

C'est bien la pire peine
De ne savoir pourquoi,
Sans amour et sans haine,
Mon coeur a tant de peine.

(*Claude Debussy Songs 1880–1904.* New York: Dover, 1981)

———————•———————

It weeps in my heart
As it rains on the town.
What is this languor
That pierces my heart?

O soft sound of the rain
On the ground and on the roofs!
For a weary heart,
Oh, the sound of the rain!

o   lə   brɥi   də  la   plɥi(ə)
**O   le   bruit   de  la   pluie!**
O   the   sound   of  the   rain!

i   lplœ rə   sã   rɛ zɔ̃
**Il   pleure   sans   raison**
It   weeps   without   reason

dã   sə   kœ   rki   se kœ rə
**Dans   ce   coeur   qui   s'écoeure**
In   this   heart   which   sickens

kwa   ny lə   tra i zɔ̃
**Quoi!   nulle   trahison?**
What!   no   betrayal?

sə   dœ   jɛ   sã   rɛ zɔ̃
**Ce   deuil   est   sans   raison**
This   mourning   is   without   reason

sɛ   bjɛ̃   la   pi rə   pɛ nə
**C'est   bien   la   pire   peine**
It is   indeed   the   worst   pain

də   nə   sa vwa   rpu rkwa
**De   ne   savoir   pourquoi,**
To   not   know   why,

sã   za mu   re   sã   ɛ nə
**Sans   amour   et   sans   haine,**
Without   love   and   without   hatred,

mɔ̃   kœ   ra   tã   də pɛ nə
**Mon   coeur   a   tant   de peine.**
My   heart   has   so much   of   pain.

It weeps without reason
In this disheartened heart.
What! There is no treason?
This sorrow is without reason.

It is far the worst pain
Not to know why,
Without love or hate,
My heart has such pain.

# III.  "L'ombre des arbres"
## *(The Shadow of the Trees)*

**Date of composition:** *6 January 1885, Paris.*
**Source:** *Paul Verlaine,* Ariettes oubliées *IX. In* Romances sans
paroles.

This is the last of the *Ariettes oubliées.* Verlaine wrote it sometime between May and June 1872, upon Rimbaud's return from
their first separation. The poem is prefaced by an epigraph from
the Baroque poet Cyrano de Bergerac's *Lettres satiriques et
amoureuses* (Satirical and Amorous Letters), which discloses
and explains the poet's fears and pessimism.

Fear of reality and despair dominate the mood of the poem,
built around one long metaphor: As the reflection of the trees
drowns in the river, so do the traveler's best hopes. What
remains of this pallid landscape of misty dreams is reality, the
reality of despair echoed by the lament of the turtledoves. The
dual play of dream and reality is staged against a shifting game of
the reflections in the water and distortions by the haze.

Debussy wrote his setting of "L'ombre des arbres" before
departing for Rome. The song reflects the mirror images in the
almost parallel structure of its two parts. Debussy created unusual modulations to convey the melancholy metaphor of landscape and soul.[34a]

# lɔ̃ brə  de  za rbr
# L'ombre des arbres
## The shadow of the trees

lə    rɔ si ɲə    lki    dy    o    dy
**Le    rossignol    qui    du    haut    d'une**
The    nightingale    that    from the    top    of a

nbrã ʃ    sə    rə ga rdə də dã    krwa
**branche    se    regarde    dedans,    croit**
branch    itself    looks    in,    thinks

ɛ trə    tɔ̃ be    dã    la    ri vjɛ r    i    lɛ
**être    tombé    dans    la    rivière. Il    est**
to have    fallen    in    the    river.    He is

to    sɔ mɛ    dœ̃    ʃɛ    ne    tu tfwa
**au    sommet    d'un    chêne et    toutefois**
at the    top    of an    oak    and yet

i    la    pœ    rdə sə    nwa je
**il    a    peur    de    se    noyer.**
he is    afraid    of    drowning.
(Cyrano de Bergerac)

lɔ̃ brə    de    za rbrə    dã    la    ri vjɛ
**L'ombre    des    arbres    dans    la    rivière**
The shadow    of the    trees    in    the    river
rã bry me ə
**embrumée**
hazy

mœ    rkɔ mə    də    la    fy me(ə)
**Meurt    comme    de    la    fumée,**
Dies    like    some    smoke,

Le rossignol qui du haut d'une
branche se regarde dedans, croit
être tombé dans la rivière. Il est
au sommet d'un chêne et
toutefois
il a peur de se noyer.
(Cyrano de Bergerac)

L'ombre des arbres dans la rivière
embrumée
    Meurt comme de la fumée,
Tandis qu'en l'air, parmi les
ramures réelles
    Se plaignent les tourterelles

Combien ô voyageur, ce paysage
blême
    Te mira blême toi-même
Et que tristes pleuraient dans les
hautes feuillées,
    Tes espérances noyées! noyées!

(*Claude Debussy Songs 1880–
1904.* New York: Dover, 1981)

———————•———————

The nightingale, from the
height of a
branch, looking down in the
river, thinks
to have fallen in it. He is
at the top of an oak and yet
he is in fear of drowning
(Cyrano de Bergerac)

tã di      kã      lε r      pa rmi    lε    ra my rə
**Tandis   qu'en   l'air,    parmi     les   ramures**
While      in      the air,  among     the   branches
re ε lə
**éelles**
real

The shadow of trees in the misty stream
  Dies like smoke,
While in the air, among the real branches,
  The turtledoves complain.

    sə      plε ɲə        lε    tu rtə rε lə
    **Se     plaignent    les   tourterelles**
    Moan                 the   turtledoves

How much, O traveler, this pallid landscape,
  Mirrored your wan self there
And how sadly grieved in the highest leaves
  Your drowned hopes!
  drowned!

kõ bjε̃     o vwa ja ʒœ r sə    pei za ʒə    blε mə
**Combien, ô voyageur, ce      paysage      blême**
How,       o traveler,   this  landscape    pallid

    tə      mi ra      blε mə    twa mε mə
    **Te     mira       blême     toi-même**
    You     reflected  wan       yourself

e      kə      tri stə   plœ rε      dã    lε    o tə
**Et    que     tristes   pleuraient  dans  les   hautes**
And    how     sad       wept        in    the   tall
fœ je(ə)
**feuillées,**
foliage,

    tε      zε spe rã sə    nwa je ə    nwa je ə
    **Tes     espérances      noyées!     noyées!**
    Your    expectations    drowned!    drowned!

# IV. "Chevaux de bois"
## (Wooden Horses)

**Date of composition:** *1885–1887.*
**Source:** *Paul Verlaine,* **Paysages Belges III.** *In* **Romances sans paroles. Sagesse** *III n° XVII.*
**Dedicated to Alfred Bachelet (first version, 1888); Mary Garden (second version, 1903).**

"Chevaux de bois" is one of the most delightful and least impressionistic of Verlaine's poems. It is a reminiscence of one of Verlaine's rambles on the Belgian roads with Rimbaud, one day in August 1872, when they came across a fair in the village of St. Gilles outside Brussels. Verlaine was strongly taken by the merry-go-rounds and went straight back to his hotel to write this dazzling poem.

At the Flemish fair, pleasures are simple and the atmosphere is full of sounds and dizziness. Blurred faces go round merrily on wooden horses, accompanied by oboes and horns. The poet is watching, feeling both the excitement and the illusory escape of the twirls. The dance of the lifeless horses becomes hopeless and absurd, until the church bell starts ringing for supper. The carousers then noisily retreat from the carnival. Breaking the joyful drumbeats from the fair, the night call of the bell becomes a dirge. The mood of the poem shifts from hearty mirth to a romantic vision of the night, followed by intimations of death. Yet the wooden horses go on turning, carrying life and excitements unendingly, mechanizing human feelings and deeds. As in most of Verlaine's poems, disenchantment supplants the vertiginous intoxication of the beginning.

Debussy's first setting of the poem was composed earlier than the other *Ariettes* and dedicated to the composer Alfred Bachelet, a friend and fellow student at the *Conservatoire.* Debussy did not use Verlaine's first version of the poem from *Ariettes oubliées,* but the second version (less two stanzas) published in *Sagesse.*[35] The vocal part of his first setting was slightly modified in two areas at the end of the song; he added to the original *Sagesse* text the epigraph from Victor Hugo's *Odes et Ballades* (which appeared in the *Romances sans paroles* version) and a final repeat of the word *tournez*, and changed *Bien* to *Rien* (stanza 4).

Debussy respected Verlaine's alternate structure of refrains and verses by contrasting two melodies. The refrains echo, each in a different key, the round-like tunes of old-fashioned carousels; their rhythm is lively yet not too fast, and every now and then drumrolls and the blare of a cornet come through, adding stridency to the striking harmonies. Even at the end of the song, when the rhythm slackens at the rise of the early stars, the melody repeats its basic design. As the rhythm picks up again for the final line, the last and softer *tournez* helps build the transition between the excitement of the beginning and the dying merriment. The song is of bold, humorous, and dizzying brilliance. It challenges the singer's diction abilities: Articulation must be precise and fast, and the production of vowel sounds very accurate. Because of the more informal style of the poem, there should be fewer optional liaisons and less sounding of the schwa.

# ʃə vo də bwa
# Chevaux de bois
## Horses of wood

| pa | rsɛ̃ | ʒil |
|----|------|-----|
| **Par** | **saint** | **Gille,** |
| By | Saint | Gille, |

| vjɛ̃ | nu | zɑ̃ |
|------|-----|-----|
| **Viens-nous-en,** | | |
| Let | us | away, |

| mɔ̃ | na ʒi |
|-----|-------|
| **Mon** | **agile** |
| My | nimble |

la lzɑ̃
**Alezan!**
Sorrel!

(V. Hugo)

| | | | | | |
|---|---|---|---|---|---|
| tu rne | tu rne | bɔ̃ | ʃə vo | də | bwa |
| **Tournez,** | **tournez,** | **bons** | **chevaux** | **de** | **bois** |
| Turn, | turn, | good | horses | of | wood |

| | | | |
|---|---|---|---|
| tu rne | sɑ̃ | tu r | tu rne |
| **Tournez** | **cent** | **tours,** | **tournez** |
| Turn | a hundred | turns, | turn |

| | |
|---|---|
| mi lə | tu r |
| **mille** | **tours** |
| a thousand | turns |

| | | | | |
|---|---|---|---|---|
| tu rne | su vɑ̃ | e | tu rne | tu ʒu r |
| **Tournez** | **souvent** | **et** | **tournez** | **toujours** |
| Turn | often | and | turn | forever |

| | | | | |
|---|---|---|---|---|
| tu rne | tu rne | o | sɔ̃ | dɛ |
| **Tournez,** | **tournez** | **au** | **son** | **des** |
| Turn, | turn | to the | sound | of the |

| |
|---|
| o bwa |
| **hautbois** |
| oboes |

| | | | | | |
|---|---|---|---|---|---|
| lɑ̃ fɑ̃ | tu | ru ʒ(ə) | e | la | mɛ rə |
| **L'enfant** | **tout** | **rouge** | **et** | **la** | **mère** |
| The child | very | ruddy | and the | | mother |

| |
|---|
| blɑ̃ ʃ(ə) |
| **blanche** |
| white |

Tournez, tournez, bons chevaux de bois
Tournez cent tours tournez mille tours
Tournez souvent et tournez toujours
Tournez, tournez au son des hautbois

L'enfant tout rouge et la mère blanche
Le gars en noir et la fille en rose
L'une à la chose et l'autre à la pose,
Chacun se paie un sou de dimanche

Tournez, tournez, chevaux de leur coeur,
Tandis qu'autour de tous vos tournois
Clignote l'oeil du filou sournois
Tournez au son du piston vainqueur!

C'est étonnant comme ça vous soûle
D'aller ainsi dans ce cirque bête:
Rien dans le ventre et mal dans la tête,
Du mal en masse et du bien en foule

Tournez dadas, sans qu'il soit besoin
D'user jamais de nuls éperons
Pour commander à vos galops ronds
Tournez, tournez, sans espoir de foin

lə  gɑ  ɑ̃  nwar  e  la  fi  jɑ̃  ro z(ə)
**Le  gars  en  noir  et  la  fille  en  rose**
The  lad  in  black  and the  girl  in  pink

ly  na la  ʃo  ze  lo  tra la
**L'une  à  la  chose  et  l'autre  à  la**
The one  at  the  thing  and the other  in  a
po z(ə)
**pose,**
pose,

ʃa kœ̃  sə  pɛ  œ̃  su  də  di mɑ̃ ʃə
**Chacun  se  paie  un  sou  de  dimanche**
Each  himself  buys  a  penny  of  Sunday

tu rne  tu rne  ʃə vo  də  lœ  rkœ r
**Tournez,  tournez,  chevaux de  leur  coeur,**
Turn,  turn,  horses  of  their  heart,

tɑ̃ di  ko tu  rdə  tu  vo  tu rnwa
**Tandis  qu'autour de  tous  vos  tournois**
While  around  of  all  your  rotations

kli ɲɔ tə  lœ  jdy  fi lu  su rnwa
**Clignote  l'oeil  du  filou  sournois**
Twinkles  the eye  of the  pickpocket  sly

tu rne  o  sõ  dy  pi stõ
**Tournez  au  son  du  piston**
Turn  to the  sound  of the  cornet
vɛ̃ kœ r
**vainqueur!**
triumphant!

Et dépêchez, chevaux de leur âme
Déjà voici que sonne à la soupe
La nuit qui tombe et chasse la troupe
De gais buveurs que leur soif affame

Tournez, tournez! Le ciel en velours
D'astres en or se vêt lentement
L'Eglise tinte un glas tristement.
Tournez au son joyeux des tambours tournez.

*(Claude Debussy Songs 1880–1904. New York: Dover, 1981)*

————————•————————

By Saint Gille,
Let's away,
My nimble
Sorrel!
                        (V. Hugo)

Turn, turn, good wooden horses,
Turn a hundred times, turn a thousand times,
Turn often and forever,
Turn, turn, to the sound of the oboes.

The red-faced child and the pale mother,
The lad in black and the girl in pink,
One down to earth and the other putting on airs,
Each one getting his Sunday pennyworth.

sɛ  te tɔ nɑ̃  kɔ mə  sa  vu  su l(ə)
**C'est étonnant comme ça vous soûle**
It is  astonishing how  that you  intoxicates

da le  (r)ɛ̃ si  dɑ̃  sə  si rkə  bɛ t(ə)
**D'aller ainsi  dans ce  cirque bête:**
To go  like that  in  this  circus  silly:

rjɛ̃  dɑ̃  lə  vɑ̃  tre  ma  ldɑ̃  la
**Rien  dans le  ventre et  mal dans la**
Nothing in  the belly  and bad  in  the
tɛ t(ə)
**tête,**
head,

dy  ma  lɑ̃ ma  se  dy  bjɛ̃  ɑ̃
**Du  mal en masse et  du  bien en**
Some bad plentiful and  some good by
fu lə
**foule**
heaps

tu rne  da da  sɑ̃  ki  lswa
**Tournez dadas,  sans  qu'il soit**
Turn  hobbyhorses, without there being
bə zwɛ̃
**besoin**
a need

dy ze  ʒa mɛ  də ny  lze pə rɔ̃
**D'user jamais de nuls éperons**
To use  ever  of any  spurs

pu  rkɔ mɑ̃ de  (r)a  vo  ga lo  rɔ̃
**Pour commander à  vos  galops ronds**
To  control  to  your gallops round

Turn, turn, horses of their hearts,
While all around your whirling,
The eyes of the sly pickpocket twinkle,
Turn to the triumphant cornet's sound.

It is astonishing how it makes you drunk
To ride like that in this silly circus!
Nothing in the belly and pain in the head,
Plenty of bad and plenty of good.

Turn, hobbyhorses,
Without ever any need of spurs
To make you continue your circular gallop,
Turn, turn, without hope of fodder.

And hurry, horses of their souls,
Already the supper bell is sounded by
The night that falls and drives away the troop
Of merry drinkers made hungry by thirst.

Turn, turn! The velvet sky
Slowly dons stars of gold.
The church tolls a mournful knell.
Turn to the joyful sound of the drums, turn.

tu rne        tu rne        sɑ̃         zɛ spwa rdə fwɛ̃
**Tournez, tournez, sans        espoir  de  foin.**
Turn,         turn,         without hope    of   fodder.


e        de pɛ ʃe        ʃə vo      də  lœ      rɑ mə
**Et        dépêchez,   chevaux de  leur  âme,**
And       hurry,        horses    of   their  soul,


de ʒa        vwa si kə        sɔ        na la  su pə
**Déjà        voici    que   sonne    à   la   soupe**
Already here        is     ringing at  the  soup


la        nɥi        ki        tɔ̃        be   ʃa sə        la
**La        nuit   qui   tombe  et   chasse        la**
The        night which falls      and disperses the
tru pə
**troupe**
troop


də        ge        by vœ        rkə   lœ        rswa
**De  gais        buveurs que leur  soif**
Of   merry drinkers that their  thirst
fa fa mə
**affame**
makes hungry


tu rne        tu rne        lə        sjɛ   lɑ̃        və lu r
**Tournez, tournez!  Le   ciel   en   velours**
Turn,         turn!   The  sky    of   velvet


da strə        zɑ̃   nɔ        rsə        vɛ        lɑ̃ tə mɑ̃
**D'astres        en  or    se    vêt   lentement**
With stars  of  gold itself  dresses slowly

le gli zə      tɛ̃    tœ̃  glɑ   tri stə mɑ̃
**L'Eglise**    **tinte**   **un**  **glas**   **tristement.**
The church  tolls   a    knell  sadly.

tu rne       o     sɔ̃    ʒwa jø  dɛ
**Tournez au**    **son**   **joyeux des**
Turn      to the  sound  joyous  of the
tɑ̃ bu r    tu rne
**tambours tournez.**
drums    turn.

# V. "Green—Aquarelle"
## (Green—Watercolor)

**Date of composition: *January 1886.***
**Source: *Paul Verlaine*, Aquarelles. *In* Romances sans paroles.**

"Green" is the first poem of what Verlaine called the "English section" of *Romances sans paroles*: his six *Aquarelles*. The date of composition is unknown but can be set sometime between October and December 1872, when Verlaine stayed in England for the first time with Rimbaud.

The meaning of the title is not altogether clear; it could be associated with the green offering of the first line, or the youthful and innocent feelings described. This love poem is a happy, tender song that holds, by its simplicity of form and content, an exceptional place in Verlaine's production. The classical correctness of the alexandrine verse brings out the clarity of imagery, simplicity of syntax, exceptional sonorities, and purity of sentiment. On a cold morning, a fervid young lover comes to his beloved, bearing gifts of fruit, flowers, leaves, and branches. Weary but loving, he begs the lovely and demure lady for a generous welcome: Let him rest his tired head on her bosom. The peaceful scene of the last verse reveals that his wishes have come true: They both repose in fulfillment of the intimacies of requited love. For once the poem does not end on a note of irony, malaise, or recrimination; it tells only of joy and satisfaction.

Debussy's setting, written at the Villa Medici, communicates the soft lyricism of the poem. Its subtle transparency conveys the freshness of a watercolor. It is a charming love song with a characteristic melody that springs forward with fervor and spontaneity, expressing the youthful eagerness of the pleading lover. The slowing of the rhythm in the last part suggests the final gratification of pleasure granted.

gri n
# Green
Green

| vwa si | dɛ | frɥi | dɛ | flœ | rdɛ |
|--------|-----|-------|------|--------|-----|
| **Voici** | **des** | **fruits** | **des** | **fleurs** | **des** |
| Here are | some | fruit | some | flowers | some |

| fœ jə | ze | dɛ | brã ʃə |
|-------|-----|-----|--------|
| **feuilles** | **et** | **des** | **branches,** |
| leaves | and | some | branches, |

| e | pɥi | vwa si | mɔ̃ | kœ | rki | nə ba |
|---|-----|--------|-----|-----|-----|-------|
| **Et** | **puis** | **voici** | **mon** | **coeur** | **qui** | **ne bat** |
| And | then | here is | my | heart | that | beats |

| kə | pu | rvu |
|----|-----|-----|
| **que** | **pour** | **vous** |
| only | for | you |

| nə | lə | de ʃi re | pɑ | a vɛ | kvo | dø |
|----|-----|----------|-----|------|-----|-----|
| **Ne** | **le** | **déchirez** | **pas** | **avec** | **vos** | **deux** |
| Not | it | rend | | not | with | your | two |

| mɛ̃ | blã ʃ(ə) |
|-----|----------|
| **mains** | **blanches,** |
| hands | white, |

| e | ka | vo | zjø | si | bo |
|---|-----|-----|------|-----|------|
| **Et** | **qu'à** | **vos** | **yeux** | **si** | **beaux** |
| And | may to | your | eyes | so | beautiful |

| lœ̃ blə | pre zã | swa | du |
|---------|--------|------|-----|
| **l'humble** | **présent** | **soit** | **doux.** |
| the humble | gift | be | pleasing. |

| ʒa ri və | tu | ku vɛ | rã kɔ rə | də | ro ze ə |
|----------|-----|-------|----------|-----|---------|
| **J'arrive** | **tout** | **couvert** | **encore** | **de** | **rosée** |
| I come | all | covered | still | with | dew |

Voici des fruits des fleurs des
feuilles et des branches
Et puis voici mon coeur qui ne
bat que pour vous
Ne le déchirez pas avec vos deux
mains blanches,
Et qu'à vos yeux si beaux
l'humble présent soit doux.

J'arrive tout couvert encore de
rosée
Que le vent du matin vient glacer
à mon front
Souffrez que ma fatigue à vos
pieds reposée
Rêve des chers instants qui la
délasseront.

Sur votre jeune sein, laissez
rouler ma tête
Toute sonore encore de vos
derniers baisers
Laissez-la s'apaiser de la bonne
tempête,
Et que je dorme un peu puisque
vous reposez.

(*Claude Debussy Songs 1880–
1904.* New York: Dover, 1981)

———————•———————

| kə | lə | vã | dy | ma tɛ̃ | vjɛ̃ | gla se |
|----|----|----|----|--------|------|--------|
| **Que** | **le** | **vent** | **du** | **matin** | **vient** | **glacer** |
| That | the | wind | of the | morning | comes | to freeze |

Here are fruit, flowers, leaves and branches,
And then here is my heart that beats for you only.
Do not rend it with your two white hands,
And let the humble gift find favor in your beautiful eyes.

| ra | mɔ̃ | frɔ̃ |
|----|----|----|
| **à** | **mon** | **front** |
| on | my | brow |

| su fre | kə | ma | fa ti g(ə) | a | vo | pje |
|--------|----|----|-----------|---|-----|-----|
| **Souffrez** | **que** | **ma** | **fatigue,** | **à** | **vos** | **pieds** |
| Allow | that | my | weariness, | at | your | feet |

| rə po ze ə |
|------------|
| **reposée** |
| rested |

I come to you still covered with the dew
That the morning wind freezes on my brow.
Suffer my weariness, rested at your feet,
To dream of the dear moments that will solace it.

| rɛ və | de | ʃɛ | rzɛ̃ stɑ̃ | ki | la |
|-------|----|----|---------|----|----|
| **Rêve** | **des** | **chers** | **instants** | **qui** | **la** |
| Dreams | of the | dear | moments | that | it |

| de la sə rɔ̃ |
|--------------|
| **délasseront.** |
| will refresh. |

On your young breast let roll my head
That still rings with your last kisses;
Let it find peace after the happy storm,
And let me sleep a while since now you repose.

| sy | rvɔ trə | ʒœ nə | sɛ̃ | le se | ru le | ma |
|----|---------|-------|-----|-------|-------|-----|
| **Sur** | **votre** | **jeune** | **sein** | **laissez** | **rouler** | **ma** |
| On | your | young | breast | allow | to roll | my |

| tɛ tə |
|-------|
| **tête** |
| head |

| tu tə | sɔ nɔ | rɑ̃ kɔ r(ə) | də | vo |
|-------|-------|-----------|----|----|
| **Toute** | **sonore** | **encore** | **de** | **vos** |
| All | resounding | still | from | your |

| dɛ rnj e | be ze |
|----------|-------|
| **derniers** | **baisers** |
| last | kisses |

le se    la   sa pe ze    də    la    bɔ nə    tɑ̃ pɛ tə

**Laissez- la s'apaiser    de    la    bonne tempête,**

Let      it   itself calm   after   the   good     storm,


e     kə    ʒə   dɔ      rmɑ̃   pø    pɥi skə

**Et     que je   dorme   un     peu   puisque**

And   let    me   sleep    a      little   since

vu     rə po ze

**vous   reposez.**

you    are resting.

# VI. "Spleen"
## (*Spleen*)

**Date of composition:** *1885–1888.*
**Source:** *Paul Verlaine,* Aquarelles. *In* Romances sans paroles.

The second of the *Aquarelles* reverts to the familiar themes of "Il pleure dans mon coeur" and "L'Ombre des arbres," although expressed in an unusual arrangement. In couplets that alternate description and introspection, Verlaine writes about despairing love and the fear of abandonment. Specific interpretations have been ascribed to the poem—in vain: The poet could be referring to either his wife or Rimbaud. Since every part of the poem remains hermetic, images and setting alike, interpretation becomes questionable and unnecessary.

Spleen is the unjustified mood of uneasiness and lassitude that overcomes the poet facing a muted and hostile nature. Neither the soft visions around him nor even his dear companion, who is the very source of his happiness, can be sympathetic to the poet's anguish. All relationship becomes temporary, and the slightest incident brings about alarm. Therefore spleen is the anxious state of a lucid but powerless heart, which is the willing and also unwilling victim of his own insecurity.

As always in Verlaine's poetry, the intensity of feelings is contained within a successfully controlled form. Repetitions of words and sounds create familiar patterns, static in the descriptive verse and dynamic in the introspective. Verlaine's mastery of his poetic material brings a fine tension to the sentiment expressed.

Debussy's setting of "Spleen" is centered around the theme of melancholy, which not only opens and ends the song but is repeated several times throughout. In the last two couplets, the theme of anxiety appears and rises, intensified by a faster tempo as the melody picks up to a B flat. The general impression is of monotony and infinite lassitude. Once again Debussy has accurately interpreted and clearly detailed Verlaine's feeling of despair.

spli n
# Spleen
Spleen

| lɛ | ro zə | ze tɛ | tu tə | ru ʒə |
|----|-------|-------|-------|-------|
| **Les** | **roses** | **étaient** | **toutes** | **rouges,** |
| The | roses | were | all | red, |

| e | lɛ | lj ɛ rə | ze tɛ | tu | nwa r |
|---|----|---------|-------|----|----|
| **Et** | **les** | **lierres** | **étaient** | **tout** | **noirs.** |
| And | the | ivy | was | all | black. |

| ʃɛ rə | pu | rpø | kə | ty | tə | bu ʒə |
|-------|-----|-----|-----|----|----|-------|
| **Chère** | **pour** | **peu** | **que** | **tu** | **te** | **bouges,** |
| Dear | for | little | that | you | yourself | move, |

| rə ne sə | tu | mɛ | de zɛ spwa r |
|----------|-----|-----|-------------|
| **Renaissent** | **tous** | **mes** | **désespoirs** |
| Return | all | my | despairs |

| lə | sjɛ | le tɛ | tro | blø | tro | tã drə |
|----|-----|-------|-----|-----|-----|--------|
| **Le** | **ciel** | **était** | **trop** | **bleu,** | **trop** | **tendre** |
| The | sky | was | too | blue, | too | tender |

| la | mɛ | rtro | vɛ | rte | lɛ | rtro | du |
|----|-----|------|-----|-----|-----|------|-----|
| **La** | **mer** | **trop** | **verte** | **et** | **l'air** | **trop** | **doux** |
| The | sea | too | green | and | the air | too | mild |

| ʒə | krɛ̃ | tu ʒu r | sə | kɛ | da tã drə |
|----|------|---------|-----|-----|-----------|
| **Je** | **crains** | **toujours** | **ce** | **qu'est** | **d'attendre** |
| I | fear | always | what | it is | to wait |

Les roses étaient toutes rouges,
Et les lierres étaient tout noirs.

Chère pour peu que tu te bouges,
Renaissent tous mes désespoirs.

Le ciel était trop bleu, trop tendre
La mer trop verte et l'air trop
doux

Je crains toujours ce qu'est
d'attendre
Quelque fuite atroce de vous

Du houx à la feuille vernie
Et du luisant buis je suis las,

Et de la campagne infinie
Et de tout, fors de vous, Hélas!

(*Claude Debussy Songs 1880–
1904.* New York: Dover, 1981)

——————— • ———————

The roses were all red
And the ivy was all black.

Dear, at your slightest move
My despair comes back.

The sky was too blue, too tender,
The sea too green and the air too
mild.

kɛlkə      fɥi      ta trɔ sə      də vu
**Quelque fuite atroce      de vous**
Some       flight   atrocious of  yours

I fear always,—ah, to wait and
wonder!
Some atrocious flight of yours.

dy      u      a      la   fœ jə      vɛ rni
**Du      houx   à      la   feuille   vernie**
Of the  holly  with the  leaf        lustrous

Of the holly with its lustrous leaf
And of the shiny boxwood I am
weary,

e      dy      lɥi zɑ̃      bɥi      ʒə sɥi la
**Et      du      luisant buis      je suis las,**
And of the shiny      boxwood I  am  weary,

And of the immense countryside,
And of everything, save you,
alas!

e      də la  kɑ̃ pa      ɲɛ̃ fi ni ə
**Et      de la  campagne infinie**
And of  the countryside infinite

e      də tu      fɔ   rdə vu      e lɑs
**Et      de tout,      fors de vous, Hélas!**
And of  everything, save of  you,    alas!

# —"Cinq Poèmes de Charles—— Baudelaire"
## *(Five Poems by Charles Baudelaire)*

**Date of composition:** *1887–1889.*
**Date of publication:** *1890.*
**Publisher:** *Librairie de l'Art Indépendant, Paris.*
**Dedicated to Etienne Dupin.**

   I.   "**Le Balcon**" (**The Balcony**)
  II.   "**Harmonie du soir**" (**Evening Harmony**)
 III.   "**Le Jet d'eau**" (**The Fountain**)
 IV.   "**Recueillement**" (**Meditation**)
  V.   "**La Mort des Amants**" (**The Death of Lovers**)

The series of Baudelaire songs marks an important turning point in Debussy's musical career. In 1888 and 1889 Debussy traveled twice to Bayreuth, invited by Etienne Dupin, a wealthy banker and music amateur. Debussy returned an enthusiastic Wagnerite from the first trip, a disillusioned one from the second. In the meantime he was composing his *Cinq Poèmes de Charles Baudelaire.* The sixteen months or so that separated the composition of the first song from the last showed both a departure from a strong Wagnerian influence and an attempt at creating a personal style. The poems and their settings were too audacious in content and form, however, to please an average audience, and the vocal range of the melodies was too intimidating for average singers. No publisher would take the risk. Therefore Debussy asked his friend Bailly, owner of the Librairie de l'Art Indépendant, whether he would consider publishing them. After some hesitation, Bailly agreed to publish the *Poèmes*, but in a limited, deluxe edition of 160 copies. Unfortunately they did not sell well, and the composer Chausson and Etienne Dupin secretly bought the unsold copies.

# I. "Le Balcon"

**Date of composition:** *January 1888.*
**Source:** *Charles Baudelaire,* **Les Fleurs du Mal, Spleen et Idéal,**
  *XXXVI, 1857.*

"Le Balcon" was inspired by precise circumstances and the
memory of Jeanne Duval, Baudelaire's mistress of many years.
The poem was written after the second breaking off of their
relationship. Jeanne was for the poet the epitome of carnal love,
both splendor and disgrace. Now that Jeanne had left him, the
poet could not bear her absence and remembered their happy
evenings by their apartment balcony. Sunset was for Baudelaire
a very sensitive moment: His solitude became all the more acute
as he had no one present with whom to share the glorious beauty
of the hour.

The poem alternates between ecstatic invocations and rich
memories. In the first strophe, Jeanne is hailed as the cherished
path to recollection, the beloved instrument of the poet's remembrance of past happiness. The next three strophes recreate
the evenings by the fire and the balcony with illuminating
nostalgia and show the poet's sensuous impregnation with every
charm of his mistress. Lovely is the sunset, deep the space,
strong life's pulsing flood, and sweet but poisonous the
woman's breath. The balcony is the link between nature and the
senses, the transition that allows the peaceful union of body and
soul. Time seems to have stopped and the everyday world to
have disappeared, as night closes in around the lovers.

The ecstasy, however, ends in the fifth strophe when the poet
regains his hold on reality: He insists on his poetic power to
evoke the past; then, in the last strophe, he wonders whether the
past can be relived at all, since the most tender intimacy of body
and mind is also poisoned. The haunting question that dooms
the exquisite moments of love to be only nostalgic vestiges
remains without answer. The last line puts aside any thought of
destruction and reaffirms the infinite beauty of human love.
Baudelaire's recollections are suffused with an intensity of feelings and sensations and a vividness of coloration. The leitmotiv
effect of the repetends confirms the incantatory power of the
memory.

Debussy's setting of "Le Balcon" has been called the most Wagnerian of the five songs because of the sumptuous, almost orchestral harmonies of the piano accompaniment. It is a monument in the vocal genre, dramatic, vibrant, superbly sensuous and passionate, rich in contrasted emotions ranging from eloquence to tenderness. The lyrical evocation is expressed in long melodic lines that respect the refrain structure and the successive moods of the poem.

## lə ba lkɔ̃
# Le Balcon
## The Balcony

mɛ rə    dɛ    su və ni r    mɛ trɛ sə    dɛ
**Mère    des   souvenirs,   maîtresse   des**
Mother  of    memories,    mistress     of
mɛ trɛ sə
**maîtresses,**
mistresses,

o  twa  tu    mɛ    ple zi r    o  twa  tu    mɛ
**O toi,  tous  mes   plaisirs!   O toi,  tous  mes**
O you,  all   my    pleasures!  O you,  all   my
də vwa r
**devoirs!**
duties!

ty    tə       ra pɛ lə ra    la   bo te    dɛ
**Tu    te       rappelleras   la   beauté  des**
You   yourself  will recall    the  beauty  of
ka rɛ sə
**caresses,**
caresses,

Mère des souvenirs, maîtresse des maîtresses,
O toi, tous mes plaisirs! ô toi, tous mes devoirs!
Tu te rappelleras la beauté des caresses,
La douceur du foyer et le charme des soirs,
Mère des souvenirs, maîtresse des maîtresses!

Les soirs illuminés par l'ardeur du charbon,
Et les soirs au balcon, voilés de vapeur rose.
Que ton sein m'était doux! que ton coeur m'était bon!
Nous avons dit souvent d'impérissables choses,
Les soirs illuminés par l'ardeur du charbon.

la      du sœ    rdy    fwaje   e    lə    ʃarmə
**La     douceur  du     foyer   et   le    charme**
The     sweetness of the hearth  and  the   charm

dɛ      swa r
**des     soirs,**
of the   evenings,

mɛ rə    də   su və ni r    mɛ trɛ sə   də
**Mère    des  souvenirs,    maîtresse  des**
Mother   of   memories,     mistress   of

mɛ trɛ sə
**maîtresses!**
mistresses!

lɛ      swa      rzi ly mi ne   pa   rla rdœ   rdy
**Les     soirs    illuminés      par  l'ardeur  du**
The     evenings illumined      by   the glow  of the

ʃa rbõ
**charbon,**
coals,

e     lɛ    swa    rzo    ba lkõ   vwa le   də
**Et    les   soirs  au     balcon,  voilés   de**
And   the   evenings on the balcony, veiled   by

va pœ   ro zə
**vapeur  rose.**
mists   pink.

kə     tõ    sɛ̃    me tɛ     du    kə    tõ
**Que    ton   sein  m'était   doux! que   ton**
How    your  breast to me was soft!  how   your

kœ    rme tɛ    bõ
**coeur m'était   bon!**
heart to me was  good!

Que les soleils sont beaux par les chaudes soirées!
Que l'espace est profond! que le coeur est puissant!
En me penchant vers toi reine des adorées,
Je croyais respirer le parfum de ton sang
Que les soleils sont beaux par les chaudes soirées!

La nuit s'épaississait ainsi qu'une cloison,
Et mes yeux dans le noir devinaient tes prunelles,
Et je buvais ton souffle, ô douceur, ô poison!
Et tes pieds s'endormaient dans mes mains fraternelles.
La nuit s'épaississait ainsi qu'une cloison.

Je sais l'art d'évoquer les minutes heureuses,
Et revis mon passé blotti dans tes genoux.
Car à quoi bon chercher tes beautés langoureuses
Ailleurs qu'en ton cher corps et qu'en ton coeur si doux?
Je sais l'art d'évoquer les minutes heureuses!

Ces serments, ces parfums, ces baisers infinis,
Renaîtront-ils d'un gouffre interdit à nos sondes,
Comme montent au ciel les soleils rajeunis
Après s'être lavés au fond des mers profondes?
Ô serments! ô parfums! ô baisers infinis!

(*Forty-three Songs for Voice and Piano.* New York: International, 1961)

nu    za vɔ̃   di    su vɑ̃    dɛ̃ pe ri sa blə
**Nous avons dit   souvent d'impérissables**
We    have    said   often    imperishable
ʃo zə
**choses,**
things,

lɛ    swa     rzi ly mi ne pa  rla rdœ   rdy
**Les soirs    illuminés par l'ardeur du**
The  evenings illumined  by   the glow  of the
ʃa rbɔ̃
**charbon.**
coals.

kə   lɛ   sɔ lɛ   jsɔ̃   bo      pa  rlɛ
**Que les soleils sont beaux    par les**
How the suns   are   beautiful  in   the
ʃo də    swa re
**chaudes soirées!**
warm    evenings!

kə    lɛ spɑ   sɛ   prɔ fɔ̃   kə   lə   kœ
**Que l'espace est profond! que le   coeur**
How the space is    deep!   how the heart
rɛ  pɥi sɑ̃
**est puissant!**
is   strong!

ɑ̃   mə    pɑ̃ ʃɑ̃   vɛ    rtwa rɛ nə  de
**En me    penchant vers   toi  reine des**
In  myself bending  toward you  queen of the
za dɔ re ə
**adorées,**
adored,

Mother of memories, mistress of mistresses,
O you, all my pleasures! O you, all my duties!
You will recall the beauty of caresses,
The sweetness of the hearth and the charm of the evenings,
Mother of memories, mistress of mistresses!

Evenings illumined by the glowing coals,
And evenings on the balcony, veiled in pink mists.
How soft was your breast, how good was your heart!
We have often said imperishable things,
On evenings illumined by the glowing coals.

How beautiful suns are in the warm evenings!
How deep is space! how strong is the heart!
Leaning toward you, most beloved among the beloved,
I thought I breathed in the perfume of your blood.
How beautiful suns are in the warm evenings!

ʒə krwajɛ rɛspire  lə  parfœ̃  də tɔ̃
**Je croyais respirer  le  parfum  de ton**
I  thought  to breathe  the  perfume  of  your
sɑ̃
**sang**
blood

The night thickened like a wall,
And my eyes in the dark divined
your pupils,
And I drank in your breath, O
sweetness, O poison!
And your feet lay asleep in my
fraternal hands.
The night thickened like a wall.

kə  lɛ  sɔlɛ  jsɔ̃  bo      pa  rlɛ
**Que les soleils sont beaux    par les**
How the suns  are  beautiful  in  the
ʃodə    swareə
**chaudes soirées!**
warm    evenings!

I know the art of evoking happy
moments,
And relive my past snuggled in
your lap.
For what's the good of seeking
your languid beauties
Elsewhere than in your own
beloved body and gentle heart?

la  nɥi  sepesisɛ    tɛ̃si  kynə  klwazɔ̃
**La  nuit  s'épaississait ainsi qu'une cloison,**
The night thickened    like  a      partition,

e   mɛ  zjø  dɑ̃  lə  nwa rdə vinɛ  tɛ
**Et  mes yeux dans le  noir devinait tes**
And my  eyes  in  the dark divined  your
pryne lə
**prunelles,**
pupils,

These vows, these perfumes,
these endless kisses,
Will they be reborn from a gulf
we cannot sound,
As the strengthened suns rise to
the sky
After being cleansed in the
bottom of the deep seas?
—O vows! O perfumes! O
endless kisses!

e   ʒə by vɛ  tɔ̃  su flə    o  du sœ r
**Et  je buvais ton  souffle, ô  douceur,**
And I  drank  your  breath,  O  sweetness,
o  pwa zɔ̃
**ô  poison!**
O  poison!

e    tɛ    pje    sɑ̃ dɔ rmɛ         dɑ̃    mɛ
**Et    tes    pieds    s'endormaient    dans mes**
And  your  feet    were falling asleep in    my
mɛ̃        fra tɛ rnɛ lə
**mains    fraternelles.**
hands    fraternal.


la    nɥi    se pe si sɛ        tɛ̃ si    ky nə    klwa zɔ̃
**La    nuit    s'épaississait ainsi    qu'une    cloison.**
The night thickened        like    a        partition.


ʒə    sɛ    la        rde vɔ ke    lɛ    mi ny tə
**Je    sais    l'art    d'évoquer    les    minutes**
I    know  the art  of evoking  the  minutes
zø rø zə
**heureuses,**
happy,


e    rə vi    mɔ̃    pɑ se    blɔ ti        dɑ̃    tɛ
**Et    revis    mon    passé    blotti        dans    tes**
And  relive  my    past    snuggled  in    your
ʒə nu
**genoux.**
lap.


ka    ra    kwa    bɔ̃    ʃɛ rʃe        tɛ    bo te
**Car    à    quoi    bon    chercher    tes    beautés**
For    to    what    good    seek        your  beauties
lɑ̃ gu rø zə
**langoureuses**
languid

a jœ        rkɑ̃     tɔ̃    ʃɛ     rkɔ r    e     kɑ̃
**Ailleurs   qu'en   ton   cher   corps   et    qu'en**
Elsewhere than in  your   dear   body   and than in

tɔ̃    kœ     rsi du
**ton   coeur si   doux?**
your   heart  so   gentle?

ʒə   sɛ      la       rde vɔ ke    le    mi ny tə
**Je   sais    l'art    d'évoquer  les   minutes**
I    know   the art  of evoking  the   minutes

zø rø zə
**heureuses!**
happy!

sɛ      sɛ rmɑ̃      sɛ      pa rfœ̃     sɛ      be ze
**Ces     serments, ces     parfums, ces     baisers**
These   vows,       these   perfumes, these   kisses

zɛ̃ fi ni
**infinis,**
endless,

rə nɛ trɔ̃    ti     ld œ̃     gu       frɛ̃ tɛ rdi   ta
**Renaîtront-ils    d'un    gouffre  interdit   à**
Will be reborn they from a   gulf        forbidden  to

no    sɔ̃ də
**nos   sondes,**
our   leads,

kɔ mə      mɔ̃ tə      to       sjɛ l   lɛ    sɔ le
**Comme    montent   au       ciel   les   soleils**
As          rise        to the  sky    the   suns

jra ʒœ ni
**rajeunis**
reinvigorated

a prɛ   sɛ trə   la ve   o   fɔ̃   dɛ
**Après s'être lavés au fond des**
After   being   washed   in the   bottom   of the
mɛ   rprɔ fɔ̃ də
**mers profondes?**
seas   deep?

o   sɛ rmã   o   pa rfœ̃   o   be ze   zɛ̃ fi ni
**—O serments! ô parfums! ô baisers infinis!**
—O   vows!   O perfumes!   O kisses   endless!

# II. "Harmonie du soir"

**Date of composition:** *January 1889.*
**Source:** *Charles Baudelaire,* **Les Fleurs du Mal, Spleen et Idéal,**
   *XLVIII. Poem first published in* **Revue Française,** *20 April*
   *1857.*

This poem was inspired by Madame Sabatier, Baudelaire's
guardian angel, muse, and madonna, whom he endowed with
every supraterrestrial charm and virtue. It was composed in the
metrical form of a *pantoum*, a Malayan verse pattern also used
by Hugo and Gautier, in which the second and fourth lines of
each stanza are repeated as the first and third of the following.
Baudelaire used this subtle and precious genre for its incantatory
effects: "Harmonie du soir" is truly a suggestive, evocative,
bewitching poem; yet, far from being a mere juxtaposition of
sensations, it is carefully composed and leads step by step to a
final mystic ecstasy. Like "Le Balcon," it is a poem of remembrance, a way of exorcising the end of love through a magical
recreation of the past.

In order to reach the beautiful memory of the beloved, the
poet borrows from the various sensory modes and their associations: The fragrance of the flowers interplays with the quivering
sound of the violin in a vertiginous and melancholy waltz of
sounds and scents, against the sad backdrop of a beautiful sunset.
The melancholy dance of perfumes, sounds, and colors lulls the
grief of the lover's tender heart, dispels fears of abysmal forget-
fulness, and induces contemplation of the remembrance. The
experience is enhanced by the reference to religious objects—
censer, altar, and ostensory or monstrance—which transforms
the incantatory sortilege into a mystical trance. As the Host, a
symbol of Christ, is offered to public adoration during Holy
Week in a monstrance placed on a temporary altar, so is the
beloved's image to the poet's adoration, like an eternal source of
life and love.

Debussy composed his setting of "Harmonie du soir" in the
same year that he visited the Oriental pavilions of the Paris
World Exhibition. The melody is built on an upward progression that parallels Baudelaire's poem. The *pantoum* repetitions

of lines are transcribed in the vocal part on a chromatic scale recalling Wagnerian harmonies.

a rmɔ ni  dy  swa r
# Harmonie du soir
## Harmony of the evening

| | | | | | | |
|---|---|---|---|---|---|---|
| vwa si | vɘ ni | rlɛ | tɑ̃ | u | vi brɑ̃ | sy |
| **Voici** | **venir** | **les** | **temps** | **où** | **vibrant** | **sur** |
| Here | come | the | times | when | trembling | on |

rsa  ti ʒɘ
**sa tige**
its stem

| | | | | |
|---|---|---|---|---|
| ʃa kɘ | flœ | rse va pɔ | rɛ̃ si | kɶ̃ |
| **Chaque** | **fleur** | **s'évapore** | **ainsi** | **qu'un** |
| Each | flower | exhales | like | a |

nɑ̃ sɑ̃ swa r
**encensoir;**
censer;

| | | | | | | |
|---|---|---|---|---|---|---|
| lɛ | sɔ̃ | ze | lɛ | pa rfɶ̃ | tu rnɘ | dɑ̃ |
| **Les** | **sons** | **et** | **les** | **parfums** | **tournent** | **dans** |
| The | sounds | and | the | perfumes | turn | in |

| | | |
|---|---|---|
| lɛ | rdy | swa r |
| **l'air** | **du** | **soir;** |
| the air | of the | evening; |

| | | | | | |
|---|---|---|---|---|---|
| va lsɘ | me lɑ̃ kɔ li | ke | lɑ̃ gu rø | vɛ rti ʒɘ |
| **Valse** | **mélancolique** | **et** | **langoureux** | **vertige!** |
| Waltz | melancholy | and | languorous | giddiness! |

Voici venir les temps où vibrant
sur sa tige
Chaque fleur s'évapore ainsi
qu'un encensoir;
Les sons et les parfums tournent
dans l'air du soir;
Valse mélancolique et
langoureux vertige!

Chaque fleur s'évapore ainsi
qu'un encensoir;
Le violon frémit comme un coeur
qu'on afflige;
Valse mélancolique et
langoureux vertige!
Le ciel est triste et beau comme un
grand reposoir.

Le violon frémit comme un coeur
qu'on afflige;
Un coeur tendre, qui hait le néant
vaste et noir!
Le ciel est triste et beau comme un
grand reposoir;
Le soleil s'est noyé dans son sang
qui se fige. . .

ʃa kə    flœ     rse va pɔ    rɛ̃ si    kœ̃
**Chaque fleur  s'évapore  ainsi  qu'un**
Each     flower  exhales    like   a
nɑ̃ sɑ̃ swa r
**encensoir;**
censer;

lə    vi jɔ lɔ̃  fre mi    kɔ      mœ̃ kœ
**Le   violon frémit  comme  un     coeur**
The   violin  quivers   as     a      heart
rkɔ̃        na fli ʒə
**qu'on    afflige;**
that one   afflicts;

va lsə  me lɑ̃ kɔ li     ke    lɑ̃ gu rø
**Valse  mélancolique et   langoureux**
Waltz  melancholy       and languorous
vɛ rti ʒə
**vertige!**
giddiness!

lə    sjɛ    lɛ   tri    ste  bo      kɔ
**Le   ciel  est  triste et   beau    comme**
The   sky   is   sad    and beautiful as
mœ̃    grɑ̃    rə po zwa r
**un   grand reposoir.**
a     large   temporary altar.

lə    vi jɔ lɔ̃  fre mi   kɔ      mœ̃ kœ
**Le   violon frémit comme  un     coeur**
The   violin  quivers as    a       heart
rkɔ̃        na fli ʒə
**qu'on    afflige,**
that one   afflicts,

Un coeur tendre, qui hait le néant vaste et noir,
Du passé lumineux recueille tout vestige!
Le soleil s'est noyé dans son sang qui se fige. . .
Ton souvenir en moi luit comme un ostensoir!

(*Forty-three Songs for Voice and Piano*. New York: International, 1961)

————————●————————

Now comes the time when, trembling on its stem,
Each flower exhales like a censer;
The sounds and perfumes turn in the evening air;
A melancholy waltz and languorous giddiness.

Each flower exhales like a censer;
The violin quivers like an afflicted heart;
A melancholy waltz and languorous giddiness!
The sky is sad and beautiful as a great altar.

The violin quivers like an afflicted heart,
A tender heart which abhors the vast and dark void!
The sky is sad and beautiful as a great altar;
The sun has drowned in its own congealing blood.

œ̃   kœ   rtɑ̃ drə ki   ɛ   lə  ne ɑ̃
**Un coeur tendre qui   hait   le  néant**
A   heart  tender which abhors the void
va   ste  nwa r
**vaste  et   noir!**
vast  and  black!

A tender heart which abhors the vast and dark void, Gathers every vestige of the luminous past! The sun has drowned in its own congealing blood. . . Your memory shines in me like an ostensory!

lə   sjɛ  lɛ  tri   ste bo   kɔ   mœ̃
**Le   ciel est triste et   beau   comme un**
The  sky is  sad  and beautiful as   a
grɑ̃   rə po zwa r
**grand reposoir;**
large  temporary altar;

lə   sɔlɛ  jsɛ  nwa je  dɑ̃  sɔ̃  sɑ̃  ki
**Le   soleil s'est noyé   dans son sang qui**
The  sun   has drowned in   its blood that
sə   fi ʒə
**se   fige.**
itself congeals.

œ̃   kœ   rtɑ̃ drə ki   ɛ   lə  ne ɑ̃
**Un coeur tendre qui   hait   le  néant**
A   heart  tender which abhors the void
va   ste
nwa r
**vasteet**
**noir,**
vast and
black,

dy       pɑ se   ly mi nø     rə kœ jə    tu
**Du        passé  lumineux  recueille  tout**
Of the   past    luminous   gathers    every
vɛ sti ʒə
**vestige!**
vestige!


lə     sɔ lɛ    jsɛ    nwa je     dɑ̃    sɔ̃   sɑ̃
**Le     soleil   s'est   noyé      dans  son  sang**
The    sun      has     drowned  in     its   blood
ki     sə       fi ʒə
**qui    se       fige. . .**
that   itself   congeals. . .


tɔ̃      su və ni      rɑ̃   mwa lɥi     kɔ
**Ton     souvenir     en   moi  luit      comme**
Your    remembrance  in    me    shines   like
mœ̃     nɔ stɑ̃ swa r
**un     ostensoir!**
an     ostensory!

# III.  "Le Jet d'eau"
## (The Fountain)

**Date of composition:** *March 1889.*
**Source:** *Charles Baudelaire,* **Les Fleurs du Mal, Les Epaves, Galanteries** *IX; poem first published in* **La Petite Revue,** *July 8, 1865.*

The inspiration of this erotic poem contrasts with the general mood of Baudelaire's poetry in that it is absolutely free of any idea or thought of sin and guilt. It is about the rise and fall of desire, and it comments on the pleasures that desire brings and the feeling of sadness that follows its gratification.

The scene takes place on a moonlit night, in the lovers' bedroom; outside, in a courtyard sheltered by trees, a fountain babbles. Differences and analogies are established at the beginning of the poem: The pleasures of love leave the woman weary and the man in voluptuous ecstasy. Their opposite reactions and feelings are reflected in the contrasted rise and fall of the water in the fountain. Then, in the second verse, sensuous desire recaptures the woman; it rises and merges into the visual image of the water that dashes into the air and immediately dies down in sadness. The last verse sums up the poet's meditation on the act of love: The rich and mature satisfaction that embraces the world around has a melancholy that reflects the poet's own melancholy. The alternating structure of stanzas and refrains, unusual in Baudelaire's poetry, provides a penetrating musicality through a choice of contrasted vocalic sounds.

Debussy used the initial version of the poem as published in *La Petite Revue*, with a variant in the refrain[35a] that suppresses the vocalic contrasts of the final version. The amorous mood of the song calls for a very fine and sustained legato. The composer here casts off the Wagnerian influence and expresses the crescendos and diminuendos of passion with great sensitivity. The seconds in the accompaniment are used to convey the sensuous babbling of the water. Stanzas and refrains are set in two distinctive ways, the vocal line being more forceful in the refrain.

## lə ʒɛ do
# Le Jet d'eau
## The Fountain

| tɛ | bo | zjø | sɔ̃ | lɑ | po |
|---|---|---|---|---|---|
| **Tes** | **beaux** | **yeux** | **sont** | **las,** | **pauvre** |
| Your | beautiful | eyes | are | weary, | poor |

| vra mɑ̃ tə | |
|---|---|
| **amante!** | |
| beloved! | |

| rɛ stə | lɔ̃ tɑ̃ | sɑ̃ | lɛ | ru vri r |
|---|---|---|---|---|
| **Reste** | **longtemps** | **sans** | **les** | **rouvrir,** |
| Stay | a long time | without | them | opening again, |

| dɑ̃ | sɛ tə | po zə | nɔ̃ ʃa lɑ̃ tə |
|---|---|---|---|
| **Dans** | **cette** | **pose** | **nonchalante** |
| In | this | pose | languid |

| u | ta | sy rpri zə | lə | ple zi r |
|---|---|---|---|---|
| **Où** | **t'a** | **surprise** | **le** | **plaisir** |
| In which | you has | surprised | the | pleasure |

| dɑ̃ | la | ku | rlə ʒɛ do | ki |
|---|---|---|---|---|
| **Dans** | **la** | **cour** | **le jet d'eau** | **qui** |
| In | the | courtyard | the fountain | which |

| ʒɑ zə |
|---|
| **jase** |
| babbles |

| e | nə | sə tɛ | ni | nɥi | ni | ʒu r |
|---|---|---|---|---|---|---|
| **Et** | **ne** | **se tait** | **ni** | **nuit** | **ni** | **jour,** |
| And | not | falls silent | either | night | or | day, |

Tes beaux yeux sont las, pauvre
amante!
Reste longtemps sans les rouvrir,
Dans cette pose nonchalante
Où t'a surprise le plaisir
Dans la cour le jet d'eau qui jase
Et ne se tait ni nuit ni jour,
Entretient doucement l'extase
Où ce soir m'a plongé l'amour.

La gerbe d'eau qui berce
    Ses mille fleurs,
Que la lune traverse
    De ses pâleurs,
Tombe comme une averse
    De larges pleurs.

Ainsi ton âme qu'incendie
L'éclair brûlant des voluptés
S'élance, rapide et hardie,
Vers les vastes cieux enchantés.
Puis, elle s'épanche, mourante,
En un flot de triste langueur,
Qui par une invisible pente
Descend jusqu'au fond de mon
coeur.

La gerbe d'eau qui berce
    Ses mille fleurs,
Que la lune traverse
    De ses pâleurs,
Tombe comme une averse
    De larges pleurs.

ã trə tjẽ    du sə mã    lε ksta zə
**Entretient doucement l'extase**
Prolongs    softly      the ecstasy

u      sə    swa    rma    plõ ʒe
**Où    ce    soir    m'a    plongé**
In which this  evening me has plunged
la mu r
**l'amour.**
the love.

la    ʒε rbə do      ki    bε rsə
**La    gerbe d'eau    qui    berce**
The    sheaf  of water that  sways

sε    mi lə    flœ r
**Ses    mille    fleurs,**
Its    thousand flowers,

kə    la    ly nə    tra vε rsə
**Que    la    lune    traverse**
Which  the  moon    penetrates

də    sε    pɑ lœ r
**De    ses    pâleurs,**
With  its    pallors,

tõ bə    kɔ    my    na vε rsə
**Tombe comme une averse**
Falls    like    a    shower

də    la rʒə    plœ r
**De    larges    pleurs.**
Of    large    tears.

O toi, que la nuit rend si belle,
Qu'il m'est doux, penché vers tes seins,
D'écouter la plainte éternelle
Qui sanglote dans les bassins!
Lune, eau sonore, nuit bénie,
Arbres qui frissonnez autour,
Votre pure mélancolie
Est le miroir de mon amour.

La gerbe d'eau qui berce
Ses mille fleurs,
Que la lune traverse
De ses pâleurs,
Tombe comme une averse
De larges pleurs.

(*Forty-three Songs for Voice and Piano.* New York: International, 1961)

———————— • ————————

Your beautiful eyes are weary, poor beloved!
Stay a long time without opening them,
In this languid pose
Where pleasure surprised you.
In the courtyard the babbling fountain
That does not keep silent night or day,
Softly prolongs the ecstasy
Into which love plunged me this evening.

The sheaf of water swaying
Its thousand flowers,
Which the moon penetrates
With its pale rays,
Falls like a shower
Of huge tears.

ɛ̃ si    tɔ̃     na mə  kɛ̃ sɑ̃ di ə
**Ainsi ton   âme    qu'incendie**
Thus   your  soul    that is set ablaze by

le klɛ     rbry lɑ̃   dɛ    vɔ ly pte
**L'éclair   brûlant des voluptés**
The flash  burning  of    sensual delights

se lɑ̃ sə    ra pi   de  a rdi ə
**S'élance, rapide et    hardie,**
Springs,   swift   and  daring,

vɛ     rlɛ  va stə  sjø    zɑ̃ ʃɑ̃ te
**Vers    les vastes cieux enchantés.**
Toward the vast    skies   enchanted.

pɥi    zɛ lə  se pɑ̃ ʃə    mu rɑ̃ tə
**Puis, elle  s'épanche, mourante,**
Then,   it    expands,   dying,

ɑ̃   nœ̃ flo   də tri stə  lɑ̃ gœ r
**En un  flot  de triste langueur,**
In  a     wave  of  sad    languor,

ki     pa   ry   nɛ̃ vi zi blə   pɑ̃ tə
**Qui   par une invisible    pente**
Which by   an    invisible    slope

de sɑ̃    ʒy sko   fɔ̃    də mɔ̃   kœ r
**Descend jusqu'au fond   de mon coeur.**
Descends to the    depths of  my   heart.

la    ʒɛ rbə do    ki  bɛ rsə
**La   gerbe d'eau   qui berce**
The  sheaf  of water that sways

Thus your soul set ablaze
By the burning flash of sensuous delight
Springs, swift and daring,
Toward the vast enchanted skies.
Then, it expands, dying,
In a wave of sad languor,
Which by an invisible slope
Descends to the depths of my heart.

The sheaf of water swaying
   Its thousand flowers,
Which the moon penetrates
   With its pale rays,
Falls like a shower
   Of huge tears.

O you, whom night makes so beautiful,
How sweet I find, leaning toward your breasts,
To listen to the endless lament
That sobs in the fountains!
Moon, resonant water, blessed night,
Trees trembling all about,
Your pure melancholy
Is the mirror of my love.

The sheaf of water swaying
   Its thousand flowers,
Which the moon penetrates
   With its pale rays,
Falls like a shower
   Of huge tears.

sɛ mi lə  flœ r
**Ses mille  fleurs,**
Its thousand flowers,

kə  la  ly nə  tra vɛ rsə
**Que la lune traverse**
Which the moon penetrates

də sɛ pɑ lœ r
**De ses pâleurs,**
With its pallors,

tɔ̃ bə kɔ  my na vɛ rsə
**Tombe comme une averse**
Falls like a shower

də la rʒə plœ r
**De larges pleurs.**
Of large tears.

o twa kə  la nɥi rɑ̃  si bɛ lə
**O toi, que la nuit rend si belle,**
O you, whom the night makes so beautiful,

ki  lmɛ  du  pɑ̃ ʃe vɛ  rtɛ
**Qu'il m'est doux, penché vers tes**
How it me is sweet, leaning toward your
sɛ̃
**seins,**
breasts,

de ku te  la plɛ̃  te tɛ rnɛ lə
**D'écouter la plainte éternelle**
To listen to the lament endless

ki    sɑ̃ glɔ tə    dɑ̃    lɛ    ba sɛ̃
**Qui   sanglote   dans   les   bassins!**
That  sobs         in     the   fountains!

ly nə    o    sɔ nɔ rə    nɥi    be ni (ə)
**Lune,   eau   sonore,   nuit   bénie,**
Moon,   water  resonant,  night  blessed,

a rbrə    ki    fri sɔ ne    zo tu r
**Arbres   qui   frissonnez   autour,**
Trees    that   tremble      all about,

vɔ trə    py rə    me lɑ̃ kɔ li ə
**Votre    pure    mélancolie**
Your     pure     melancholy

ɛ    lə    mi rwa    rdə    mɔ̃    na mu r
**Est   le   miroir   de   mon   amour.**
Is    the   mirror   of    my    love.

la    ʒɛ rbə do    ki    bɛ rsə
**La    gerbe d'eau    qui   berce**
The   sheaf of water  that  sways

sɛ    mi lə    flœ r
**Ses   mille   fleurs,**
Its   thousand flowers,

kə    la    ly nə    tra vɛ rsə
**Que   la   lune   traverse**
Which  the  moon   penetrates

də    sɛ    pɑ lœ r
**De    ses   pâleurs,**
With   its   pallors,

tɔ̃ bə      kɔ        my   na vɛ rsə
**Tombe  comme  une  averse**
Falls     like      a     shower

              də   la rʒə    plœ r
              **De  larges  pleurs.**
              Of  large    tears.

# IV. "Recueillement"
## (Meditation)

**Date of composition: *1889*.**
**Source: *Charles Baudelaire*, Nouvelles Fleurs du Mal, *VII;*
  poem first published in Revue Européenne, *November 1,
  1861*.**

Baudelaire wrote "Recueillement" in the fall of 1861 after he left
Jeanne Duval. Following a stormy twenty-year relationship,
their parting was bitter. Baudelaire was then on the brink of
suicide, ill and penniless. He had never been so lonely and he
expressed this unbearable feeling in "Recueillement." One moment of the day, though, assuaged his overwrought sensitivity:
Dusk, which he had previously felt disquieting, now provided
some alleviation to his nerves.

Writing in a meditative mood, the poet addresses his Sorrow
as one would a restless child. His Sorrow had impatiently waited
for the Evening to come; now the Evening has come bringing
peace to the chosen few and worries to the miserable multitude.
The poet, therefore, takes his Sorrow by her hand so as to part
from the multitude's servile addiction to Pleasure. He invites
Her to contemplate a past grown dear and quaint for which he
feels no remorse, only calm Regret. When the Sun finally dis-
appears under an arch—perhaps the arch of a river bridge in the
city—the poet urges his Sorrow to listen to the slow majestic
steps of the long-awaited gentle Night that comes down to
soothe the poet's struggle.

"Recueillement" is an allegory with abstractions marked by
capital letters, expressing the conflict of the poet's Christian
conscience torn between good and evil. It is also one of the most
musical and harmonious of Baudelaire's poems: In sonnet form,
it has repeated effects of liquid and nasal sounds, particularly in
the two tercets. The composition of a sonnet calls for a double
movement: The two quatrains invite a meditation, away from
the evil crowd, while the two tercets invite a contemplation of a
smiling past and peaceful future. The turning point is the bold
enjambment of the ninth line that stresses the poet's urge to

break away from passions and announces his deep submission and ensuing rest.

This is perhaps the most beautiful of the five Baudelaire songs. The opening of Debussy's sombre and dramatic melody has an intense Wagnerian mood. Debussy, however, departs from the *Tristan* atmosphere toward the end of the piece, where a more personal touch appears in the simple progression of chords that, softly and suggestively, accompanies the vocal line. The slow and moving melody of the beginning quickens to a vindictive passion against the profligates in the turbulent city. Next it becomes softer and expressive to evoke visions of the past. Finally it welcomes the arrival of the Night, at first with solemnity, then with serenity.

## rə kœ jmã
# Recueillement
## Meditation

| | | | | | |
|---|---|---|---|---|---|
| swa | sa ʒ(ə) | o | ma | du lœ r | e |
| **Sois** | **sage,** | **ô** | **ma** | **Douleur,** | **et** |
| Be | good, | O | my | Sorrow, | and |

| | | |
|---|---|---|
| tjɛ̃ twa | ply | trã ki lə |
| **tiens-toi** | **plus** | **tranquille.** |
| keep yourself | more | still. |

| | | | | |
|---|---|---|---|---|
| ty | re kla mɛ | lə | swa r | i |
| **Tu** | **réclamais** | **le** | **Soir;** | **il** |
| You | were calling for the | | Evening; | it |

| |
|---|
| lde sã |
| **descend;** |
| is falling; |

| |
|---|
| lə vwa si |
| **le voici:** |
| it is here: |

Sois sage, ô ma Douleur, et tiens-toi plus tranquille.
Tu réclamais le Soir; il descend; le voici:
Une atmosphère obscure enveloppe la ville,
Aux uns portant la paix, aux autres le souci.

Pendant que des mortels la multitude vile,
Sous le fouet du Plaisir, ce bourreau sans merci,
Va cueillir des remords dans la fête servile,
Ma Douleur, donne-moi la main; viens par ici,

y    na tmɔ sfɛ    rɔ psky    rɑ̃ və lɔ pə    la
**Une atmosphère obscure enveloppe la**
An   atmosphere   obscure    envelops      the
vi lə
**ville,**
city,

o    zœ̃    pɔ rtɑ̃    la    pɛ    o    zo trə
**Aux uns   portant   la   paix,  aux  autres**
To   some   bringing   the  peace,  to   others
lə   su si
**le   souci.**
the  worry.

pɑ̃ dɑ̃    kə    de    mɔ rtɛ    la    my lti ty də
**Pendant que des mortels la   multitude**
While   of    the   mortals   the   multitude
vi lə
**vile,**
base,

su    lə    fwɛ    dy    ple zi r    sə
**Sous  le   fouet  du   Plaisir,   ce**
Under  the  whip   of   Pleasure,   this
bu ro    sɑ̃    mɛ rsi
**bourreau  sans    merci,**
tormentor  without  mercy,

va    kœ ji    rdɛ    rə mɔ    rdɑ̃    la
**Va   cueillir  des   remords  dans  la**
Goes  to gather  some  remorse  in    the
fɛ tə    sɛ rvi lə
**fête     servile,**
festival  servile,

Loin d'eux. Vois se pencher les
défuntes Années,
Sur les balcons du ciel, en robes
surannées;
Surgir du fond des eaux le Regret
souriant;

Le Soleil moribond s'endormir
sous une arche,
Et, comme un long linceul
traînant à l'Orient,
Entends, ma chère, entends la
douce Nuit qui marche.

(*Forty-three Songs for Voice
and Piano.* New York:
International, 1961)

————————•————————

Be good, O my Sorrow, and
keep more still,
You were calling for the
Evening; it is falling; here it is:
An obscure atmosphere envelops
the city,
Bringing peace to some, to others
worry.

While the base multitude of
mortals,
Under the whip of Pleasure, this
merciless tormentor,
Goes to gather remorse in the
servile festival,
My Sorrow, give me your hand;
come this way,

Far from them. See the dead
Years leaning
Over the balconies of heaven, in
outmoded dresses;
Smiling Regret rising from the
depths of the waters;

| ma | du lœr | dɔ nə | mwa | la | mɛ̃ | vjɛ̃ |
|---|---|---|---|---|---|---|
| **Ma** | **Douleur,** | **donne-moi** | **la** | **main;** | **viens** |
| My | Sorrow, | give | me | the | hand; | come |

| pa | ri si |
|---|---|
| **par** | **ici,** |
| this | way, |

The dying Sun going to sleep under an arch,
And, like a long shroud trailing toward the East,
Hear, my dear, hear the gentle Night progressing.

| lwɛ̃ | dø | | vwa | sə pã ʃe | lɛ |
|---|---|---|---|---|---|
| **Loin** | **d'eux.** | | **Vois** | **se pencher** | **les** |
| Far | from them. | See | leaning | | the |

| de fœ̃ tə | za ne ə |
|---|---|
| **défuntes** | **Années,** |
| dead | Years, |

| sy | rlɛ | ba lkɔ̃ | dy | sjɛ | lã | rɔ bə |
|---|---|---|---|---|---|---|
| **Sur** | **les** | **balcons** | **du** | **ciel,** | **en** | **robes** |
| Over | the | balconies | of the | sky, | in | dresses |

| sy ra ne (ə) |
|---|
| **surannées;** |
| outmoded; |

| sy rʒi | rdy | fɔ̃ | dɛ | zo | lə |
|---|---|---|---|---|---|
| **Surgir** | **du** | **fond** | **des** | **eaux** | **le** |
| Rising | from the | depths | of the | waters | the |

| rə grɛ | su rijã |
|---|---|
| **Regret** | **souriant;** |
| Regret | smiling; |

| lə | sɔ lɛ | jmɔ ri bɔ̃ | sã dɔ rmi | rsu | zy |
|---|---|---|---|---|---|
| **Le** | **Soleil** | **moribond** | **s'endormir** | **sous** | **une** |
| The | Sun | dying | going to sleep | under | an |

| na rʃə |
|---|
| **arche,** |
| arch, |

e     kɔ      mœ̃ lɔ̃    lɛ̃ sœ    ltrɛ nɑ̃   ta
**Et,   comme  un   long  linceul  traînant  à**
And,  like    a    long  shroud   trailing  to

lɔ rijɑ̃
**l'Orient,**
the East,

ɑ̃ tɑ̃       ma   ʃɛ rə   ɑ̃ tɑ̃     la   du sə
**Entends, ma  chère,  entends  la   douce**
Hear,      my   dear,   hear     the  gentle

nɥi    ki    ma rʃə
**Nuit   qui   marche.**
Night  which  is progressing.

# V. "La Mort des Amants"
## *(The Death of Lovers)*

**Date of composition:** *December 1887.*
**Source:** *Charles Baudelaire,* **Les Fleurs du Mal, La Mort** *CXXI;*
   *poem first published in* **Le Messager de l'Assemblée,** *9 April,*
   *1851.*

This sonnet is the first of three poems on Death from the last
section of the *Flowers of Evil.* The idea of Death is perceived by
Baudelaire in the tradition of the Spiritualistic Romanticism of
the 1830's, Death being not the end of life but its ultimate
achievement, the only gate to knowledge. To that purpose, the
poet envisions the details of the ceremony that will lead the
lovers into their mystical communion. The voluptuous decor
made up of Baudelaire's favorite props (deep couches, scented
beds, exotic blooms, torches and mirrors) prepares the lovers'
souls and hearts for their union in death. Then on an enchanting
night, one supreme look will pass between the lovers, laden
with an extended farewell to life. Parting will not be without
regret; but immortality, introduced by a joyful and familiar
Angel, will dispel fears. The flames of love will then be eternally
revived, the communion of souls and hearts being total. The
poem keeps the dual theme of Love and Death inseparable and
expresses Baudelaire's hopes for an extraordinary Rebirth after
Death.
   "La Mort des Amants" is the earliest of Debussy's settings of
Baudelaire. The three parts of the song richly depict the sensual
atmosphere of love, the apotheosis of passion and the hereafter,
on a full melodic line supported by a luxurious accompaniment.
The five–bar transition of the vocal line between the second and
third parts prepares for a sublimated evocation of the hereafter in
which terrestrial passion becomes spiritual love.

la mɔ rde za mɑ̃
# La Mort des Amants
## The Death of the Lovers

| nu | zɔ rɔ̃ | de | li | plɛ̃ | dɔ dœ |
|---|---|---|---|---|---|
| **Nous** | **aurons** | **des** | **lits** | **pleins** | **d'odeurs** |
| We | shall have | some | beds | filled | with scents |

rle ʒɛ rə
**légères,**
light,

| dɛ | di vɑ̃ | prɔ fɔ̃ | kɔ mə | dɛ |
|---|---|---|---|---|
| **Des** | **divans** | **profonds** | **comme** | **des** |
| Some | divans | deep | as | some |

tɔ̃ bo
**tombeaux,**
tombs,

| e | de trɑ̃ ʒə | flœ | rsy rdɛ | ze ta ʒɛ rə |
|---|---|---|---|---|
| **Et** | **d'étranges** | **fleurs** | **sur des** | **étagères,** |
| And | some strange | flowers | on some | shelves, |

| e klo zə | pu | rnu | su | dɛ | sjø | ply |
|---|---|---|---|---|---|---|
| **Ecloses** | **pour** | **nous** | **sous** | **des** | **cieux** | **plus** |
| Blooming | for | us | under | some | skies | more |

bo
**beaux.**
beautiful.

| y zɑ̃ | ta lɑ̃ vi | lœ | rʃa lœ | rdɛ rnjɛ rə |
|---|---|---|---|---|
| **Usant** | **à l'envi** | **leurs** | **chaleurs** | **dernières,** |
| Using up | emulously | their | ardors | last, |

Nous aurons des lits pleins
d'odeurs légères,
Des divans profonds comme des
tombeaux,
Et d'étranges fleurs sur des
étagères,
Ecloses pour nous sous des cieux
plus beaux.

Usant à l'envi leurs chaleurs
dernières,
Nos deux coeurs seront deux
vastes flambeaux,
Qui réfléchiront leurs doubles
lumières
Dans nos deux esprits, ces
miroirs jumeaux.

Un soir fait de rose et de bleu
mystique,
Nous échangerons un éclair
unique,
Comme un long sanglot, tout
chargé d'adieux;

Et plus tard un ange,
entr'ouvrant les portes,
Viendra ranimer, fidèle et
joyeux,
Les miroirs ternis et les flammes
mortes.

(*Forty-three Songs for Voice
and Piano.* New York:
International, 1961)

no   dø   kœ   rsə rɔ̃   dø   va stə
**Nos deux coeurs seront deux vastes**
Our  two  hearts  will be  two  huge
flɑ̃ bo
**flambeaux,**
torches,

ki   re fle ʃi rɔ̃   lœ   rdu blə   ly mjɛ rə
**Qui réfléchiront leurs doubles lumières**
That  will reflect  their  two  lights

dɑ̃   no   dø   zɛ spri   sɛ   mi rwa
**Dans nos deux esprits, ces miroirs**
In  our  two  spirits,  these  mirrors
rʒy mo
**jumeaux.**
twin.

œ̃   swa   rfɛ   də ro   ze   də blø
**Un soir fait de rose et de bleu**
One  evening  made  of  rose  and of  blue
mi sti kə
**mystique,**
mystic,

nu   ze ʃɑ̃ ʒə rɔ̃   œ̃   ne klɛ   ry ni kə
**Nous échangerons un éclair unique,**
We  shall exchange  a  flash of light  single,

kɔ   mœ̃ lɔ̃   sɑ̃ glo   tu   ʃa rʒe
**Comme un long sanglot, tout chargé**
Like  a  long  sob,  all  laden
da djø
**d'adieux;**
with farewells;

We shall have beds filled with light: scents,
Divans deep as tombs,
And, on shelves, strange flowers
That bloomed for us under fairer skies.

Vying with each other to consume their last ardors
Our two hearts will be two huge torches,
That will reflect their double light
In our two souls, these twin mirrors.

On an evening of rose and mystic blue,
We shall exchange a single flash of light,
Like a long sob laden with parting;

And later an Angel, half-opening the doors,
Will come, faithful and joyous, to revive
The tarnished mirrors and the dead flames.

e      ply    ta     rɑ̃    nɑ̃ ʒə   ɑ̃ tru vrɑ̃      lɛ
**Et     plus   tard   un    ange,  entr'ouvrant les**
And    more   late   an    Angel, half-opening  the

pɔ rtə
**portes,**
doors,


vjɛ̃ dra     ra ni me      fi dɛ    le     ʒwa jø
**Viendra    ranimer,     fidèle   et    joyeux,**
Will come  to reanimate, faithful  and  joyous,


lɛ     mi rwa    rtɛ rni    e     lɛ    flɑ mə
**Les    miroirs  ternis     et    les   flammes**
The    mirrors  tarnished  and   the   flames

mɔ rtə
**mortes.**
dead.

# -"La Belle au Bois dormant"——
## (The Sleeping Beauty)

**Date of composition:** *1882–1890.*
**Date of publication:** *1902.*
**Publisher:** *Société nouvelle d'Editions musicales, Paris.*
**Source:** *Vincent Hyspa.*

The classic seventeenth-century tale of the Sleeping Beauty remains inscribed in the memory of every Frenchman since childhood. Hyspa rewrote this popular story in the form of a ballad. The knightly lover, a moon-colored helmet on his sunlit hair, gallops through the woods at dusk toward the Sleeping Beauty. This dashing young man, though valiant and charming, has holes in his doublet and spurs his steed furiously, leaving traces of blood on his passage. The reader already suspects some dubious business. Truly the narrator's voice soon awakens the Beauty: This mysterious gallant lover has stolen her ring!

The story does not conclude or moralize: Did the knight actually steal the ring? Did he do it for a love keepsake? or out of greed? No one knows or will know. Each strophe ends in a two-line refrain which, with variants, enjoins the Beauty to sleep. The last refrain, however, provides a dramatic contrast when it begs the Beauty to wake up.

Léon Vallas noted that the song was written soon after Debussy returned to Paris from his Russian trip (1881), along with "Paysage sentimental" (Sentimental Landscape) and "Voici que le printemps" (Here Comes Spring). This may explain the association instantly made between Borodin and this song. There is, however, no Borodin connotation in the dominant theme of the Debussy piece, which is borrowed from the popular French round "Nous n'irons plus au bois" (We will no longer go to the woods). The song was very likely touched up some twelve years later, before being presented for publication in 1893. It was finally published only in 1902. Debussy's setting flows as easily and simply as Hyspa's ballad. Two alternating themes present the dynamic silhouette of the knight and the resting Beauty. The last bars take a dramatic turn when the story evolves to its brutal ending.

# la bɛ lo bwa dɔrmɑ̃
# La Belle au Bois dormant
## The Beauty in the Wood sleeping

| dɛ | tru | a | sɔ̃ | pu rpwɛ̃ | vɛ rmɛ j |
|----|-----|---|-----|----------|----------|
| **Des** | **trous** | **à** | **son** | **pourpoint** | **vermeil,** |
| Some | holes | in | his | doublet | vermilion, |

| ə | ʃə va lje | va | pa rla | bry nə |
|---|-----------|----|--------|--------|
| **Un** | **Chevalier** | **va** | **par la** | **brune,** |
| A | knight | goes | in the | dusk, |

| lɛ | ʃə vø | tu | plɛ̃ | də sɔ lɛ j |
|----|-------|----|------|------------|
| **Les** | **cheveux** | **tout** | **pleins** | **de soleil** |
| The | hair | all | full | of sun |

| su | zɶ̃ | ka skə | ku lɶ | rdə ly nə |
|----|-----|--------|-------|-----------|
| **Sous** | **un** | **casque** | **couleur** | **de lune** |
| Under | a | helmet | color | of moon |

| dɔ rme | tu ʒu r | dɔ rme | zo | bwa |
|--------|---------|--------|----|----|
| **Dormez** | **toujours,** | **dormez** | **au** | **bois,** |
| Sleep | on, | sleep | in the | wood, |

| la no | la | bɛl | a | vɔ trə | dwa |
|-------|----|----|---|--------|-----|
| **L'anneau** | **la** | **belle,** | **à** | **votre** | **doigt.** |
| The ring, | the | Beauty, | on | your | finger. |

| dɑ̃ | la | pu sje rə | de | ba ta jə |
|-----|----|-----------|----|----|
| **Dans** | **la** | **poussière** | **des** | **batailles** |
| In | the | dust | of the | battles |

| i | la | ty e | lwa ja le | drwa |
|---|----|----|-----------|------|
| **Il** | **a** | **tué** | **loyal et** | **droit** |
| He has | killed | loyal | and | direct |

Des trous à son pourpoint vermeil,
Un chevalier va par la brune,
Les cheveux tout pleins de soleil
Sous un casque couleur de lune

Dormez toujours, dormez au bois,
L'anneau la belle, à votre doigt.

Dans la poussière des batailles
Il a tué loyal et droit,
En frappant d'estoc et de taille
Ainsi que frapperait un roi.

Dormez au bois, où la verveine,
Fleurit avec la marjolaine

Et par les monts et par la plaine
Monté sur son grand destrier
Il court, il court à perdre haleine
Et tout droit sur ses étriers

Dormez la belle au bois rêvez
Qu'un prince vous épouserez.

Dans la forêt des lilas blancs
Sous l'éperon d'or qui l'excite
Son destrier perle de sang
Les lilas blancs et va plus vite

Dormez au bois, dormez la belle
Sous vos courtines de dentelle

ã    fra pã    dɛ stɔ    ke    də    ta jə
**En frappant d'estoc et de taille**
By   striking   with cut   and   with   thrust

ɛ̃ si    kə    fra pə rɛ    tœ̃ rwa
**Ainsi que frapperait un roi.**
Just   as    would strike a   king.

dɔ rme    zo    bwa    u    la    vɛ rvɛ nə
**Dormez au    bois,   où    la    verveine,**
Sleep    in the   wood,   where   the   verbena,

flœ ri    (t)a vɛ    kla    ma rʒɔ lɛ nə
**Fleurit avec    la    marjolaine.**
Blooms   with    the    marjoram.

e    pa    rlɛ mɔ̃    ze    pa    rla plɛ nə
**Et    par   les   monts et    par   la   plaine**
And   over   the   hills   and   over   the   dale

mɔ̃ te    sy    rsɔ̃    grã    dɛ stri je
**Monté    sur   son   grand   destrier**
Mounted   on   his   tall   steed

i    lku r    i    lku    ra    pɛ    rdra lɛ nə
**Il    court, il   court à    perdre   haleine**
He   runs,   he   runs   until   losing   breath

e    tu    drwa    sy    rsɛ    ze tri je
**Et    tout   droit   sur   ses   étriers**
And   all   erect   on   his   stirrups

dɔ rme    la    bɛ    lo    bwa    rɛ ve
**Dormez la    belle   au    bois,   rêvez**
Sleep    the   Beauty   in the   Wood,   dream

Mais il a pris l'anneau vermeil
Le chevalier qui par la brune
A des cheveux pleins de soleil
Sous un casque couleur de lune

Ne dormez plus, la belle au bois
L'anneau n'est plus à votre doigt.

*(Forty-three Songs for Voice and Piano.* New York: International, 1961)

———————— ● ————————

With holes in his vermilion doublet
A knight goes by in the dusk,
His hair touched with sunlight,
Under his moon-colored helmet.

Sleep on, sleep in the wood,
With the ring on your finger,
Beauty.

In the dust of battles
He has killed, loyal and direct,
Striking with cuts and thrusts
As a king would strike.

Sleep in the wood, where the verbena
Blooms with the marjoram.

And over hill and dale,
Astride his tall charger,
He runs on and on, breathlessly,
Standing straight in his stirrups.

Sleep, Beauty in the Wood, dream
That you will marry a prince.

kɶ̃     prɛ̃ sə    vu     ze pu zə re
**Qu'un   prince   vous   épouserez.**
That a    prince    you     will marry.

dɑ̃     la    fɔ rɛ   dɛ     li lɑ    blɑ̃
**Dans   la   forêt   des     lilas   blancs**
In      the   forest   of the   lilacs   white

su      le pə rɔ̃    dɔ      rki     lɛ ksi tə
**Sous   l'éperon   d'or    qui     l'excite**
Under   the spur    of gold   which   it prods

sɔ̃     dɛ stri je   pɛ rlə      də sɑ̃
**Son   destrier   perle      de   sang**
His     steed      sheds beads   of   blood

lɛ     li lɑ   blɑ̃     e     va     ply     vi tə
**Les   lilas   blancs,   et     va     plus   vite**
The    lilacs   white,    and   goes   more   swiftly

dɔ rme    zo     bwa    dɔ rme    la    bɛ lə
**Dormez   au     bois,    dormez   la    belle**
Sleep      in the   wood,   sleep     the   Beauty

su     vo     ku rti nə    də dɑ̃ tɛ lə
**Sous   vos    courtines de   dentelle.**
Under   your   curtains    of   lace.

mɛ    zi   la   pri     la no     vɛ rmɛ j
**Mais   il    a     pris    l'anneau   vermeil**
But    he   has   taken   the ring    vermilion

lə    ʃə va lje    ki     pa   rla   bry nə
**Le   chevalier   qui   par   la   brune,**
The   knight     who   in    the   dusk,

In the forest of white lilacs,
Under the prod of the golden spur,
His charger sheds blood beads
On the white lilacs, and runs
more swiftly.

Sleep in the wood, sleep, Beauty,
Under your curtains of lace.

But he has taken the vermilion ring,
The knight who in the dusk
Has hair touched with sunlight,
Under his moon-colored helmet.

Sleep no more, Beauty in the Wood,
The ring is no longer on your finger.

a    dɛ    ʃə vø    plɛ̃    də sɔlɛj
**A    des    cheveux pleins de soleil**
Has some hair         full    of sun

su    zœ̃ ka skə    ku lœ    rdə ly nə
**Sous    un casque    couleur de    lune**
Under a    helmet    color    of moon

nə    dɔrme    ply    la    bɛ    lo    bwa
**Ne    dormez    plus, la    belle    au    bois,**
Don't sleep    more, the Beauty in the Wood,

la no    nɛ    ply    za    vɔ trə dwa
**L'anneau n'est plus    à    votre doigt.**
The ring    notis    longer    on    your    finger.

# "Les Angélus"
## *(The Angelus)*

**Date of composition:** *1891.*
**Date of publication:** *1891.*
**Publisher:** *J. Hamelle, Paris.*
**Source:** *Grégoire Le Roy,* Mon coeur pleure d'autrefois. *In* La Chanson du Pauvre. *Poem probably written between 1886 and 1888.*

Church bells ring three times a day in the Roman Catholic rites: at sunrise, noon, and sunset. They call for devotional exercise to commemorate the Annunciation. As messengers of the Incarnation, they restore hopes for redemption in humankind. They once inspired the poet of "Les Angélus" with fresh confidence, renewed energies; today, though, his grieving soul does not respond to the call. Instead it seeks the darkness of the evening. The only bell it hears is the death toll. The healing power of religious rites becomes powerless and empty. Le Roy's lyricism remains subdued; his melancholy is vague and his longing for his past happiness rather muted.

Debussy's setting calls for an equal restraint in emotion and a similar tone of resignation. The entire song is accompanied by harmonies of bells delicately annotated.

# le zɑ̃ ʒe ly s
## Les Angélus
### The Angelus

klɔ ʃə    kre tjɛ nə    pu    rlɛ ma ti nə
**Cloches chrétiennes pour les matines,**
Bells    Christian    for    the   matins,

sɔ nɑ̃    to    kœ    rde spe re   (r)ɑ̃ kɔ r
**Sonnant au    coeur d'espérer encore!**
Ringing  to the heart  to hope   more!

ɑ̃ ʒe ly    zɑ̃ ʒe li ze    dɔ rɔ rə
**Angélus angélisés   d'aurore!**
Angelus  made angelic by dawn!

lɑs    u    sɔ̃    vo    pri jɛ rə kɑ li nə
**Las! où   sont vos  prières câlines?**
Alas! where are   your  prayers comforting?

vu    ze tje də    si    du sə    fɔ li ə
**Vous étiez de   si    douces folies!**
You  were some such sweet  follies!

e    ʃɑ̃ tə rɛ lə    da mu    rprɔ ʃɛ nə
**Et  chanterelles  d'amours prochaines!**
And highest strings of loves   coming!

o ʒu rdɥi    su və rɛ    nɛ ma pɛ nə
**Aujourd'hui souveraine est ma peine,**
Today    supreme    is  my grief,

e    tu tə    ma ti nə  za bɔ li ə
**Et  toutes matines abolies.**
And all    matins  abolished.

Cloches chrétiennes pour les matines,
Sonnant au coeur d'espérer encore!
Angélus angelisés d'aurore!
Las! Où sont vos prières calines?

Vous étiez de si douces folies!
Et chanterelles d'amours prochaines!
Aujourd'hui souveraine est ma peine,
Et toutes matines abolies.

Je ne vis plus que d'ombre et de soir;
Les las angélus pleurent la mort,
Et là, dans mon coeur résigné, dort
La seule veuve de tout espoir.

*(Forty-three Songs for Voice and Piano.* New York: International, 1961)

—————— • ——————

Christian bells for matins,
Ringing, asking the heart to keep on hoping!
Angelus bells made angelic by the dawn!
Alas! where are your comforting prayers?

ʒə  nə      vi  ply           kə  dɔ̃          bre də
**Je  ne      vis plus          que d'ombre et  de**
I    don't  live any more  but  in shadow and  in

swa r
**soir;**
evening;

lɛ  lɑ      zɑ̃ʒe ly  splœ rə   la  mɔ r
**Les las      angélus pleurent la  mort,**
The weary  angelus  cry         the death,

e  la      dɑ̃  mɔ̃  kœ   re zi ɲe  dɔ r
**Et  là,      dans mon coeur résigné, dort**
And there, in    my    heart resigned, sleeps

la  sœ lə      vœ və      də tu    tɛ spwa r
**La  seule      veuve      de tout espoir.**
The single bell deprived of all      hope.

You rang such sweet follies!
And on a high pitch, sang of
loves to come!
Today my grief is supreme,
And all matins abolished.

I now live only in shadow and
evening;
The weary angelus bemoan the
dead,
And there, in my resigned heart,
sleeps
The single bell deprived of all
hope.

# ————"Dans le Jardin"————
## *(In the Garden)*

**Date of composition:** *1891 (Lesure; Wenk; Grove), 1903 (Cobb; Lockspeiser).*
**Date of publication:** *1905*
**Publisher:** *J. Hamelle, Paris.*
**Source:** *Paul Gravollet, Les Frissons, N° 5, p. 20. (Paris: J. Hamelle, 1905).*

While peeping through a hedge, the poet saw a young girl in a garden. The lovely sight charmed him and, despite painful scratches from the bramble thorns, he stood there, staring and appraising her minutely. Her eyes, brow, hair, body, voice, and motions were entrancing, all the more subjugated as she was no longer a child but not yet a woman. The poem is a charming tribute to the early bloom of girlhood when adolescent gracefulness remains fragile and untouched. The poet's indiscretion is redeemed by the spontaneousness of his emotion.

Debussy's song retains the graceful atmosphere of the poem. It flows serenely along a succession of chords. However, it does not stand out as one of his most inspired songs.

## dɑ̃ l(ə) ʒa rdɛ̃
# Dans le jardin
## In the garden

| | | | | |
|---|---|---|---|---|
| ʒə | rə ga rdɛ | dɑ̃ | lə | ʒa rdɛ̃ |
| **Je** | **regardais** | **dans** | **le** | **jardin** |
| I | looked | into | the | garden |

| | | | | |
|---|---|---|---|---|
| fy rti f | o tra vɛ | rdə la | ɛ | |
| **Furtif** | **au travers** | **de la** | **haie;** | |
| Furtive | through | of the | hedge; | |

| | | | | |
|---|---|---|---|---|
| ʒə | te | vy | ɑ̃ fɑ̃ | e | su dɛ̃ |
| **Je** | **t'ai** | **vue,** | **enfant!** | **et** | **soudain,** |
| I | you have | seen, | child! | and | suddenly, |

| | | | | |
|---|---|---|---|---|
| mɔ̃ | kœ | rtrɛ sa ji | ʒə | tɛ mɛ |
| **Mon** | **coeur** | **tressaillit:** | **je** | **t'aimais!** |
| My | heart | quivered: | I | you loved! |

| | | | |
|---|---|---|---|
| ʒə | me gra ti ɲɛ | o | ze pi nə |
| **Je** | **m'égratignais** | **aux** | **épines,** |
| I | got scratched | from the | thorns, |

| | | | | | |
|---|---|---|---|---|---|
| mɛ | dwa | sɛ ɲɛ | (t)a vɛ klɛ | my rə |
| **Mes** | **doigts** | **saignaient** | **avec** | **les** | **mûres,** |
| My | fingers | bled | with | the | brambles, |

| | | | | |
|---|---|---|---|---|
| e | ma su frɑ̃ | se tɛ | di vi nə |
| **Et** | **ma souffrance** | **était** | **divine:** |
| And | my suffering | was | divine: |

| | | | | |
|---|---|---|---|---|
| ʒə | vwa jɛ tɔ̃ | frɔ̃ | də ga mi nə |
| **Je** | **voyais ton** | **front** | **de** | **gamine,** |
| I | saw | your | brow | of little girl, |

Je regardais dans le jardin
Furtif au travers de la haie;
Je t'ai vue, enfant! et soudain,
Mon coeur tressaillit: je t'aimais!

Je m'égratignais aux épines,
Mes doigts saignaient avec les
mûres,
Et ma souffrance était divine:
Je voyais ton front de gamine,
Tes cheveux d'or et ton front pur!

Grandette et pourtant puérile,
Coquette d'instinct seulement,
Les yeux bleus ombrés de longs
cils
Qui regardent tout gentiment,
Un corps un peu frêle et
charmant,
Une voix de mai, des gestes
d'avril!

Je regardais dans le jardin,
Furtif, au travers de la haie;
Je t'ai vue, enfant! et soudain,
Mon coeur tressaillit: je t'aimais!

(*Forty-three Songs for Voice and Piano.* New York: International, 1961)

————————— • —————————

I looked into the garden,
Furtively, through the hedge;
I saw you, child! and suddenly,
My heart trembled: I loved you!

tɛ   ʃə vø   dɔ   re   tɔ̃   frɔ̃   py r
**Tes cheveux d'or et ton front pur!**
Your hair of gold and your brow pure!

The thorns scratched me,
My fingers bled from the brambles,
And my pain was divine:
I saw your girlish brow,
Your golden hair and your pure brow!

grɑ̃ dɛ   te   pu rtɑ̃   pɥe ri lə
**Grandette et pourtant puérile,**
Fairly grown and yet childlike,

kɔ kɛ tə   dɛ̃ stɛ̃   sœ lə mɑ̃
**Coquette d'instinct seulement,**
Coquettish by instinct only,

Fairly grown and yet like a child,
A coquette only by instinct,
Your blue eyes shaded by long lashes,
Which gaze about very sweetly,
A body a little frail and lovely,
A May-like voice, April-like gestures!

lɛ   zjø   blø   (z)ɔ̃ bre   də lɔ̃   si l
**Les yeux bleus ombrés de longs cils**
The eyes blue shaded by long lashes

ki   rə ga rdə   tu   ʒɑ̃ ti mɑ̃
**Qui regardent tout gentiment,**
Which gaze about very sweetly,

I looked into the garden,
Furtively, through the hedge;
I saw you, child! and suddenly,
My heart trembled: I loved you!

œ̃   kɔ   rœ̃   pø   frɛ   le   ʃa rmɑ̃
**Un corps un peu frêle et charmant,**
A body a little frail and charming,

y nə   vwa   də mɛ   dɛ   ʒɛ stə   da vri l
**Une voix de mai, des gestes d'avril!**
A voice of May, some gestures of April!

ʒə   rə ga rdɛ   dɑ̃   lə   ʒa rdɛ̃
**Je regardais dans le jardin,**
I looked into the garden,

fy rti f   o tra vɛ   rdə la   ɛ
**Furtif, au travers de la haie;**
Furtive, through of the hedge;

ʒə  te        vy   ɑ̃ fɑ̃     e    su dɛ̃
**Je  t'ai       vue, enfant!  et   soudain,**
I   you have  seen,  child!    and  suddenly,

mɔ̃   kœ    rtrɛ sa ji   ʒə  tɛ mɛ
**Mon  coeur tressaillit:  je   t'aimais!**
My    heart  quivered:    I    you loved!

<br>

<br>

*(Deux Romances)*

# I. "Romance"

*(Romance)*

**Date of composition:** *1891 (1886).*[36]
**Date of publication:** *1891.*
**Publisher:** *A. Durand & Fils, Paris.*
**Source:** *Paul Bourget, "Amour." In* Les Aveux *II, 1882.*

"Romance" is one of five poems of the same title. The melancholy theme of bygone love and days underlies the two rhetorical questions that make up Bourget's short lyrical poem: Where has the sweet love of yesterday gone? Is it truly gone forever? To enrich his theme, the poet uses one metaphor in the entire poem: The lily, the aesthetes' chosen flower, not only is the symbol of the beloved's unsullied soul, but it bewitches the lover with its voluptuous scents. The last two lines of the poem may imply that where there was sweet fragrance and bliss, there is now regret and unrest. Yet the atmosphere of the poem remains mildly melancholy and peaceful.

Debussy submitted his settings of "Romance" and "Les Cloches" to his publisher without specific titles. The publisher added the titles. Judging from the style of the two pieces, particularly of "Romance," it is to be assumed that they were composed at an earlier date than 1891 as it appears on the score; they are likely to belong to the Vasnier cycle of earlier settings from Bourget. The ample phrasing of the melody pleasantly conveys the voluptuous languor and charm of the poem.

rɔ mɑ̃ s
# Romance
Romance

| lɑ | me va pɔ re e | su frɑ̃ tə |
|---|---|---|
| **L'âme** | **évaporée et** | **souffrante,** |
| The soul | evanescent and | suffering, |

| la mə | du sə | lɑ | mɔ dɔ rɑ̃ tə |
|---|---|---|---|
| **L'âme** | **douce,** | **l'âme** | **odorante** |
| The soul | gentle, | the soul | fragrant |

| dɛ | li | sdi vɛ̃ | kə | ʒe | kœ ji |
|---|---|---|---|---|---|
| **Des** | **lys** | **divins** | **que** | **j'ai** | **cueillis** |
| Of the | lilies | divine | that | I have | picked |

| dɑ̃ | lə | ʒa rdɛ̃ | də | ta | pɑ̃ se |
|---|---|---|---|---|---|
| **Dans** | **le** | **jardin** | **de** | **ta** | **pensée,** |
| In | the | garden | of | your | thought, |

| u | dɔ̃ | lɛ | vɑ̃ | lɔ̃ ti | lʃa se |
|---|---|---|---|---|---|
| **Où** | **donc** | **les** | **vents** | **l'ont-ils** | **chassée,** |
| Where | then | the | winds | it have they | driven, |

| sɛ | tɑ | ma dɔ ra blə | dɛ | li s |
|---|---|---|---|---|
| **Cette** | **âme** | **adorable** | **des** | **lys?** |
| This | soul | adorable | of the | lilies? |

| nɛ ti | lply | zœ̃ | pa rfœ̃ | ki |
|---|---|---|---|---|
| **N'est-il** | **plus** | **un** | **parfum** | **qui** |
| Not is there | any longer | a | fragrance | that |

| rɛ stə |
|---|
| **reste** |
| remains |

L'âme évaporée et souffrante,
L'âme douce, l'âme odorante
Des lys divins que j'ai cueillis
Dans le jardin de ta pensée,
Où donc les vents l'ont-ils chassée,
Cette âme adorable des lys?

N'est-il plus un parfum qui reste
De la suavité céleste
Des jours où tu m'enveloppais
D'une vapeur surnaturelle
Faite d'espoir, d'amour fidèle,
De béatitude et de paix?

(*Forty-three Songs for Voice and Piano.* New York: International, 1961)

———————•———————

The evanescent and suffering soul,
The gentle soul, the fragrant soul
Of the divine lilies I gathered
In the garden of your thoughts,
Where have the winds driven
This adorable soul of the lilies?

Is there not any fragrance left
From the celestial sweetness
Of the days when you enveloped me
In a supernatural vapor
Of hope, of faithful love,
Of bliss and peace?

də   la   sya vi te    se lɛ stə
**De   la   suavité    céleste**
Of   the   sweetness  celestial

dɛ        ʒu      r(z)u   ty    mɑ̃ və lɔ pɛ
**Des        jours   où    tu    m'enveloppais**
From the   days    when  you   me enveloped

dy nə   va pœ   rsy rna ty rɛ lə
**D'une   vapeur   surnaturelle**
From a   vapor    supernatural

fɛ tə       dɛ spwa r   da mu    rfi dɛ lə
**Faite       d'espoir,   d'amour   fidèle,**
Made up   of hope,   of love    faithful,

də   be a ti ty (d) (d)e   də   pɛ
**De   béatitude   et    de   paix?**
Of   bliss           and   of   peace?

# II. "Les Cloches"
## *(The Bells)*

**Date of composition:** *1891 (1886).*[37]
**Date of publication:** *1891.*
**Publisher:** *A. Durand & Fils, Paris.*
**Source:** *Paul Bourget,* Dilettantisme. *In* Les Aveux *II, 1882.*

This vision of spring is dominated by the sound of bells. Airily ringing in the fair sky, bells salute the advent of spring but bring back to the poet's mind memories of bygone days. Their fervid rhythm recalls the pious hymns and the white flowers of the church altar. Religious feeling is here reduced to the sentimental recollection of pleasant sounds and sights. Bells are voices of happiness gone forever, and the budding foliage represents the passing of time. The poet sadly comments on the vanishing of happy days: Faded leaves cannot revive the past; they only appear to do so.

Debussy's delicate setting recaptures the nostalgia of the poem. Accompanied by a background of bells, the melody flows gently and expressively without ever becoming louder or faster. Happy memories should not be disturbed.

## le klɔʃ
# Les Cloches
## The Bells

| lɛ | fœ jə | su vrɛ | sy | rlə | bɔ | rdɛ |
|---|---|---|---|---|---|---|
| **Les** | **feuilles** | **s'ouvraient** | **sur** | **le** | **bord** | **des** |
| The | leaves | were opening | on | the | side | of the |

brã ʃə
**branches,**
branches,

de li ka tə mã
**Délicatement,**
Delicately,

| lɛ | klɔ ʃə | tẽ tɛ | le ʒɛ rə | ze |
|---|---|---|---|---|
| **Les** | **cloches** | **tintaient,** | **légères** | **et** |
| The | bells | were ringing, | light | and |

frã ʃə
**franches,**
pure,

| dã | lə | sjɛ | l kle mã |
|---|---|---|---|
| **Dans** | **le** | **ciel** | **clément.** |
| In | the | sky | mild. |

| ri tmi | ke | fɛ rvã | kɔ | my |
|---|---|---|---|---|
| **Rythmique** | **et** | **fervent** | **comme** | **une** |
| Rhythmical | and | fervent | as | an |

nã ti jɛ nə
**antienne,**
antiphon,

Les feuilles s'ouvraient sur le
bord des branches,
    Délicatement,
Les cloches tintaient, légères et
franches,
    Dans le ciel clément.

Rythmique et fervent comme
une antienne,
    Ce lointain appel
Me remémorait la blancheur
chrétienne
    Des fleurs de l'autel.

Ces cloches parlaient d'heureuses
années,
    Et dans le grand bois
Semblaient reverdir les feuilles
fanées
    Des jours d'autrefois.

(*Forty-three Songs for Voice
and Piano.* New York:
International, 1961)

———————•———————

The leaves opened on the sides of
the branches,
    Delicately,
The bells rang lightly and openly,
    In the mild sky.

| sə | lwɛ̃ tɛ | na pɛ l |
|----|---------|---------|
| **Ce** | **lointain** | **appel** |
| That | distant | call |

Rhythmical and fervent as an antiphon,
 That distant call
Reminded me of the Christian whiteness
 Of the altar flowers.

| mə | rə me mɔ rɛ | la | blɑ̃ ʃœ | rkre tjɛ nə |
|----|-------------|-----|---------|-------------|
| **Me** | **remémorait** | **la** | **blancheur** | **chrétienne** |
| Me | reminded | the | whiteness | Christian |

| | dɛ | flœ | rdə | lo tɛ l |
|---|-----|-----|-----|---------|
| | **Des** | **fleurs** | **de** | **l'autel.** |
| | Of the | flowers | of | the altar. |

Those bells spoke of happy years,
 And, in the large wood,
The faded leaves seemed to turn green again
 From the bygone days.

| sɛ | klɔ ʃə | pa rlɛ | dø rø zə |
|----|--------|--------|----------|
| **Ces** | **cloches** | **parlaient** | **d'heureuses** |
| These | bells | were speaking | of happy |

| za ne ə |
|---------|
| **années,** |
| years, |

| | e | dɑ̃ | lə | grɑ̃ | bwa |
|---|-----|-----|-----|------|-----|
| | **Et,** | **dans** | **le** | **grand** | **bois,** |
| | And, | in | the | large | wood, |

| sɑ̃ blɛ | rə vɛ rdi | rlɛ | fœ jə |
|---------|-----------|-----|-------|
| **Semblaient** | **reverdir** | **les** | **feuilles** |
| Seemed | to turn green again | the | leaves |

| fa ne ə |
|---------|
| **fanées** |
| faded |

| | dɛ | ʒu | rdo trə fwa |
|---|-----|-----|-------------|
| | **Des** | **jours** | **d'autrefrois.** |
| | From the | days | gone by. |

# "Fêtes galantes"
## (first series)

**Date of composition:** *1891.*
**Date of publication:** *1903.*
**Publisher:** *E. Fromont, Paris.*
**Source:** *Paul Verlaine,* Fêtes galantes, *1869.*

  I. "En sourdine" (Muted).
 II. "Fantoches" (Marionettes).
III. "Clair de lune" (Moonlight).

This first series of *Fêtes galantes* shows a definite turn in Debussy's style of writing. No trace remains of the rhetorical eloquence of his earliest songs. He is now facing new modes of expression that consist in a simpler vocal line, subtler nuances of color in the accompaniment, and a tighter grip on the emotions.

# I. "En sourdine"
## (Muted)

**Dedicated to Madame Robert Godet.**

Verlaine's poem was introduced on p.69.

Debussy's second version of "En sourdine," written nine years after the first, is totally different. It opens slowly and dreamily and remains so throughout to express, with delicate sensibility, the muted atmosphere of the poem.

Whereas the voice recites the text in a soft expression and bears very lightly on the uninflected syllables, the accompaniment carries the texture of the poem: The silence of the forest is broken by the reiterated theme of the nightingale, the waves of the grass rippled by the lulling wind.

Madame Godet, to whom Debussy dedicated the song, was the wife of Robert Godet, a journalist and musicologist who became a close friend of Debussy in 1888.

# ɑ̃ su rdin
## En sourdine
## Muted

ka lmə  dɑ̃  lə  də mi ʒu r
**Calmes dans le demi-jour**
Calm   in   the  half-light

kə  lɛ  brɑ̃ ʃə  o tə  fɔ̃
**Que les branches hautes font,**
That the branches high  make,

pe ne trɔ̃   bjɛ̃  nɔ  tra mu r
**Pénétrons   bien  notre amour**
Let us penetrate well  our   love

də  sə  si lɑ̃ sə  prɔ fɔ̃
**De  ce  silence  profond**
With this silence deep

fɔ̃ dɔ̃  no  zɑ mə  no  kœ r
**Fondons nos âmes, nos coeurs**
Let us fuse our  souls, our hearts

ze  no  sɑ̃  sɛ kstɑ zje
**Et  nos sens  extasiés**
And our senses raptured

pa rmi  lɛ  va gə  lɑ̃ gœ r
**Parmi les vagues langueurs**
Amid  the vague  languors

dɛ  pɛ̃  (z)e dɛ  za rbu zje
**Des pins et des arbousiers.**
Of the pines and the arbutus.

Calmes dans le demi-jour
Que les branches hautes font,
Pénétrons bien notre amour
De ce silence profond.

Fondons nos âmes, nos coeurs
Et nos sens extasiés
Parmi les vagues langueurs
Des pins et des arbousiers.

Ferme tes yeux à demi,
Croise tes bras sur ton sein,
Et de ton coeur endormi
Chasse à jamais tout dessein.

Laissons-nous persuader
Au souffle berceur et doux
Qui vent à tes pieds rider
Les ondes de gazon roux.

Et quand, solennel, le soir,
Des chênes noirs tombera
Voix de notre désespoir,
Le rossignol chantera.

*(Forty-three Songs for Voice and Piano.* New York: International, 1961)

———————•———————

Calm in the half-light
Made by the high branches,
Let us permeate our love
With this deep silence.

fε rmə  tε     zjø   (z)a dəmi
**Ferme  tes    yeux  à     demi,**
Close    your   eyes  half-way,

krwa zə  tε     bra   sy   rtɔ̃   sɛ̃
**Croise  tes    bras  sur  ton   sein,**
Cross    your   arms  on   your  breast,

e      də    tɔ̃    kœ     rɑ̃ dɔ rmi
**Et    de    ton   coeur  endormi**
And   from  your  heart  drowsy

ʃa     sa     ʒa mε   tu    de sɛ̃
**Chasse  à     jamais  tout  dessein.**
Banish  for   ever    all   design.

le sɔ̃      nu      pε rsy a de
**Laissons-nous   persuader**
Let ourselves    be persuaded

o      su flə   bε rsœ   re   du
**Au    souffle  berceur  et   doux**
By the  wind    lulling   and  soft

ki     vjɛ̃    (t)a tε    pje    ri de
**Qui    vient   à    tes   pieds  rider**
Which  comes  at   your  feet   ripple

lε    zɔ̃ də   də   gɑ zɔ̃    ru
**Les ondes  de   gazon  roux.**
The  waves  of   russet  lawn.

e     kɑ̃     sɔ la nεl   lə   swa r
**Et    quand,  solennel,  le   soir,**
And   when,   solemn,    the  evening,

Let us fuse our souls, our hearts
And our raptured senses
Into the vague languors
Of the pines and arbutus.

Close your eyes half-way,
Cross your arms on your breast,
And from your drowsy heart
Forever banish all design.

Let ourselves be persuaded
By the lulling soft wind
That comes, at your feet, to ripple
The waves of russet lawn.

And when, solemnly, the evening
Falls from the black oaks,
The voice of our despair,
The nightingale, will sing.

| dε | ʃɛ nə | nwa | rtɔ̃ bə ra |
|----|-------|-----|-----------|
| **Des** | **chênes** | **noirs** | **tombera** |
| From the | oaks | black | will fall |

| vwa | də | nɔ trə | de zɛ spwa r |
|-----|-----|--------|--------------|
| **Voix** | **de** | **notre** | **désespoir,** |
| Voice | of | our | despair, |

| lə | rɔ si ɲɔ | lʃɑ̃ tə ra |
|----|----------|-----------|
| **Le** | **rossignol** | **chantera.** |
| The | nightingale | will sing. |

# II. "Fantoches"
## *(Marionettes)*

**Date of composition:** *8 January 1882; revised in 1891.*
**Dedicated to Madame Lucien Fontaine.**

"Fantoches" is nothing but a dazzling jest in four octosyllabic triplets. The poem resembles "Pantomime" in form and setting, but its mood is explicitly established and defined by Verlaine from the beginning by the title: None of the characters are to be taken seriously; they are puppets and nothing else. Even the languorous love call of the nightingale in the last tercet is humoristic. The short scenes from the Italian comedy are skillfully and daintily presented. No satirical intent, hidden meaning, or melancholy underlie them. The maiden who in "Pantomime" was left dreaming of voluptuous pleasures, here appears very determined to satisfy her longings, even with the most outlandish lover, in this case the extravagant Spanish pirate. The poem is fun and folly.

Debussy's first version of "Fantoches" (1882) was his very first attempt at setting Verlaine's poems; dedicated to Madame Vasnier, it was never published. The second version is but a slight revision of the original score, this time dedicated to another friend, Madame Lucien Fontaine: Like her sister-in-law, Mme. Arthur Fontaine, she sang in the choral group founded by her husband and directed by Debussy.

Thorough identification is achieved between the tone of the poem and Debussy's setting. Verlaine's preciosity of language finds musical expression in the details of the vocal part and accompaniment, particularly when the doctor's daughter appears. Debussy contrives to endow commonplace characters and situations with a farcical dimension. The whole song dashes airily and spiritedly and ends with a short ironic melisma.[37a]

# fɑ̃ tɔ ʃ
# **Fantoches**
## Marionettes

| | | | |
|---|---|---|---|
| ska ra mu | ʃe | pu ltʃi nɛ lla | |
| **Scaramouche** | **et** | **Pulcinella** | |
| Scaramouche | and | Pulcinella | |

Scaramouche et Pulcinella
Qu'un mauvais dessein
rassembla
Gesticulent noirs sous la lune,
la la la. . .

| | | | |
|---|---|---|---|
| kɶ̃ | mɔ vɛ | de sɛ̃ | ra sɑ̃ bla |
| **Qu'un** | **mauvais** | **dessein** | **rassembla** |
| Whom an | evil | plot | brought together |

Cependant l'excellent docteur
Bolonais cueille avec lenteur
Des simples parmi l'herbe brune

| | | | | |
|---|---|---|---|---|
| ʒɛ sti ky lə | nwa | rsy | rla ly nə | la la la |
| **Gesticulent** | **noirs** | **sur** | **la** **lune,** | **la la la...** |
| Gesticulate | black | against | the moon, | la la la. . . |

Lors sa fille, piquant minois
Sous la charmille, en tapinois
Se glisse demi-nue la la la. . . en
quête

| | | | |
|---|---|---|---|
| sə pɑ̃ dɑ̃ | lɛ ksɛ lɑ̃ | dɔ ktɶ | |
| **Cependant** | **l'excellent** | **docteur** | |
| Meanwhile | the excellent | doctor | |

De son beau pirate espagnol
Dont un amoureux rossignol
Clame la détresse à tue-tête.
La la la.

| | | | |
|---|---|---|---|
| rbɔ lɔ nɛ | kɶ | ja vɛ | klɑ̃ tɶ |
| **Bolonais** | **cueille** | **avec** | **lenteur** |
| Bolognese | picks | with | slowness |

(*Forty-three Songs for Voice
and Piano.* New York:
International, 1961)

| | | | | |
|---|---|---|---|---|
| rdɛ | sɛ̃ plə | pa rmi | lɛ rbə | bry nə |
| **Des** | **simples** | **parmi** | **l'herbe** | **brune** |
| Some | simples | among | the grass | dark |

Scaramouche and Pulcinella,[38]
Whom an evil plot broght
together,
Gesticulate, black shadows on
the moon, la la la. . .

| | | | | |
|---|---|---|---|---|
| lɔ | rsa fi jə | pi kɑ̃ | mi nwa | |
| **Lors** | **sa fille,** | **piquant** | **minois** | |
| Then | his daughter, | saucy | countenance | |

Meanwhile the excellent doctor
From Bologna[39] slowly picks
Simples[40] among the dark grass.

su la ʃa rmi jə ɑ̃ ta pi nwa
**Sous la charmille, en tapinois**
Under the bower, slyly

sə gli sə də mi ny ə la la la ɑ̃ kɛ tə
**Se glisse demi-nue la la la. . . en quête**
Steals in half-naked la la la. . . in quest

də sɔ̃ bo pi ra tɛ spa ɲɔ l
**De son beau pirate espagnol**
Of her handsome pirate Spanish

dɔ̃ tœ̃ na mu rø rɔ si ɲɔ l
**Dont un amoureux rossignol**
Of whom a lovelorn nightingale

kla mə la de trɛ sa ty tɛ tə
**Clame la détresse à tue-tête.**
Proclaims the distress at the top of his voice.

la la la
**La la la.**
La la la.

Then his daughter, of saucy countenance,
Under the bower, slyly
Steals in, half-naked, la la la. . . in quest

Of her handsome Spanish pirate
Whose distress a lovelorn nightingale
Proclaims at the top of his voice.
La la la.

# III. "Clair de lune"
## *(Moonlight)*
## (second version)

### Dedicated to Madame Arthur Fontaine

Verlaine's poem was introduced on p. 83.

Debussy dedicated this song to Madame Arthur Fontaine, at whose house he was a frequent caller and who sang in the amateur choir that Debussy directed from 1893 to 1904. The Fontaines were admirers and friends of Debussy.

This version of "Clair de lune" is altogether different from the first version. It has been praised as utterly original and shows Debussy's fascination with the pentatonic scale of the *gamelan*. Still there are no bold harmonic innovations: In the melodic line of this version Debussy communicates the subtle melancholy of the poem, whereas the modal coloring of the accompaniment renders the sweet sadness and beauty of the moonlight scene in the park.

klɛ rdə ly n

# Clair de lune

*Light of moon*

| vɔ | trɑ | mɛ | tœ̃ | pe i za ʒə | ʃwa zi |
|----|-----|-----|-----|------------|--------|
| **Votre** | **âme** | **est** | **un** | **paysage** | **choisi** |
| Your | soul | is | a | landscape | chosen |

| kə | vɔ̃ | ʃa rmɑ̃ | ma skə | ze |
|----|-----|--------|--------|-----|
| **Que** | **vont** | **charmant** | **masques** | **et** |
| Which | go | charming | masquers | and |

bɛ rga ma skə
**bergamasques**
bergamasquers

| ʒu ɑ̃ | dy ly | te | dɑ̃ sɑ̃ | e | ka zi |
|-------|-------|-----|--------|-----|-------|
| **Jouant** | **du luth** | **et** | **dansant** | **et** | **quasi** |
| Playing | the lute | and | dancing | and | almost |

| tri stə | su | lœ | rde gi zə mɑ̃ |
|---------|-----|-----|---------------|
| **Tristes** | **sous** | **leurs** | **déguisements** |
| Sad | beneath | their | disguises |

fɑ̃ ta skə
**fantasques**
fantastic

| tu | tɑ̃ | ʃɑ̃ tɑ̃ | sy | rlə | mɔ də | mi nœ r |
|----|-----|--------|-----|-----|-------|---------|
| **Tout** | **en** | **chantant** | **sur** | **le** | **mode** | **mineur** |
| While | in | singing | in | the | mode | minor |

| la mu | rvɛ̃ kœ | re | la | vi | ɔ pɔ rty nə |
|-------|---------|-----|-----|-----|-------------|
| **L'amour** | **vainqueur** | **et** | **la** | **vie** | **opportune** |
| The love | victorious | and | the | life | opportune |

Votre âme est un paysage choisi
Que vont charmant masques et
bergamasques
Jouant du luth et dansant et quasi
Tristes sous leurs déguisements
fantasques

Tout en chantant sur le mode
mineur
L'amour vainqueur et la vie
opportune,
Ils n'ont pas l'air de croire à leur
bonheur,
Et leur chanson se mêle au clair de
lune,

Au calme clair de lune triste et
beau,
Qui fait rêver les oiseaux dans les
arbres
Et sangloter d'extase les jets d'eau
Les grands jets d'eau sveltes
parmi les marbres.

(*Forty-three Songs for Voice
and Piano.* New York:
International, 1961)

———————— • ————————

Your soul is a chosen landscape
Charmed by masquers and
bergamasquers,
Playing the lute and dancing and
almost
Sad beneath their fantastic
disguises.

| i | lnɔ̃ | pɑ | le | rdə | krwa | ra | lœ |
|---|---|---|---|---|---|---|---|
| **Ils** | **n'ont** | **pas** | **l'air** | **de** | **croire** | **à** | **leur** |
| They | do | not | seem | to | believe | | in their |

| rbɔ nœ r |
|---|
| **bonheur,** |
| happiness, |

While singing in the minor mode
Of victorious love and the
opportunities of life,
They do not seem to believe in
their happiness,
And their songs blend with the
moonlight.

| e | lœ | rʃɑ̃ sɔ̃ | sə mɛ | lo | klɛ |
|---|---|---|---|---|---|
| **Et** | **leur** | **chanson** | **se mêle** | **au** | **clair** |
| And | their | song | mingles | with the | light |

| rdə | ly nə |
|---|---|
| **de** | **lune,** |
| of | moon, |

With the calm moonlight, sad
and beautiful,
That makes the birds dream in
the trees
And the fountains sob with
ecstasy,
The tall slender fountains among
the marbles.

| o | ka lmə | klɛ | rdə | ly nə | tri | ste |
|---|---|---|---|---|---|---|
| **Au** | **calme** | **clair** | **de** | **lune** | **triste** | **et** |
| With the | calm | light | of | moon | sad | and |

| bo |
|---|
| **beau,** |
| beautiful, |

| ki | fɛ | rɛ ve | le | zwa zo | dɑ̃ | le |
|---|---|---|---|---|---|---|
| **Qui** | **fait** | **rêver** | **les** | **oiseaux** | **dans** | **les** |
| That | makes | dream | the | birds | in | the |

| za rbrə |
|---|
| **arbres** |
| trees |

| e | sɑ̃ glɔ te | dɛ ksta zə | le | ʒɛ | do |
|---|---|---|---|---|---|
| **Et** | **sangloter** | **d'extase** | **les** | **jets** | **d'eau** |
| And | sob | with ecstasy | the | fountains, |

lɛ    grã    ʒɛ do    svɛltə    pa rmi    lɛ
**Les  grands jets d'eau sveltes  parmi   les**
The    tall    fountains  slender  among   the

ma rbrə
**marbres.**
marbles.

# ————— "Trois mélodies" —————
## (Three Melodies)

Date of composition: *1891.*
Date of publication: *1901.*
Publisher: *J. Hamelle, Paris.*
Source: *Paul Verlaine,* Sagesse III, IV, IX, XIII, 1881.

I. "La Mer est plus belle" (The Sea Is Fairer).
II. "Le Son du cor s'afflige" (The Sound of the Horn Mourns).
III. "L'Echelonnement des haies" (The Spacing-out of the Hedgerows).

The poems from *Sagesse* are for the most part of religious inspiration, although some were written before Verlaine's conversion. In the third section of the volume, from which Debussy selected his *Three Melodies*, the repenting poet proclaims his discovery of wisdom: Wary of human passions, he now favors landscapes over civilization, where he can praise God's benevolence and harmony.

Verlaine's gifts as a landscape painter are fully developed in these three poems on the sea, the hedgerows in the meadows, and a winter evening. They are exquisite bits of nature description that reveal the poet's entrancement with English scenery.

Debussy's *Three Melodies* are the last settings of Verlaine poems in a period of his life that was predominantly influenced by Symbolism and Verlaine in particular. They combine musical richness and respect for the texts. Debussy changed the order of Verlaine's poems, placing the melancholy hibernal scene of "Le Son du cor" in between the happier moods of "La Mer" and "L'Echelonnement des haies."

# I. "La Mer est plus belle"

**Dedicated to Ernest Chausson.**

Verlaine wrote this poem in 1877 at Bournemouth on the southern coast of England, where he was a French and Latin master in a Catholic private school. Although he found the position untenable, in his leisure time Verlaine was free to walk out alone, and the miles of sea with their foreground of gorse-covered cliffs were very inspiring. The maladjusted poet was then seeking refuge in the Church and finding in its permanence and security motherly qualities that soothed him. Religious themes therefore pervade this poem: The grandiose sea, more majestic than cathedrals, is the mother of all sinners, inflexible yet forgiving, angry yet equitable, a figure of authority and love, a divine healing power for man's suffering soul. At this point the poem is not without a hint of drama and exhibitionism, by which the poet humbles himself and delights in stressing his unworthiness.

The lively tempo of Debussy's melody triumphantly proclaims the beauty and majesty of the sea. After evoking in contrasted moods both its anger and understanding, the melody slows and softly comforts despondent mortals. The last stanza gives rise to an elegiac song in celebration of the loveliness and benevolence of the waters. The rich harmonies of the accompaniment depict the grandeur of the sea, whereas the contrasted rhythms set off its mood and power.

# la mɛ rɛ ply bɛ l
# Le Mer est plus belle
## The Sea is more beautiful

| la | mɛ | rɛ | ply | bɛ lə |
|----|----|----|-----|-------|
| **La** | **mer** | **est** | **plus** | **belle** |
| The sea | | is | more | beautiful |

| kɛ | lɛ | ka te dra lə |
|----|----|-------------|
| **Que** | **les** | **cathédrales,** |
| Than | the | cathedrals, |

| nu ri sə | fi dɛ lə |
|----------|----------|
| **Nourrice** | **fidèle,** |
| Wet nurse | faithful, |

La Mer est plus belle
Que les cathédrales,
Nourrice fidèle,
Berceuse de râles,
La mer sur qui prie
La Vierge Marie!

Elle a tous les dons
Terribles et doux.
J'entends ses pardons,
Gronder ses courroux
Cette immensité
N'a rien d'entêté

bɛ rsø zə   də  rɑ lə
**Berceuse de râles,**
Rocker    of  death-rattles,

la   mɛ  rsy  rki   pri
**La  mer  sur  qui  prie**
The sea  over  which prays

la   vjɛ rʒə  ma ri ə
**La  Vierge Marie!**
The Virgin  Mary!

ɛ    la   tu   lɛ   dɔ̃
**Elle a   tous les dons**
It  has  all   the qualities

tɛ ri blə    ze   du
**Terribles  et   doux.**
Terrible   and  sweet.

ʒɑ̃ tɑ̃    sɛ   pa rdɔ̃
**J'entends ses  pardons,**
I hear     its  pardons,

grɔ̃ de    sɛ   ku ru
**Gronder ses  courroux**
Roaring   its  wrath

sɛ    ti mɑ̃ si te
**Cette immensité**
This    immensity

na   rjɛ̃    dɑ̃ tɛ te
**N'a  rien   d'entêté**
Has  nothing of willful

Oh! si patiente,
Même quand méchante!
Un souffle ami hante
La vague, et nous chante:
"Vous, sans espérance,
Mourez sans souffrance!"

Et puis, sous les cieux
Qui s'y rient plus clairs,
Elle a des airs bleus,
Roses, gris et verts. . .
Plus belle que tous,
Meilleure que nous!

(*Forty-three Songs for Voice
and Piano.* New York:
International, 1961)

———————— ● ————————

The sea is fairer
Than cathedrals,
A faithful wet nurse,
A rocker of death-rattles,
The sea over which
The Virgin Mary prays.

It has all qualities,
Terrible and sweet.
I hear its pardons
And its wrath roar.
This immensity
Is without willfulness.

Oh! so patient,
Even when malicious!
A friendly breath haunts
The wave and sings to us:
"You, without hope,
May you die without suffering!"

o   si  pa si ã tə
**Oh! si patiente,**
Oh!  so  patient,

mɛ mə  kã    me ʃã tə
**Même  quand  méchante!**
Even  when  malicious!

œ̃  su    fla mi  ã tə
**Un souffle ami    hante**
A   breath  friendly haunts

la  va gə  e   nu  ʃã tə
**La  vague, et  nous chante:**
The wave,  and us   sings:

vu    sã    ze spe rã sə
**"Vous, sans    espérance,**
"You,  without hope,

mu re  sã    su frã sə
**Mourez sans    souffrance!"**
Die    without suffering!"

e   pɥi  su   lɛ  sjø
**Et  puis, sous  les  cieux**
And then, beneath the skies

ki   si  ri ə  ply  klɛ r
**Qui  s'y  rient plus  clairs,**
Which in it smile more bright,

ɛ   la  dɛ   zɛ  rblø
**Elle a   des  airs bleus,**
It   has  some airs  blue,

And then, beneath the skies
Which reflect in it a brighter
smile,
It looks blue,
Pink, gray and green. . .
Fairer than all
And better than us!

ro zə      gri    ze    vɛ r
**Roses,    gris    et     verts. . .**
Pink,      gray   and   green. . .

ply      bɛ lə        kə      tu s
**Plus    belle        que    tous,**
More     beautiful    than   all,

mɛ jœ rə      kə      nu
**Meilleure    que    nous!**
Better         than   us!

# II. "Le Son du cor s'afflige"

**Dedicated to Robert Godet**

The winter scene in this poem is all sounds and sights, in a rolling landscape of country and woods. The north wind blows by gusts, pushing long trails of snow across the vivid redness of the sunset. Away in the woods a hunting horn sounds a doleful tone, which is joined by the plaintive howling of a wolf. The evening drags out, mild, almost autumnal, uneventful; it lulls the uniform landscape into a tranquil tediousness.

In this seemingly descriptive poem, there is no overt subjectivity. Sensations are juxtaposed and superimposed, associations are striking, although unusual at times; long harmonious sentences are evenly broken with and within each line of this almost perfectly classical sonnet. One admires Verlaine's craft as a landscape painter. Then a closer reading of the poem evokes familiar notes: The "landscape" of the last verse recalls the "chosen landscape" of the soul in "Mandoline." The hunting horn and the wolf are common themes of inspiration in French Romantic poetry. Verlaine's poem becomes entirely symbolic: The poet's soul (the wolf), a prey to his woeful memories (the hunting horn), grieves in agony; but the agony seems to be assuaged, and the poet's feelings find solace in the soft uneventful passing of time. The poem was written in 1872, before Verlaine's conversion and during his wild passion for Rimbaud, and it recaptures some of the moods of the *Ariettes oubliées*.

Debussy dedicated the song to Robert Godet, a Swiss journalist and musicologist whom he had met two years before. They went to Bayreuth together and formed one of the best and longest friendships in Debussy's life. This song, like the other two of the series, was composed for a mezzo-soprano and lends itself well to the mellowness of this voice range. The slowly unwinding melody, alternately in minor and major modes, expresses the nuances of the poem, allowing an expressive legato to convey the mournful beauty of the winter sunset.

# lə sɔ̃ dy kɔ rsa fli ʒ
## Le Son du cor s'afflige
### The Sound of the horn mourns

| lə | sɔ̃ | dy | kɔ | rsa fli | ʒə | vɛ | rlɛ |
|----|-----|----|----|---------|-----|-----|-----|
| **Le** | **son** | **du** | **cor** | **s'afflige** | | **vers** | **les** |
| The | sound | of the | horn | mourns | | toward | the |

bwa
**bois**
woods

| dy nə | du lœ | rɔ̃ | vø | krwa | rɔ rfə li nə |
|-------|-------|-----|-----|------|--------------|
| **D'une** | **douleur** | **on** | **veut** | **croire** | **orpheline** |
| Of a | grief | one | wishes | to believe | orphan |

| ki | vjɛ̃ | mu ri | ro | ba | də la |
|----|------|-------|-----|-----|-------|
| **Qui** | **vient** | **mourir** | **au** | **bas** | **de la** |
| Which | comes | to die | at the | foot | of the |

kɔ li nə
**colline**
hill

| par mi | la | bi | zɛ rɑ̃ | tɑ̃ | ku |
|--------|-----|-----|--------|-----|-----|
| **Parmi** | **la** | **bise** | **errant** | **en** | **courts** |
| In | the | north wind | roving | in | short |

rza bwa
**abois.**
howlings.

| la mə | dy | lu | plœ rə | dɑ̃ | sɛ tə | vwa |
|-------|-----|-----|--------|-----|-------|-----|
| **L'âme** | **du** | **loup** | **pleure** | **dans** | **cette** | **voix** |
| The soul | of the | wolf | weeps | in | that | voice |

| ki | mɔ̃ | ta vɛ | klə sɔ lɛ | jki | de kli nə |
|----|-----|-------|-----------|-----|-----------|
| **Qui** | **monte** | **avec** | **le soleil** | **qui** | **décline** |
| Which | rises | with | the sun | that | declines |

Le son du cor s'afflige vers les bois
D'une douleur on veut croire orpheline
Qui vient mourir au bas de la colline
Parmi la bise errant en courts abois.

L'âme du loup pleure dans cette voix
Qui monte avec le soleil qui décline
D'une agonie on veut croire câline
Et qui ravit et qui navre à la fois.

Pour faire mieux cette plainte assoupie
La neige tombe à longs traits de charpie
A travers le couchant sanguinolent,

Et l'air a l'air d'être un soupir d'automne
Tant il fait doux par ce soir monotone
Où se dorlote un paysage lent.

*(Forty-three Songs for Voice and Piano.* New York: International, 1961)

dy  na gɔ ni ɔ̃  vø  krwa rə  kɑ li nə
**D'une agonie on veut croire câline**
In an   agony   one  wishes  to believe  caressing

e  ki  ra vi  e  ki  nɑ  vra
**Et qui ravit et qui navre à**
And which entrances and which distresses at

la  fwa
**la fois.**
the  time.

pu  rfɛ  rmjø  sɛ tə  plɛ̃  ta su pi ə
**Pour faire mieux cette plainte assoupie**
To   make  better  this  lament  lulled

la  nɛ ʒə  tɔ̃  ba lɔ̃  trɛ  də  ʃa rpi ə
**La neige tombe à longs traits de charpie**
The  snow  falls  in  long  trails  of  rags

a  tra vɛ  rlə  ku ʃɑ̃  sɑ̃ gi nɔ lɑ̃
**A travers le couchant sanguinolent,**
Across   the  sunset   blood-red,

e  lɛ  ra  lɛ  rdɛ  trœ̃  su pi
**Et l'air a l'air d'être un soupir**
And the air has the air of being a  sigh

rdo tɔ nə
**d'automne**
of autumn

tɑ̃  ti  lfɛ  du  pa  rsə  swa  rmɔ nɔ tɔ nə
**Tant il fait doux par ce soir monotone**
So  it  is  mild  on  this  evening monotonous

u  sə  dɔ rlɔ  tœ̃  pe i za ʒə  lɑ̃
**Où se dorlote un paysage lent.**
Where itself nestles  a  landscape  sluggish.

The sound of the horn mourns away toward the woods,
Of a sorrow you wish to believe one and only
Which comes to die out at the foot of the hill
Amidst the short howlings of the roving north wind.

The soul of the wolf weeps in this voice
Which rises with the declining sun,
In an agony you wish to believe soothing,
Both enrapturing and distressing.

To enhance this lulled lament,
The snow falls in long trails of rags
Across the blood-red sunset,

And the air seems to be an autumnal sigh,
So mild is this monotonous evening
That enfolds the sluggish landscape.

# III.  "L'Echelonnement des haies"

**Dedicated to Robert Godet**

Verlaine was released from prison in January 1875, confessed and absolved, yearning to forgive and to be forgiven. He went off to Paris, but there underwent a succession of failures, trying to ingratiate himself with both his wife and Rimbaud. He then fled to England in March and obtained a teaching position at a grammar school in Stickney, Lincolnshire. The year he spent there was calm and relatively happy on the surface; the atmosphere was so pleasant, in fact, that he started to think about settling definitely in England. He was healthy, read a lot, walked across magnificent sheep pastures, and wrote poetry.

"L'Echelonnement des haies," also entitled "Paysage au Lincolnshire" (Landscape in Lincolnshire), is a watercolor of fine lines and delicate hues. Against a pale blue sky, rows of hedges stretch out to the horizon, while colts and ewes play in the verdant meadows among trees and windmills. The light mist makes the rural landscape shift its contours and objects: Hedges roll like sea waves, trees and mills float on the grass, colts frolic briskly. Sensations are fresh and aerial. It is Sunday, a transparent and incredible Sunday of early spring, Easter Sunday, perhaps, since bells ring in the sky. Verlaine's poem is unusually vibrant and elated. Reality becomes impalpable and almost uncertain, as if the poet insisted on remaining deaf and blind to the true reality: One wonders what storms are dormant behind the spell of the vision and moment.

The pastoral setting of the poem inspired Debussy to a lively and luminous version. The song abounds in graceful happiness: Waves of sound burst out in a brisk rhythm. The use of the pentatonic scale depicts the rustic scene. The staccatos of the melody set off the playful mood of the poem, whereas the smooth ending of the song expresses the soul's elation and quietude.

# le ʃə lɔ nmã de ɛ
# L'Echelonnement des haies
## The Spacing out of the hedgerows

| le ʃə lɔ nə mã | | de | ɛ |
|---|---|---|---|
| **L'échelonnement** | **des** | | **haies** |
| The spacing out | | of the | hedgerows |

| mu tɔ | | na lɛ̃ fi ni | mɛ |
|---|---|---|---|
| **Moutonne** | | **à l'infini,** | **mer** |
| Froths | | infinitely, | sea |

| rklɛ rə | dã | lə | bru ja | | rklɛ r |
|---|---|---|---|---|---|
| **Claire** | **dans** | **le** | **brouillard** | | **clair** |
| Clear | in | the | fog | | clear |

| ki | sã | bɔ̃ | lɛ | ʒœ nə | bɛ |
|---|---|---|---|---|---|
| **Qui** | **sent** | **bon** | **les** | **jeunes** | **baies.** |
| Which | smells | nice | the | young | berries. |

| dɛ | za rbrə | ze | dɛ | mu lɛ̃ |
|---|---|---|---|---|
| **Des** | **arbres** | **et** | **des** | **moulins** |
| Some | trees | and | some | mills |

| sɔ̃ | le ʒe | sy | rlə | vɛ | rtã drə |
|---|---|---|---|---|---|
| **Sont** | **légers** | **sur** | **le** | **vert** | **tendre** |
| Are | light | on | the | green | delicate |

| u | vjɛ̃ | se ba | | tre | se tã drə |
|---|---|---|---|---|---|
| **Où** | **vient** | **s'ébattre** | | **et** | **s'étendre** |
| Where | comes | to gambol | | and | stretch |

| la ʒi li te | | dɛ | pu lɛ̃ |
|---|---|---|---|
| **L'agilité** | | **des** | **poulains.** |
| The agility | | of the | colts. |

L'échelonnement des haies
Moutonne à l'infini, mer
Claire dans le brouillard clair
Qui sent bon les jeunes baies.

Des arbres et des moulins
Sont légers sur le vert tendre
Où vient s'ébattre et s'étendre
L'agilité des poulains.

Dans ce vague d'un Dimanche
Voici se jouer aussi
De grandes brebis aussi
Douces que leur laine blanche.

Tout à l'heure déferlait
L'onde roulée en volutes,
De cloches comme des flûtes
Dans le ciel comme du lait.

(*Forty-three Songs for Voice and Piano*. New York: International, 1961)

• 

The spacing out of the
hedgerows
Is frothing endlessly, sea-like
And clear in the clear mist,
Fragrant with young berries.

Trees and windmills
Are light on the delicate green
Where come to frolic and stretch
The agile colts.

| dã | sə | va gə | dœ̃ | di mã ʃə |
|---|---|---|---|---|
| **Dans** | **ce** | **vague** | **d'un** | **Dimanche** |
| In | this | vagueness | of a | Sunday |

On this vague Sunday,
Here come also to play
Large ewes as
Soft as their white wool.

| vwa si | sə | ʒu e | ro si |
|---|---|---|---|
| **Voici** | **se** | **jouer** | **aussi** |
| Here | are | playing | also |

Just now there broke
A wave, rolling in curls,
Of flute-like bells
In the milk-white sky.

| də | grã də | brə bi | o si |
|---|---|---|---|
| **De** | **grandes** | **brebis** | **aussi** |
| Some | large | ewes | as |

| du sə | kə | lœ | rlɛ nə | blã ʃə |
|---|---|---|---|---|
| **Douces** | **que** | **leur** | **laine** | **blanche.** |
| Soft | as | their | wool | white. |

| tu | ta | lœ rə | de fɛ rlɛ |
|---|---|---|---|
| **Tout** | **à** | **l'heure** | **déferlait** |
| Just | | now | broke |

| lõ də | ru le ə | ã | vɔ ly tə |
|---|---|---|---|
| **L'onde,** | **roulée** | **en** | **volutes,** |
| The wave, | rolled | in | curls, |

| də | klɔ ʃə | kɔ mə | dɛ | fly tə |
|---|---|---|---|---|
| **De** | **cloches** | **comme** | **des** | **flutes** |
| Of | bells | like | some | flutes |

| dã | lə | sjɛ l | kɔ mə | dy | lɛ |
|---|---|---|---|---|---|
| **Dans** | **le** | **ciel** | **comme** | **du** | **lait.** |
| In | the | sky | like | some | milk. |

# ———"Proses Lyriques"———
## *(Lyrical Prose)*

**Date of publication:** *1895.*
**Publisher:** *E. Fromont, Paris.*

  I. **"De rêve"** (Of Dream).
 II. **"De grève"** (Of Strand).
III. **"De fleurs"** (Of Flowers).
IV. **"De soir"** (Of Evening).

The *Proses Lyriques* are considered a first step toward the *Pelléas et Mélisande* atmosphere. Their texts have often been criticized: Too many influences were found, and some of their images and sound effects were regarded as regrettable. Nevertheless, not only are they Debussy's personal attempt at poetry, but they also embody his concern with the technical association between poetry and music, and more specifically with experiments with free verse. In addition, they convey his interest in the aesthetic ideas of his time and carry the Symbolist preoccupation with sadness and boredom, along with the harmful role of memory and the power of nostalgia. Two themes derived from Laforgue's works are particularly prominent, those of innocence and boredom. The Baudelairian influence is also strongly felt, specially in "De rêve" and "De fleurs."

Debussy submitted the four poems to the poet Henri de Régnier for judgment; Régnier, in turn, recommended two of them, "De rêve" and "De grève," for publication in his friend Viélé-Griffin's review *Entretiens politiques et littéraires* (Political and Literary Talks). The songs are very lyrical and demanding in the vocal line. The accompaniment offers orchestral effects of a rich nature.

# I. "De rêve"

**Date of composition:** *1892.*
**Dedicated to Vital Hocquet.**

This poem was published in the *Entretiens Politiques et Litté-raires* of December 1892. The themes of the poem are of Decadent inspiration and recall, in particular, the Symbolist poem of Henri de Régnier, "Songe de la forêt" (Dream of the Forest). In the dreamy atmosphere of an autumnal forest, reminiscent of *Parsifal,* legendary figures appear on a tender night: A regal woman passes by, followed by laughing maidens and valiant knights on their way to the Grail. But the grass of the clearing is sparse, trees are shedding their golden leaves and fail to comfort the disconsolate woman. One hears the maidens' laughter die down with the breeze, and the knights' helmets have suddenly lost their shine. A pale tremor arises under the moon, souls sigh beneath the trees, and only memories are left from the days of beauty, merrymaking, and heroism: The poet's melancholy soul now grieves at the faded dream of a glorious past.

The song was dedicated to Vital Hocquet, the plumbing contractor and music amateur whom Debussy met at the *Chat Noir.* It has two tempos and two musical themes that intertwine the ideas of regret and remembrance. The remembrance theme culminates halfway through with the evocation of the knights of the Grail; at this point a horn calls three times, then echoes away to the end of the song. The vocal line offers many opportunities for legato.

# də rɛ v
# **De rêve**
## Of dream

| la | nɥi | a | dɛ | du sœ | rdə fa mə |
|----|-----|---|----|-------|-----------|
| **La** | **nuit** | **a** | **des** | **douceurs** | **de femme** |
| The | night | has | some | sweetnesses | of    woman |

| e | lɛ | vjø | za rbrə | su | la | ly nə |
|---|----|-----|---------|----|----|----|
| **Et** | **les** | **vieux** | **arbres,** | **sous** | **la** | **lune** |
| And | the | old | trees, | under | the | moon |

| dɔ r |
|------|
| **d'or,** |
| of gold, |

| sɔ̃ ʒə |
|--------|
| **Songent!** |
| Dream! |

| a | sɛ lə | ki | vjɛ̃ | də | pɑ se | la | tɛ |
|---|-------|----|------|----|-------|----|----|
| **A** | **celle** | **qui** | **vient** | **de** | **passer,** | **la** | **tête** |
| To | her | who | has | just | passed, | the | head |

| tɑ̃ pɛ rle ə |
|-------------|
| **emperlée,** |
| pearled, |

| mɛ̃ tə nɑ̃ | na vre ə | a | ʒa mɛ |
|-----------|----------|---|-------|
| **Maintenant** | **navrée,** | **à** | **jamais** |
| Now | heartbroken, | for | ever |

| na vre ə |
|----------|
| **navrée,** |
| heartbroken, |

| i | lnɔ̃ | pɑ | sy | lɥi | fɛ rə | si ɲə |
|---|------|----|----|----|-------|-------|
| **Ils** | **n'ont** | **pas** | **su** | **lui** | **faire** | **signe. . .** |
| They | did | not | know | her | beckon. . . |

La nuit a des douceurs de femmes
Et les vieux arbres, sous la lune
d'or,
Songent!
A celle qui vient de passer, la tête
emperlée,
Maintenant navrée, à jamais
navré,
Ils n'ont pas su lui faire signe. . .

Toutes! Elles ont passé: les Frêles,
les Folles,
Semant leur rire au gazon grêle,
aux brises frôleuses la caresse
charmeuse des hanches
fleurissantes.
Hélas! de tout ceci, plus rien
qu'un blanc frisson.

Les vieux arbres sous la lune d'or
pleurent leurs belles feuilles d'or!
Nul ne leur dédiera plus la fierté
des casques d'or
Maintenant ternis! à jamais
ternis.
Les chevaliers sont morts
Sur le chemin du Grâal!

| tu tə | ε lə | zɔ̃ | pɑ se | lε | frε lə | lε |
|-------|------|-----|-------|-----|--------|-----|
| **Toutes!** | **Elles** | **ont** | **passé:** | **les** | **Frêles,** | **les** |
| All! | They | have | passed: | the | Frail, | the |

| fɔ lə | | | | | | |
|-------|--|--|--|--|--|--|
| **Folles,** | | | | | | |
| Foolish, | | | | | | |

| sə mɑ̃ | lœ | ri | ro | gɑ zɔ̃ | grε lə |
|--------|-----|-----|-----|--------|--------|
| **Semant** | **leur** | **rire** | **au** | **gazon** | **grêle,** |
| Casting | their | laughter | to the | grass | thin, |

| o | bri zə | | | | |
|---|--------|--|--|--|--|
| **aux** | **brises** | | | | |
| to the | breezes | | | | |

| fro lø zə | la | ka rε sə | ʃa rmø zə | de |
|-----------|-----|----------|-----------|-----|
| **frôleuses** | **la** | **caresse** | **charmeuse** | **des** |
| grazing | the | caress | alluring | of the |

| ɑ̃ ʃə | | | | |
|-------|--|--|--|--|
| **hanches** | | | | |
| hips | | | | |

| flœ ri sɑ̃ tə |
|--------------|
| **fleurissantes** |
| blossoming |

| e lɑ s | də tu | sə si | ply | rjɛ̃ | kœ̃ |
|--------|-------|-------|-----|------|-----|
| **Hélas!** | **de tout** | **ceci,** | **plus** | **rien** | **qu'un** |
| Alas! | of all | this, | left | nothing | but a |

| blɑ̃ | fri sɔ̃ | |
|------|---------|--|
| **blanc** | **frisson. . .** | |
| pale | tremor. . . | |

La nuit a des douceurs de femmes,
Des mains semblent frôler les âmes, mains si folles, si frêles,
Au temps où les épées chantaient pour Elles!
D'étranges soupirs s'élèvent sous les arbres.
Mon âme c'est du rêve ancien qui t'étreint!

*(Forty-three Songs for Voice and Piano.* New York: International, 1961)

———————— • ————————

The night has a woman's sweetness
And the old trees, under the golden moon,
Dream!
To Her who has just passed, her head pearled,
Now heartbroken, forever heartbroken,
They did not know how to beckon.

All of them! They have passed: the Frail, the Foolish,
Casting their laughter to the thin grass, to the grazing breezes the alluring caress of their blossoming hips.
Alas! of all this nothing is left but a pale tremor. . .

lɛ      vjø    za rbrə  su       ia    ly nə    dɔ r
**Les   vieux  arbres   sous     la    lune     d'or**
The     old    trees    under    the   moon     of gold
plœ rə
**pleurent**
weep

lœ      rbɛ lə    fœ jə      dɔ r
**leurs belles    feuilles   d'or!**
their   beautiful leaves     of gold!

ny     lnə   lœ    rde di ra       ply     la    fjɛ rte
**Nul  ne    leur  dédiera         plus    la    fierté**
No     one   their will dedicate   more    the   pride
dɛ
**des**
of the

ka skə     dɔ r
**casques   d'or**
helmets    of gold

mɛ̃ tə nɑ̃       tɛ rni       a      ʒa mɛ     tɛ rni
**Maintenant   ternis,      à      jamais    ternis.**
Now            tarnished,   for    ever      tarnished.

lɛ    ʃə va lje      sɔ̃    mɔ r
**Les chevaliers     sont   morts**
The   knights        are    dead

sy    rlə   ʃə mɛ̃     dy    gra l
**Sur  le    chemin    du    Grâal!**
On    the   path      to the Grail!

The old trees under the golden
moon weep for their beautiful
golden leaves!
No one will dedicate to them
evermore the pride of the golden
helmets
Now tarnished, forever
tarnished.
The knights have died
On the road to the Grail.

The night has a woman's
sweetness,
Hands seem to graze the souls,
hands so foolish, so frail,
In the days when swords sang for
Them!
Strange sighs rise under the trees.
My soul, this is some ancient
dream that grips you!

la   nɥi   a   dɛ   du sœ      rdə fa mə
**La   nuit   a   des   douceurs   de   femme,**
The   night   has   some   sweetnesses   of   woman,

dɛ   mɛ̃   sɑ̃ blə   fro le   lɛ   zɑ mə
**Des   mains semblent   frôler   les   âmes,**
Some   hands   seem   to graze   the   souls,
mɛ̃
**mains**
hands

si   fɔ lə   si   frɛ lə
**si   folles,   si   frêles,**
so   foolish,   so   frail,

o   tɑ̃   u   lɛ   ze pe ə   ʃɑ̃ tɛ
**Au   temps   où   les   épées   chantaient**
At the   time   when the   swords   sang
pu   rɛ lə
**pour   Elles!**
for   Them!

de trɑ̃ ʒə   su pi   rse lɛ və   su   lɛ
**D'étranges   soupirs   s'élèvent   sous   les**
Strange   sighs   rise   under   the
za rbrə
**arbres.**
trees.

mɔ̃   nɑ mə se   dy   rɛ   vɑ̃ si jɛ̃ ki
**Mon   âme   c'est   du   rêve   ancien qui**
My   soul   this is some   dream   ancient   which
te trɛ̃
**t'étreint!**
you grips!

# II. "De grève"

**Date of composition:** *1892.*
**Dedicated to Raymond Bonheur.**

The seascape of this impressionistic poem is captured in three successive moments: before, during, and after a squall. Debussy recreates scenes reminiscent of Verlaine's *Aquarelles* and the sea watercolors of the British painter Turner. At dusk, waves ripple and chatter like little girls coming out of school; then a squall comes to scatter the waves and cause a commotion among them. But the compassionate moon rises and pacifies them. The final appeasement is broken only by the distant chimes from floating churches. Color tones are given in the repeated verse, white representing calm and green representing torment. The choice of the word *soie* (silk) calls for background sounds as the waves rustle like the silk dresses of frenzied little girls. The innocent evocation derives its poetic loveliness from this charming comparison.

"De grève" was dedicated to Raymond Bonheur, a fellow student of Debussy's at the Paris Conservatory. Some Debussyists consider it one of Debussy's most perfect songs and the finest of his *Proses Lyriques*.[41] Contrasts must be established between the chattering agitation of the beginning, the foreboding cloud formation and the abrupt violence of the squall in the second part, and the final appeasement. The varying texture of the accompaniment conveys the changes of color and light of the English watercolor.

də grɛ v
## De grève
Of strand

sy     rla  mɛ    rlɛ  kre py sky lə  tɔ̃ bə
**Sur   la   mer   les  crépuscules     tombent,**
Over   the  sea   the  twilights       fall,

swa   blɑ̃     ʃe fi le ə
**Soie  blanche  effilée.**
Silk   white    frayed.

lɛ    va gə    kɔ mə    də    pə ti tə   fɔ lə
**Les   vagues   comme de    petites    folles**
The   waves    like     some   little     silly girls

ʒɑ zə     pə ti tə  fi jə   sɔ rtɑ̃     də  le kɔ lə
**Jasent,    petites   filles  sortant    de l'école,**
Chatter,   little    girls   coming out of   school,

pa rmi   lɛ   fru fru    də  lœ   rɔ bə
**Parmi   les  froufrous  de  leur  robe**
Amid    the  swishings  of   their  dress

swa   vɛ     rti ri ze ə
**Soie  verte  irisée!**
Silk   green  iridescent!

lɛ    ny a ʒə   gra və   vwa ja ʒœ r
**Les   nuages,   graves   voyageurs,**
The   clouds,   solemn   travelers,
sə kɔ̃ sɛ rtə
**se concertent**
consult

Sur la mer les crépuscules
tombent,
Soie blanche effilée.
Les vagues comme de petites
folles
Jasent, petites filles sortant de
l'école,
Parmi les froufrous de leur robe,
Soie verte irisée!

Les nuages, graves voyageurs, se
concertent sur le prochain orage,
Et c'est un fond vraiment trop
grave à cette anglaise aquarelle.
Les vagues, les petites vagues, ne
savent plus où se mettre, car voici
la méchante averse.
Froufrous de jupes envolées,
Soie verte affolée.

Mais la lune, compatissante à
tous!
Vient apaiser ce gris conflit
Et caresse lentement ses petites
amies qui s'offrent comme lèvres
aimantes
A ce tiède et blanc baiser.
Puis,
Plus rien. . .
Plus que les cloches attardées des
flottantes églises!
Angélus des vagues,
Soie blanche apaisée!

(*Forty-three Songs for Voice
and Piano.* New York:
International, 1961)

sy rlə prɔ ʃɛ nɔ ra ʒə
**sur le prochain orage,**
on the impending storm,

e sɛ tœ̃ fɔ̃ vrɛ mã tro
**Et c'est un fond vraiment trop**
And this is a background truly too

gra və
**grave**
dark

a sɛ tã glɛ za kwa rɛ lə
**à cette anglaise aquarelle.**
for this English watercolor.

lɛ va gə lɛ pə ti tə va gə nə
**Les vagues, les petites vagues ne**
The waves, the little waves, don't

sa və
**savent**
know

ply zu sə mɛ trə ka rvwa si
**plus où se mettre, car voici**
any longer where to go, for here comes

la me ʃã ta vɛrsə
**la méchante averse,**
the malicious shower,

fru fru də ʒy pə zã vɔ le ə
**Froufrous de jupes envolées,**
Swishings of skirts flying,

swɑ vɛ rta fɔ le ə
**Soie verte affolée.**
Silk green bewildered.

Over the sea twilights fall,
Frayed white silk.
Waves like little silly girls
Chatter, like little girls coming
out of school,
Amid the swishing of their
dresses,
Iridescent green silk!

Clouds, solemn travelers,
consult over the impending
storm,
And it is truly too dark a
background for this English
watercolor.
Waves, the little waves, no
longer know where to go, for
here comes the malicious
shower,
Swishing of flying skirts,
Bewildered green silk.

But the moon, compassionate to
all!
Comes to pacify this gray conflict
And slowly caresses its little
friends who offer themselves like
loving lips
To this warm white kiss.
Then,
Nothing more. . .
Only the belated bells of the
floating churches!
Angelus of the waves,
Smoothed white silk!

mɛ      la     ly nə    kɔ̃ pa ti sɑ̃       ta    tu s
**Mais    la     lune,    compatissante à    tous!**
But     the    moon,    compassionate to   all!

vjɛ̃        ta pe ze   sə     gri    kɔ̃ fli
**Vient     apaiser    ce     gris    conflit**
Comes     to pacify   this    gray   conflict

e       ka rɛ sə    lɑ̃ tə mɑ̃      sɛ     pə ti tə    za mi (ə)
**Et      caresse     lentement  ses    petites    amies**
And     caresses    slowly        its     little      friends

ki      sɔ frə                kɔ mə    lɛ vrə    zɛ mɑ̃ tə
**qui    s'offrent            comme    lèvres    aimantes**
who     themselves offer   like       lips       loving

a       sə     tjɛ     de     blɑ̃     be ze
**A      ce     tiède   et     blanc   baiser.**
To      this    warm    and    white   kiss.

pɥi
**Puis,**
Then,

ply      rjɛ̃
**Plus    rien. . .**
More    nothing. . .

ply      kə     lɛ     klɔ ʃə      za ta rde ə    dɛ
**Plus    que    les    cloches    attardées     des**
More    than    the    bells       belated        of the

flɔ tɑ̃ tə      ze gli zə
**flottantes    églises!**
floating       churches!

ɑ̃ ʒe ly     sdɛ     va gə
**Angélus   des     vagues,**
Angelus   of the  waves,

swɑ     blɑ̃     ʃa pe ze (ə)
**Soie   blanche apaisée!**
Silk    white    smoothed!

# III.  "De fleurs"

**Date of composition:** *June 1893.*
**Dedicated to Madame E. Chausson.**

The *Art Nouveau* floral imagery of this poem suggestively blends with reminiscences of Baudelaire's *Fleurs du Mal* (Flowers of Evil) and Maeterlinck's *Serres Chaudes* (Hothouses). The Baudelairian theme of boredom is associated here with the hot vapid atmosphere of a greenhouse, where the poet's soul is dissolving, suffocated by the evil flowers of tediousness. The sun that breeds heavy scents overpowers the poet's dreams and drowns his creativity. Irises and lilies despoil his soul, which, now unable to pray or cry, perishes in the deadly heat of the hothouse. May salvation come again with renewed inspiration to break all delusions and evil thoughts and restore fresh energy! Unfortunately, it is but a mirage. The poet's soul is doomed to unrelieved sorrow and boredom.

The inescapability of the poet's predicament is reinforced by the intolerably stuffy atmosphere of the greenhouse. The dramatic efforts of the creative soul in its struggle against adverse forces are artfully evoked by the stifling confinement of the glass panes. The sun, commonly revered as a source of life, is here shown consuming the poet's soul, whose creative energies long for the soothing darkness that fosters dreams.

The melody was dedicated to Madame Chausson, wife of the composer Ernest Chausson who provided Debussy with great support. The tonal harmonies of the major and minor chords and the slow tempo of the beginning recreate the poem's mood of boredom; a good legato is called for in the melodic line. The song becomes dramatic, somewhat grandiloquent as it conveys the exacerbated thoughts of the poet. It dies away as the succession of minor and major triads reappears to suggest the soul's resignation to boredom.

## də flœ r
# De fleurs
## Of flowers

| | | | | | |
|---|---|---|---|---|---|
| dɑ̃ | lɑ̃ nɥi | si | de zɔ le mɑ̃ | vɛ r | də |
| **Dans** | **l'ennui** | **si** | **désolément** | **vert** | **de** |
| In | the boredom | so | desolately | verdant | of |
| la | sɛ rə | | | | |
| **la** | **serre** | | | | |
| the | hothouse | | | | |

| | | | | | |
|---|---|---|---|---|---|
| də du lœ r | | lɛ | flœ | rzɑ̃ la sə | mɔ̃ |
| **de douleur,** | | **les** | **Fleurs** | **enlacent** | **mon** |
| of sorrow, | | the | Flowers | entwine | my |
| kœ r | də | | | | |
| **coeur** | **de** | | | | |
| heart | with | | | | |

| | | | |
|---|---|---|---|
| lœ | rti ʒə | me ʃɑ̃ tə | |
| **leurs** | **tiges** | **méchantes.** | |
| their | stems | wicked. | |

| | | | | | |
|---|---|---|---|---|---|
| ɑ | kɑ̃ | rə vjɛ̃ drɔ̃ | o tu | rdə | ma |
| **Ah!** | **Quand** | **reviendront** | **autour** | **de** | **ma** |
| Ah! | When | will return | about | of | my |
| tɛ tə | lɛ | | | | |
| **tête** | **les** | | | | |
| head | the | | | | |

| | | | | |
|---|---|---|---|---|
| ʃɛ rə | mɛ̃ | si | tɑ̃ drə mɑ̃ | de zɑ̃ la sø zə |
| **chères** | **mains** | **si** | **tendrement** | **désenlaceuses?** |
| dear | hands | so | tenderly | disentwining? |

Dans l'ennui si désolément vert de la serre de douleur, les Fleurs enlacent mon coeur de leurs tiges méchantes.
Ah! quand reviendront autour de ma tête les chères mains si tendrement désenlaceuses?

Les grands Iris violets violèrent méchamment tes yeux, en semblant les refléter,
Eux qui furent l'eau du songe où plongèrent mes rêves si doucement enclos en leur couleur;
Et les lys, blancs jets d'eau de pistils embaumés, ont perdu leur grâce blanche
Et ne sont plus que pauvres malades sans soleil!

Soleil! ami des fleurs mauvaises,
Tueur de rêves!
Tueur d'illusions, ce pain béni des âmes misérables!
Venez!
Venez!
Les mains salvatrices!
Brisez les vitres de mensonges,
Brisez les vitres de maléfice,
Mon âme meurt de trop de soleil!

lɛ      grɑ̃      zi ri    svjɔ lɛ
**Les    grands    Iris     violets**
The     tall      Irises   violet

vjɔ lɛ rə    me ʃa mɑ̃      tɛ      zjø     ɑ̃
**Violèrent    méchamment  tes      yeux,   en**
Violated     wickedly                your    eyes,   while
sɑ̃ blɑ̃     lɛ      rə fle te
**semblant    les     refléter,**
seeming      them    reflect,

ø      ki      fy rə    lo      dy      sɔ̃ ʒə    u
**Eux    qui     furent   l'eau    du      songe    où**
They    that    were     the water  of the  dream    where
plɔ̃ ʒɛ rə
**plongèrent**
plunged

mɛ      rɛ və     si      du sə mɑ̃      tɑ̃ klo      ɑ̃      lœ
**mes    rêves     si      doucement     enclos      en      leur**
my      dreams    so      softly                  enclosed  in      their
rku lœ r
**couleur;**
color;

e       lɛ      li s     blɑ̃      ʒɛ      do       də pi sti
**Et      les     lys,     blancs    jets    d'eau     de pistils**
And     the     lilies,  white     jets    of water  of pistils
lzɑ̃ bo me
**embaumés,**
fragrant,

ɔ̃      pɛ rdy    lœ      rg rɑ sə    blɑ̃ ʃə
**ont    perdu     leur     grâce       blanche**
have    lost      their    grace       white

Mirages!
Plus ne refleurira la joie de mes
yeux
Et mes mains sont lasses de prier,
Mes yeux sont las de pleurer!
Eternellement ce bruit fou des
pétales noirs de l'ennui tombant
goutte à goutte sur ma tête
Dans le vert de la serre de
douleur!

*(Forty-three Songs for Voice
and Piano.* New York:
International, 1961)

———————●———————

In the boredom of sorrow's
hothouse, so desolately verdant,
the Flowers entwine my heart
with their wicked stems.
Ah! When will come again about
my head the dear hands that so
tenderly disentwine?

The tall violet Irises
Wickedly violated your eyes
while seeming to reflect them,
They that were the water of the
dream in which my dreams
plunged, so softly enclosed in
their color;
And the lilies, white fountains of
fragrant pistils, have lost their
white grace
And are now only poor invalids
without sun!

| e | nə | sɔ̃ | ply | kə | po vrə | ma la də |
|---|---|---|---|---|---|---|
| **Et** | **ne** | **sont** | **plus** | **que** | **pauvres** | **malades** |
| And | not | are | more | than | poor | invalids |

| sɑ̃ | | sɔ lɛ j |
|---|---|---|
| **sans** | | **soleil!** |
| without | | sun! |

| sɔ lɛ j | a mi | dɛ | flœ | rmɔ vɛ zə |
|---|---|---|---|---|
| **Soleil!** | **ami** | **des** | **fleurs** | **mauvaises,** |
| Sun! | friend | of the | flowers | evil, |

| ty œ | rdə | rɛ və |
|---|---|---|
| **Tueur** | **de** | **rêves!** |
| Killer | of | dreams! |

| ty œ | rdi ly zi ɔ̃ | sə | pɛ | be ni | dɛ |
|---|---|---|---|---|---|
| **Tueur** | **d'illusions** | **ce** | **pain** | **béni** | **des** |
| Killer | of illusions | this | bread | blessed | of the |

| zɑ mə | mi ze ra blə |
|---|---|
| **âmes** | **misérables!** |
| souls | wretched! |

| və ne | və ne | lɛ | mɛ̃ | sa lva tri sə |
|---|---|---|---|---|
| **Venez!** | **Venez!** | **Les** | **mains** | **salvatrices!** |
| Come! | Come! | the | hands | salvaging! |

| bri ze | lɛ | vi trə | də | mɑ̃ sɔ̃ ʒə |
|---|---|---|---|---|
| **Brisez** | **les** | **vitres** | **de** | **mensonge,** |
| Break | the | panes | of | delusion, |

| bri ze | lɛ | vi trə | də | ma le fi sə |
|---|---|---|---|---|
| **Brisez** | **les** | **vitres** | **de** | **maléfice,** |
| Break | the | panes | of | maleficence, |

Sun! friend of evil flowers,
Slayer of dreams!
Slayer of illusions, blessed bread
of wretched souls!
Come! Come! Hands of
salvation!
Break the glass panes of delusion,
Break the glass panes of
maleficence,
My soul is dying of too much
sun!

Mirages! The joy of my eyes will
never blossom again
And my hands are weary of
praying,
My eyes are weary of weeping!
Eternally this insane sound of
boredom's black petals falling,
drop by drop, on my head
In the verdure of sorrow's
hothouse!

mɔ̃    na mə   mœ    rdə  tro    də  sɔlɛj
**Mon âme    meurt    de    trop  de  soleil!**
My    soul    dies    of    too    of  sun!


mi ra ʒə    ply    nə    rə flœ ri ra        la
**Mirages! Plus    ne    refleurira        la**
Mirages!    More    never    will blossom again    the
ʒwa    də    mɛ    zjø
**joie    de    mes    yeux**
joy    of    my    eyes


e    mɛ    mɛ̃    sɔ̃    la sə    də pri je
**Et    mes    mains    sont    lasses    de prier,**
And    my    hands    are    weary    of    praying,


mɛ    zjø    sɔ̃    la        də    plœ re
**Mes    yeux    sont    las        de    pleurer!**
My    eyes    are    weary    of    crying!


e tɛ rnɛ lə mã    sə    brɥi    fu        dɛ
**Eternellement ce    bruit    fou        des**
Eternally            this    sound    insane    of the
pe ta lə    nwa
**pétales    noirs**
petals    black


rdə    lã nɥi    tɔ̃ bã    gu        ta    gu tə    sy
**de    l'ennui    tombant    goutte    à    goutte    sur**
of    boredom    falling    drop    by    drop    on
rma    tɛ tə
**ma    tête**
my    head


dã    lə    vɛ    rdə la    sɛ rə        də    du lœ r
**Dans le    vert    de    la    serre        de    douleur!**
In    the    green    of    the    hothouse    of    sorrow!

# IV. "De soir"

**Date of composition:** *July 1893.*
**Dedicated to Henry Lerolle.**

The Sunday observance is commonly associated with boredom and, as such, is the occasion for mockery of bourgeois mediocrity. Debussy may have been inspired by the ten or so "Sunday" poems written by the young Symbolist poet Jules Laforgue. His version, however, departs from the Symbolist irony and presents a cheerful picture of Sundays in France.

The first part shows some of the traditional activities of the late nineteenth-century urban Sunday afternoon: children's games and rounds, bustling crowds in the train stations frantically waving to one another. The excitement of exploring the outskirts of Paris has been brilliantly illustrated by the contemporary painters Claude Monet and Edouard Manet. In the same amused vein, one cannot help but recall the merry picnics on the grass, boating expeditions, and convivial feasting in rustic inns offered to pleasure-hungry Parisians by the railroads, that magnificent invention of the century.

By the middle of the poem, however, the mood changes to light mockery: Debussy implies that this beautiful invention is turning people and nature into a mechanized universe. What has happened to the good old Sundays? The tone of the poem becomes more personal and melancholy: As the night closes in and Sunday moves away, the poet turns meditative and nostalgic. Religious connotations enter his mind in contrast to the human bustle of the day. The beauty of the vast sky alone lulls one into sleep and peace. Finally a prayer rises to the heraldic figure of the Virgin Mary, asking indulgence for the city dwellers' souls. The childlike exaltation of the beginning of the poem evolves into a touching evocation of the tender night.

The melody was dedicated to Henry Lerolle: A painter and Chausson's brother-in-law, he was well connected with the influential society of the time to which he introduced Debussy. Freshness and dynamism characterize the first part of the song. Church bells are charmingly interrupted by the theme of an old folk tune popular among French children ("La tour, prends garde": Tower, watch out). The rhythm accelerates to evoke the dazzling speed of the train rides, then calms down as the poet recalls the Sundays of old. A nocturnal scene of solemn stillness prepares for the final prayer to the Virgin Mary, accompanied by faint chimes of church bells in a slower tempo.

## də swa r
# De soir
# Of evening

| di mã ʃə | sy | rlɛ | vi lə |
|---|---|---|---|
| **Dimanche** | **sur** | **les** | **villes,** |
| Sunday | over | the | towns, |

| di mã ʃə | dã | lɛ | kœ r |
|---|---|---|---|
| **Dimanche** | **dans** | **les** | **coeurs!** |
| Sunday | in | the | hearts! |

| di mã ʃə | ʃe | lɛ | pə ti tə | fi jə | ʃã tã |
|---|---|---|---|---|---|
| **Dimanche** | **chez** | **les** | **petites** | **filles** | **chantant** |
| Sunday | among | the | little | girls | singing |

| dy nə | vwa |
|---|---|
| **d'une** | **voix** |
| in a | voice |

| ɛ̃ fɔ rme | dɛ | rɔ̃ də | zɔ psti ne (ə) | u |
|---|---|---|---|---|
| **informée** | **des** | **rondes** | **obstinées** | **où** |
| knowing | some | rounds | persistent | where |

| də | bɔ nə | tu r |
|---|---|---|
| **de** | **bonnes** | **Tours** |
| some | good | Towers |

| nã | nɔ̃ | ply | kə | pu | rkɛ lkə | ʒu r |
|---|---|---|---|---|---|---|
| **n'en** | **ont** | **plus** | **que** | **pour** | **quelques** | **jours!** |
| not | have | longer | than | for | a few | days! |

Dimanche sur les villes,
Dimanche dans les coeurs!
Dimanche chez les petites filles
chantant d'une voix informée des
rondes obstinées où de bonnes
Tours n'en ont plus que pour
quelques jours!

Dimanche, les gares sont folles!
Tout le monde appareille pour
des banlieues d'aventure en se
disant adieu avec des gestes
éperdus!

Dimanche les trains vont vite,
dévorés par d'insatiables tunnels;
Et les bons signaux des routes
échangent d'un oeil unique des
impressions toutes mécaniques.

Dimanches, dans le bleu de mes
rêves où mes pensées tristes de
feux d'artifices manqués
Ne veulent plus quitter le deuil de
vieux Dimanches trépassés.

di mã ʃə    lɛ    ga rə    sɔ̃    fɔ lə
**Dimanche, les gares sont folles!**
Sunday,    the stations are    frantic!

tu    lə mɔ̃    da pa rɛ jə   pu    rdɛ
**Tout le monde appareille pour des**
Everybody    takes off    for    some
bã ljø    da vã ty rə
**banlieues d'aventure**
suburbs    of adventure

ã    sə    di zã   ta djø   a vɛ   kdɛ
**en se    disant adieu   avec   des**
to   each other saying   goodbye with   some
ʒɛ stə    ze pɛ rdy
**gestes    éperdus!**
gestures   distracted!

di mã ʃə    lɛ    trɛ̃    vɔ̃    vi tə   de vɔ re
**Dimanche les trains vont vite, dévorés**
Sunday    the trains   go    fast,   devoured

pa    rdɛ̃ sa si a blə   ty nɛ l
**par d'insatiables tunnels;**
by    insatiable    tunnels;

e    lɛ   bɔ̃    si ɲo    dɛ    ru tə
**Et   les bons signaux des    routes**
And   the good signals    of the roads
e ʃã ʒə    dœ̃
**échangent d'un**
exchange    with an

Et la nuit à pas de velours vient
endormir le beau ciel fatigué, et
c'est Dimanche dans les avenues
d'étoiles; la Vierge or sur argent
laisse tomber les fleurs de
sommeil!

Vite, les petits anges
Dépassez les hirondelles afin de
vous coucher forts d'absolution!
Prenez pitié des villes,
Prenez pitié des coeurs,
Vous, la Vierge or sur argent!

(*Forty-three Songs for Voice
and Piano*. New York:
International, 1961)

———————— ● ————————

Sunday over the towns,
Sunday in the hearts!
Sunday among the little girls
singing, with knowing voices,
persistent rounds in which kind
Towers have only a few days left!

On Sunday, the stations are
frantic!
Every one takes off for the
suburbs of adventure bidding
farewell to one another with
distracted gestures!

On Sunday, trains go fast,
devoured by insatiable tunnels;
And the kind road signals
exchange with their single eye
utterly mechanical impressions.

| nœ | jy ni kə | de | zɛ̃ prɛ si ɔ̃ | tu tə |
|---|---|---|---|---|
| **oeil** | **unique** | **des** | **impressions** | **toutes** |
| eye | single | some | impressions | utterly |

| me ka ni kə |
|---|
| **mécaniques.** |
| mechanical. |

| di mɑ̃ ʃə | dɑ̃ | lə | blø | də | mɛ | rɛ və |
|---|---|---|---|---|---|---|
| **Dimanche,** | **dans** | **le** | **bleu** | **de** | **mes** | **rêves** |
| Sunday, | in | the | blue | of | my | dreams |

| u | mɛ |
|---|---|
| **où** | **mes** |
| where | my |

| pɑ̃ se | tri stə | də | fø | da rti fi sə |
|---|---|---|---|---|
| **pensées** | **tristes** | **de** | **feux** | **d'artifices** |
| thoughts | saddened | by | fireworks | |

| mɑ̃ ke |
|---|
| **manqués** |
| missed |

| nə | vœ lə | ply | ki te | lə | dœ j | də |
|---|---|---|---|---|---|---|
| **Ne** | **veulent** | **plus** | **quitter** | **le** | **deuil** | **de** |
| Not will | | longer | go out | of | mourning | for |

| vjø | di mɑ̃ ʃə | tre pa se |
|---|---|---|
| **vieux** | **Dimanches** | **trépassés.** |
| the old | Sundays | bygone. |

| e | la | nɥi | a | pɑ | də | və lu r | vjɛ̃ |
|---|---|---|---|---|---|---|---|
| **Et** | **la** | **nuit** | **à** | **pas** | **de** | **velours** | **vient** |
| And | the | night | with | steps | of | velvet | comes |

| tɑ̃ dɔ rmi r |
|---|
| **endormir** |
| to send to sleep |

On Sunday, in the blue of my dreams in which my thoughts, saddened by missed fireworks, Will no longer stop mourning for the old bygone Sundays.

And the night with velvet steps comes down to send the beautiful and weary sky to sleep, and it is Sunday in the avenues of stars; the Virgin Mary, gold upon silver, drops the flowers of sleep!

Hurry, little angels Outfly the swallows so as to go to bed, strengthened by absolution! Take pity on the towns, Take pity on the hearts You, Virgin Mary gold upon silver!

lə  bo           sjɛl  fa ti ge     e    sɛ
**le  beau        ciel  fatigué,  et   c'est**
the  beautiful  sky    tired,      and  it is

di mɑ̃ ʃə       dɑ̃    lɛ
**Dimanche  dans  les**
Sunday         in      the


za və ny  de twa lə    la   vjɛ r3ə    ɔ     rsy
**avenues  d'étoiles;  la   Vierge   or   sur**
avenues  of stars;     the  Virgin   gold  upon

ra r3ɑ̃   lɛ sə
**argent  laisse**
silver    lets


tɔ̃ be     lɛ   flœ      rdə  sɔ mɛ j
**tomber  les  fleurs  de   sommeil!**
fall       the  flowers  of    sleep!


vi tə     lɛ   pə ti     zɑ̃ 3ə
**Vite,   les  petits   anges**
Hurry,   the  little     angels


de pa se   lɛ   zi rɔ̃ dɛ lə    a fɛ̃       də  vu
**Dépassez  les  hirondelles  afin      de  vous**
Overtake   the  swallows      in order  to  go
ku ʃe
**coucher**
to bed


fɔ                rda psɔ ly si jɔ̃
**forts             d'absolution!**
strengthened   by absolution!


prə ne    pi tje   dɛ     vi lə
**Prenez  pitié   des    villes,**
Take      pity     on the  towns,

prə ne   pi tje   dɛ     kœ r
**Prenez pitié  des     coeurs,**
Take     pity    on the hearts,

vu      la   vjɛ rʒə   ɔ     rsy   ra rʒɑ̃
**Vous, la   Vierge   or    sur   argent!**
You,    the  Virgin   gold  upon  silver!

# —"Les Chansons de Bilitis"——
## (The Songs of Bilitis)

**Date of publication:** *1899.*
**Publisher:** *E. Fromont, Paris.*
**Source:** *"Bucoliques en Pamphylie"* Nos 20, 21, 44. In Les
  Chansons de Bilitis.
**Dedicated to Madame M. V. Peter.**
**First performance:** *Paris, Société Nationale de musique, 17
  March 1900. (Blanche Marot, accompanied by Debussy).*

  I. "La flûte de Pan" (Pan's flute).
 II. "La Chevelure" (The Hair).
III. "Le Tombeau des Naïades" (The Tomb of the Naïads).

The *Songs of Bilitis* exemplify a new phase in Debussy's
aesthetics, inasmuch as they present a more restrained and precise style. They have the simplicity of line of a classical medal, as
if Debussy attempted to transcribe the luminous beauty of
Greece. Each of the three songs has a unity of composition and
sobriety of expression that suggest direct emotion. It took about
ten years for them to reach a wide audience.

  The fictitious daughter of a Greek and a Phoenician, Bilitis
lived her early years in Pamphylia with her mother and sisters. It
is an austere country of deep forests, petrifying springs, salted
lakes, and silent valleys. Flocks grazed on the slopes of the
Taurus. Bilitis ran and played in the meadows, offered sacrifices
to the water nymphs, and often talked to them. Her pastoral life
ended one day when she met a young shepherd; then she felt the
mysterious awakening of her senses.

# I. "La flûte de Pan"

**Date of composition:** *22 June, 1897.*

  One evening at dusk, Bilitis left her mother's house on a
pretext and met her young friend, the shepherd. He was going
to teach her to play the flute he had given her for the festival of
Hyacinthus.[42] Bilitis sat on his lap, trembling a bit while he
played softly. They were so close that there was no need to
speak. Their lips wandered and joined, by turns, on the flute.
Silence settled on the scene; the frogs' song rose. The girl

became suddenly aware that it was late; her mother would never accept her excuse.

The poem is a song of innocent sensuality. Neither fear nor guilt comes to interfere with Bilitis' first encounter with love. She gives herself utterly and genuinely to the thrilling moment. The little story she has told her mother is candid and enticing. Erotic implications are exquisitely mingled with a spontaneous sincerity of feelings.

Debussy wrote a charming melody, suggestive in its simplicity, naive but passionate. The vocal line unfolds in smooth curves and precipitates its tempo only at the end of the song to stress Bilitis' confusion. The narrow note intervals imply that the song is more to be whispered than sung. The accompaniment creates an exquisite mood of enchantment: The flute theme spirals sensuously around Bilitis, and the frogs' song enhances the calm beauty of the nocturnal scene. The *mélodie* was dedicated to Madame M. V. Peter, to whom Debussy was briefly attracted.

## la flyt də pã
## La flûte de Pan
## The flute of Pan

| pu | rlə | ʒu | rdɛ | zi a sẽ ti (ə) | i | lma |
|----|-----|-----|-----|----------------|---|-----|
| **Pour** | **le** | **jour** | **des** | **Hyacinthies,** | **il** | **m'a** |
| For | the | of | Hyacinthus, | he | me has | |

dɔ ne
**donné**
given

Pour le jour des Hyacinthies, il m'a donné une syrinx faite de roseaux bien taillés, unis avec la blanche cire qui est douce à mes lèvres comme le miel.

| y nə | si rẽ ks | fɛ tə | də | ro zo | bjẽ | tɑ je |
|------|----------|-------|-----|-------|-----|-------|
| **une** | **syrinx** | **faite** | **de** | **roseaux** | **bien** | **taillés,** |
| a | syrinx | made | from | reeds | well | cut, |

y ni
**unis**
joined

Il m'apprend à jouer, assise sur ses genoux; mais je suis un peu tremblante. Il en joue après moi, si doucement que je l'entends à peine.

za vɛ kla blɑ̃ ʃə si rə ki ɛ du sa
**avec la blanche cire qui est douce à**
with the white wax which is sweet to

mɛ lɛ vrə
**mes lèvres**
my lips

kɔ mə lə mjɛ l
**comme le miel.**
like the honey.

i lma prɑ̃ ta ʒu e a si zə sy rsɛ
**Il m'apprend à jouer, assise sur ses**
He me teaches to play, seated on his

ʒə nu
**genoux;**
lap;

mɛ ʒə sɥi zœ̃ pø trɑ̃ blɑ̃ tə i lɑ̃
**mais je suis un peu tremblante. Il en**
but I am a bit trembling. He it

ʒu a prɛ mwa
**joue après moi,**
plays after me,

si du sə mɑ̃ kə ʒə lɑ̃ tɑ̃ za pɛ nə
**si doucement que je l'entends à peine.**
so softly that I it hear barely.

nu na vɔ̃ rjɛ̃ na nu di rə
**Nous n'avons rien à nous dire,**
We have nothing to each other tell,

tɑ̃ nu
**tant nous**
so we

Nous n'avons rien à nous dire, tant nous sommes près l'un de l'autre; mais nos chansons veulent se répondre, et tour à tour nos bouches s'unissent sur la flûte.

Il est tard; voici le chant des grenouilles vertes qui commence avec la nuit. Ma mère ne croira jamais que je suis restée si longtemps à chercher ma ceinture perdue.

*(Forty-three Songs for Voice and Piano.* New York: International, 1961)

————————•————————

For Hyacinthus' day, he gave me a syrinx made of carefully cut reeds, joined with white wax which is sweet to my lips like honey.

He teaches me to play, seated on his lap; but I tremble a little. He plays it after me, so softly that I can barely hear him.

We have nothing to tell each other, so close are we one to the other; but our songs wish to answer each other, and by turns our mouths join on the flute.

It is late; here is the song of the green frogs that begins with the night. My mother will never believe that I have stayed so long searching for my lost belt.

sɔ mə　　prɛ　lœ̃　　də lo trə　　mɛ
**sommes près l'un　de l'autre;　mais**
are　　　close the one to　the other;　but

no　　ʃɑ̃sɔ̃　vœ lə
**nos　chansons veulent**
our　songs　wish


sə　　　　re pɔ̃ drə　e　tu　　ra tu　　rno
**se　　　répondre,　et　tour　à　tour　nos**
each other answer,　　and turn　by turn　our

bu ʃə
**bouches**
mouths


sy ni sə　　sy　rla　fly tə
**s'unissent sur la　flûte.**
join　　　　on　the flute.


i　lɛ　ta r　vwa si　lə　ʃɑ̃　　dɛ
**Il　est　tard;　voici　le　chant　des**
It　is　late;　here is　the　song　of the

grə nu jə
**grenouilles**
frogs


vɛ rtə　ki　　kɔ mɑ̃　　sa vɛ kla nɥi
**vertes　qui　commence avec la　nuit.**
green　which begins　　with the　night.

ma　mɛ rə　　nə
**Ma　mère　　ne**
My　mother　not

krwa ra    ʒa mɛ    kə    ʒə    sɥi    rɛ ste    si
**croira    jamais    que    je    suis    restée    si**
will believe    ever    that    I    have    stayed    so

lɔ̃ tɑ̃
**longtemps**
long

a    ʃɛ rʃe    ma    sɛ̃ ty rə    pɛ rdy ə
**à    chercher    ma    ceinture    perdue.**
to    search    my    belt    lost.

# II. "La Chevelure"

**Date of composition:** *July 1897.*

"La Chevelure" tells a story within a story: Bilitis relives a moment of intimacy with her lover during which he had related a dream. In his dream, Bilitis' tresses of hair were intertwined so closely around their bodies that they became one mass of hair, one body and one soul. Then, when the account of the dream was over, the lover tenderly touched and looked at Bilitis, who modestly but acquiescently lowered her eyes.

Two levels of feeling appear in the poem: the ardent love of the dream and the eloquent tenderness of the subsequent scene. Because the dream is only reconstructed, it does not have the vividness of actual vision; thus is preserved the emotional unity of the poem, told from the point of view of the chaste young girl. Such purity of tone does not preclude, however, a current of passionate tension and subtle sensuality from passing between the lovers. The beauty of the poem comes from the simplicity of its vocabulary, the elegant suggestiveness of its imagery, and the musicality of its sinuous sentences.

Debussy's setting first appeared in *L'Image* of October 1897, with illustrations by Van Dongen. The structure of the song makes very apparent the duality of the time sequences and feelings of the poem, marked by differences in tempo and vocal intensity. The low tessitura of the vocal part suggests Bilitis' restrained emotions, whereas its chant-like melodic line conveys the density of the evocation.

# la ʃə vly r
# La Chevelure
# The Hair

| i | lma | di | sɛ tə | nɥi | ʒe |
|---|---|---|---|---|---|
| **Il** | **m'a** | **dit:** | **"Cette** | **nuit,** | **j'ai** |
| He | me has | said: | "This | night, | I have |

| rɛ ve |
|---|
| **rêvé.** |
| dreamt. |

| ʒa vɛ | ta | ʃə və ly | ro tu | rdə mɔ̃ | ku |
|---|---|---|---|---|---|
| **J'avais** | **ta** | **chevelure** | **autour** | **de mon** | **cou.** |
| I had | your | hair | around | of my | neck. |

| ʒa vɛ | tɛ | ʃə vø | kɔ | mɶ̃ kɔ lje |
|---|---|---|---|---|
| **J'avais** | **tes** | **cheveux** | **comme** | **un collier** |
| I had | your | hair | like | a collar |

| nwa |
|---|
| **noir** |
| black |

| ro tu | rdə | ma | ny k | e | sy | rma |
|---|---|---|---|---|---|---|
| **autour** | **de** | **ma** | **nuque** | **et** | **sur** | **ma** |
| around | of | my | nape | and | over | my |

| pwa tri nə |
|---|
| **poitrine.** |
| chest. |

| ʒə | lɛ | ka rɛ sɛ | e | se tɛ | lɛ |
|---|---|---|---|---|---|
| **"Je** | **les** | **caressais,** | **et** | **c'étaient** | **les** |
| "I | them | caressed, | and | they were | the |

| mjɛ̃ |
|---|
| **miens;** |
| mine; |

Il m'a dit: "Cette nuit, j'ai rêvé. J'avais ta chevelure autour de mon cou. J'avais tes cheveux comme un collier noir autour de ma nuque et sur ma poitrine.

"Je les caressais, et c'étaient les miens; et nous étions liés pour toujours ainsi, par la même chevelure la bouche sur la bouche, ainsi que deux lauriers n'ont souvent qu'une racine.

"Et peu à peu, il m'a semblé, tant nos membres étaient confondus, que je devenais toi-même ou que tu entrais en moi comme mon songe."

Quand il eut achevé, il mit doucement ses mains sur mes épaules, et il me regarda d'un regard si tendre, que je baissai les yeux avec un frisson.

(*Forty-three Songs for Voice and Piano.* New York: International, 1961)

He said to me: "Last night, I had a dream. I had your hair around my neck like a black collar around my nape and over my chest.

| e | nu | ze tjɔ̃ | li je | pu | rtu ʒu | rzɛ̃ si |
|---|---|---|---|---|---|---|
| **et** | **nous** | **étions** | **liés** | **pour** | **toujours** | **ainsi,** |
| and | we | were | joined | for | ever | thus, |

"I caressed them, and they were mine; and we were joined forever this way, by the same hair, mouth upon mouth, just as two laurels often have only one root.

| pa | rla | mɛ mə | ʃə və ly rə | la | bu ʃə | sy |
|---|---|---|---|---|---|---|
| **par** | **la** | **même** | **chevelure** | **la** | **bouche** | **sur** |
| by | the | same | hair | | the | mouth | upon |

| rla | bu ʃə |
|---|---|
| **la** | **bouche,** |
| the | mouth, |

"And little by little, it seemed to me, so intermingled were our limbs, that I was becoming you or that you were entering into me like my dream."

| ɛ̃ si | kə | dø | lɔ rje | nɔ̃ | su vɑ̃ |
|---|---|---|---|---|---|
| **ainsi** | **que** | **deux** | **lauriers** | **n'ont** | **souvent** |
| just | as | two | laurels | have | often |

| ky nə | ra si nə |
|---|---|
| **qu'une** | **racine.** |
| only one | root. |

When he finished, he gently put his hands on my shoulders, and he looked at me with so tender a look that I lowered my eyes with a shiver.

| e | pø | a | pø | i | lma | sɑ̃ ble |
|---|---|---|---|---|---|---|
| **"Et** | **peu** | **à** | **peu,** | **il** | **m'a** | **semblé,** |
| "And | little | by | little, | it | me has | seemed, |

| tɑ̃ | no | mɑ̃ brə | ze tɛ | kɔ̃ fɔ̃ dy |
|---|---|---|---|---|
| **tant** | **nos** | **membres** | **étaient** | **confondus,** |
| so | our | limbs | were | intermingled, |

| kə | ʒə | də və nɛ | twa mɛ mə | u | kə | ty |
|---|---|---|---|---|---|---|
| **que** | **je** | **devenais** | **toi-même** | **ou** | **que** | **tu** |
| that | I | became | yourself | or | that | you |

| ɑ̃ trɛ | zɑ̃ | mwa | kɔ mə | mɔ̃ | sɔ̃ ʒə |
|---|---|---|---|---|---|
| **entrais** | **en** | **moi** | **comme** | **mon** | **songe."** |
| entered | into | me | like | my | dream." |

kɑ̃    ti  ly  ta ʃə ve  i  lmi
**Quand il eut achevé, il mit**
When  he had finished, he put

du sə mɑ̃
**doucement**
gently


sɛ  mɛ̃  sy  rmɛ  ze po lə  e  i  lmə
**ses mains sur mes épaules, et il me**
his hands on my shoulders, and he me


rə ga rda dœ̃  rə ga  rsi  tɑ̃ drə  kə  ʒə
**regarda d'un regard si tendre, que je**
looked with a look so tender, that I


be se  lɛ  zjø  a vɛ  kœ̃  fri sɔ̃
**baissai les yeux avec un frisson.**
lowered the eyes with a shiver.

# III.  "Le Tombeau des Naïades"

**Date of composition: *23 August 1898*.**

   This last poem of the "Bucoliques" strikes a desolate note:
After the tender warmth of the twilight and the nocturnal enchantment of Bilitis' adolescent songs, now comes the wintry
season foreshadowing her adult years. Bilitis is seen wandering
helplessly in the woods; her sandal-covered feet trudging in the
snow, she stumbles against the indifferent cold in utter confusion. She is looking for some evidence of life, yet no life appears
in this crystalline transparency of ice, snow, and frost. "Everyone is dead," announces her companion cruelly, and, besides,
the tracks on the snow do not belong to a satyr[43] but to a plain
he-goat! When they arrive at the tomb, the young man dismays
her by breaking the ice of the spring, shattering her hopes of
finding the Naiads.[44]
   The slow tempo of Debussy's setting, the repetitive theme of
the accompaniment depict Bilitis' march in the snow, whereas
the weary expression given by the composer to the vocal part
recreates the girl's confusion and desolation. The second part of
the song opposes, in the dialogue, the chilled world of today to
the fluidity of sweet memories. The third part marks a contrast
when the vocal line ascends and the tempo accelerates to relate
the young man's defiance. Debussy concludes his song by re-
suming the initial theme of the piano accompaniment, which
prolongs the frieze-like effect of Bilitis' walk against the backdrop of the frozen woods.

lə tɔ̃bo de najad
## Le Tombeau des Naïades
The Tomb of the Naiads

| lə lɔ̃ | dy | bwa | ku vɛ | rdə | ʒi vrə |
|--------|-----|------|---------|------|--------|
| **Le long** | **du** | **bois** | **couvert** | **de** | **givre,** |
| Along | the | wood | covered | with | frost, |

ʒə ma rʃɛ    mɛ   ʃə vø   də vɑ̃   ma
**je marchais; mes cheveux devant ma**
I   walked;   my   hair    across  my

bu ʃə
**bouche**
mouth


sə    flœ ri sɛ          də    pə ti   gla sɔ̃
**se   fleurissaient   de    petits  glaçons,**
itself blossomed       with  little   icicles,


e    mɛ    sɑ̃ da lə    ze tɛ    lu rdə    də
**et   mes   sandales   étaient  lourdes   de**
and  my    sandals     were     heavy     with


nɛ ʒə    fɑ̃ ʒø        ze    tɑ se
**neige   fangeuse    et    tassée.**
snow     muddy       and   packed.


        i    lmə   di    kə     ʃɛ rʃə    ty
        **Il   me    dit:  "Que   cherches-tu?"** —
        He   me    said: "What   seek      you?"—

ʒə   sɥi
**"Je  suis**
"I   follow


la   tra sə   dy    sa ti rə   sɛ    pə ti   pɑ
**la   trace   du    satyre.   Ses   petits  pas**
the  track   of the satyr.    His   little   steps

fu rʃy
**fourchus**
cloven

Le long du bois couvert de givre, je marchais; mes cheveux devant ma bouche se fleurissaient de petits glaçons et mes sandales étaient lourdes de neige fangeuse et tassée.

Il me dit: "Que cherches-tu?"— "Je suis la trace du satyre. Ses petits pas fourchus alternent comme des trous dans un manteau blanc." Il me dit: "Les satyres sont morts.

"Les satyres et les nymphes aussi. Depuis trente ans il n'a pas fait un hiver aussi terrible. La trace que tu vois est celle d'un bouc. Mais restons ici, où est leur tombeau."

Et avec le fer de sa houe il cassa la glace de la source où jadis riaient les Naïades. Il prenait de grands morceaux froids, et les soulevant vers le ciel pâle, il regardait au travers.

(*Forty-three Songs for Voice and Piano.* New York: International, 1961)

●

Along the frost-covered wood, I walked; my hair across my mouth blossomed with little icicles, and my sandals were heavy with packed muddy snow.

za ltɛ rnə   kɔ mə   dɛ     tru     dɑ̃   zœ̃
**alternent  comme   des    trous   dans  un**
alternate    like    some   holes   in    a

mɑ̃ to
**manteau**
cloak


blɑ̃         i     lmə di   lɛ     sa ti rə   sɔ̃
**blanc."   Il    me dit:   "Les   satyres    sont**
white."     He    me said:  "The   satyrs     are

mɔ r
**morts."**
dead."


        lɛ     sa ti rə   ze    lɛ    nɛ̃ fə   zo si
        **"Les  satyres    et    les   nymphes  aussi.**
        "The   satyrs     and   the   nymphs   too.

də pɥi
**Depuis**
For


trɑ̃        tɑ̃     i    lna    pɑ     fɛ     tœ̃    ni vɛ
**trente    ans    il   n'a    pas    fait   un     hiver**
thirty     years  there has   not    been   a      winter


ro si      tɛ ri blə   la    tra sə   kə    ty     vwa    ɛ
**aussi     terrible.   La    trace    que   tu     vois   est**
so         terrible.   The   track    that  you    see    is


sɛ lə      dœ̃    bu k    me     rɛ stɔ̃    zi si
**celle     d'un   bouc.   Mais   restons   ici,**
that       of a   he-goat. But   let us stay  here,


u          ɛ      lœ     rtɔ̃ bo
**où        est    leur   tombeau."**
where      is     their  tomb."


He said to me: "What are you seeking?"—"I am following the track of the satyr. His little cloven footprints alternate like holes in a white cloak." He said to me: "The satyrs are dead."

"The satyrs and the nymphs too. In thirty years there has not been such a terrible winter. The tracks that you see are those of a he-goat. But let us stay here, where their tomb is."

And with the head of his hoe he broke the ice of the spring where the Naiads used to laugh. He took large cold pieces, and raising them to the pale sky, he looked through them.

e  a vɛ klə fɛ  rdə sa u  i
**Et  avec le  fer  de  sa  houe il**
And with the head of his hoe  he

lkɑ sa
**cassa**
broke

la  glɑ sə də la  su  rsu  ʒɑ di sri jɛ
**la  glace de la  source où  jadis riaient**
the ice  of the source where once laughed

lɛ  na ja də  i  lprə nɛ  də  grɑ̃
**les  Naïades. Il  prenait de  grands**
the  Naiads.  He took  some large
mɔ rso
**morceaux**
pieces

frwa  e  lɛ  su lə vɑ̃  vɛ  rlə
**froids, et  les  soulevant vers  le**
cold,  and them raising  toward the

sjɛ  lpɑl  i  lrə gɑ rdɛ  to tra vɛ r
**ciel  pâle, il  regardait au travers.**
sky  pale, he looked  through.

# ——"Trois Chansons de France"-
## (Three Songs of France)

**Date of composition:** *1904.*
**Date of publication:** *1904.*
**Publisher:** *A. Durand, Paris.*
**Sources:** *Charles d'Orléans,* **Poésies;** *Tristan L'Hermite,* **Le Promenoir des deux Amants.**

I. "Rondel: Le temps a laissié son manteau" (Rondel: The Time Has Shed Its Cloak).
II. "La Grotte" (The Grotto).[45]
III. "Rondel: Pour ce que Plaisance est morte" (Rondel: Because Pleasure Is Dead).

The Middle Ages were almost over and chivalry was a code of the past when a prince of the French royal house sang of his aristocratic melancholy with unrivaled elegance. Charles d'Orléans lived in an era of national disasters, spent years in prison abroad, yet he found peace and escape from disillusion in the innocent evocation of nature and the seasons. Occasionally a more tragic and profound vein turned his finely chiseled poetic forms into lyrical poems of striking modernity. The two rondels selected by Debussy expressed these diverse moods. The rondel as a poetic form was in great vogue between the fourteenth and the sixteenth century. It consists of thirteen lines, the first and second of which recur as a refrain after the sixth, and the first alone is repeated once more in a refrain to end the poem.

## I. "Le Temps a laissié son manteau"

Charles d'Orléans shared the medieval sensitivity to seasonal changes and sang of spring as a time of renewed joy and hope. He was most intrigued by the effect of nature and its seasons upon the soul but, unlike the troubadours and trouvères, avoided the traditional descriptive formulas and preferred to draw his images from the resources of his imagination. Here he welcomes the arrival of spring as a change of garments. The coarse outer cloak of blustery winter is cast off for the soft, light, and bright fabrics of spring. The sunlight plays on the embroidery and on the brooks and fountains as well. Myriad sounds join the visual festival, making of Nature a consummate creator of exquisite beauty. Given the formal restrictions of the rondel, the poet's descriptions are highly selective and revolve around the sensuous richness of the evocation.

The structure of the rondel form must have disconcerted Debussy, who chose to keep the stanzas symmetrical and, to this effect, repeated only the first line of the refrain.[45a] The joyful and lively rhythm of his song, however, is precisely attuned to the poem's elated mood.

## lə tã a le se sɔ̃ mã to
# Le Temps a laissié son manteau
## The Time has shed its cloak

| lə | tã | a | le se | sɔ̃ | mã to |
|----|-----|-----|--------|-----|--------|
| **Le** | **temps** | **a** | **laissié** | **son** | **manteau** |
| The | time | has | shed | its | cloak |

| də | vã | də | frwa dy | re | də | plyi ə |
|----|-----|-----|----------|-----|-----|--------|
| **De** | **vent,** | **de** | **froidure** | **et** | **de** | **pluye,** |
| Of | wind, | of | cold | and | of | rain, |

| e | sɛ | vɛ ty | də | brɔ də ri ə |
|----|-----|--------|-----|--------------|
| **Et** | **s'est** | **vestu** | **de** | **broderye,** |
| And | has | clothed | in | embroidery, |

| də | sɔ le | jre jã | klɛ | re | bo |
|----|--------|---------|-----|-----|-----|
| **De** | **soleil** | **raiant,** | **cler** | **et** | **beau.** |
| In | sun | shining, | clear | and | lovely. |

| i | lni | ja | bɛ tə | nə | wa zo |
|----|------|-----|--------|-----|--------|
| **Il** | **n'y a** | **beste** | **ne** | **oiseau** |
| There | not is | beast | nor | bird |

Le temps a laissié son manteau
De vent, de froidure et de pluye,
Et s'est vestu de broderye,
De soleil raiant, cler et beau.

Il n'y a beste ne oiseau
Qui en son jargon ne chante ou crye
Le temps a laissié son manteau.

Rivière, fontaine et ruisseau
Portent en livrée jolye
Goultes d'argent d'orfaverie
Chascun s'abille de nouveau,
Le temps a laissié son manteau.

(*Claude Debussy Songs 1880–1904.* New York: Dover, 1981)

———————•———————

The time has shed its cloak
Of wind, cold and rain
And has put on embroidery,
Clear and lovely shining sun.

| ki | ɑ̃ | sɔ̃ | ʒa rgɔ̃ | nə | ʃɑ̃ | tu | kri ə |
|----|-----|-----|---------|-----|--------|-----|-------|
| **Qui** | **en** | **son** | **jargon** | **ne** | **chante** | **ou** | **crye** |
| That | in | its | language | not | sings | or | cries |

There is no beast or bird
That in its language does not sing
or cry:
The time has shed its cloak.

| lə | tɑ̃ | a | le se | sɔ̃ | mɑ̃ to |
|----|-----|-----|--------|-----|--------|
| **Le** | **temps** | **a** | **laissié** | **son** | **manteau.** |
| The | time | has | shed | its | cloak. |

Stream, fountain and brook
Wear in pretty livery
Drops of silver jewelry.
Everyone dresses anew.
The time has shed its cloak.

| ri vjɛ rə | fɔ̃ tɛ | ne | rɥi so |
|-----------|--------|-----|--------|
| **Rivière,** | **fontaine** | **et** | **ruisseau** |
| Stream, | fountain | and | brook |

| pɔ rtə | tɑ̃ | li vre | ʒɔ li ə |
|--------|-----|--------|---------|
| **Portent,** | **en** | **livrée** | **jolye** |
| Wear, | in | livery | pretty |

| gu tə | da rʒɑ̃ | dɔ rfa və ri ə |
|-------|---------|----------------|
| **Goultes** | **d'argent** | **d'orfaverie** |
| Drops | of silver | of jewelry |

| ʃa kœ̃ | sa bi jə | də nu vo |
|--------|----------|----------|
| **Chascun** | **s'abille** | **de nouveau,** |
| Everyone | dresses | anew, |

| lə | tɑ̃ | a | le se | sɔ̃ | mɑ̃ to |
|----|-----|-----|--------|-----|--------|
| **Le** | **temps** | **a** | **laissié** | **son** | **manteau.** |
| The | time | has | shed | its | cloak. |

# III. "Rondel: Pour ce que Plaisance est morte"

This introspective poem relates the poet's distress now that the times of pleasure have gone. The rainy day of May incarnates his soul's discomfort, and mourning is the only suitable attire for his mood. The access to merry adventures is now closed, just as the access to the fields is flooded by the rain.

Whereas in the first poem the restraint of the rondel form kept the poet's emotions hidden behind the description, here intimate feelings are openly expressed, thus giving a movingly human dimension to the rondel. Moreover, Charles d'Orléans' undisguised revelation of his distress departs from the medieval concept of self-awareness through social relationships and announces the introspective quest of self of the Romantic and of modern man. Yet the poet in mourning does not elaborate and wishes not to expand on his distress with complacency. He merely states his mood, with dignity, as he feels befits a nobleman. This restrained emotion has been sensed and respected by Debussy, who set the rondel with sobriety and delicacy of feeling.

pu rsə kə plɛ zɑ̃ sɛ mɔrt
## Pour ce que Plaisance est morte
Because Pleasure is dead

| pu | rsə | kə | plɛ zɑ̃ | sɛ | mɔ rtə |
|----|-----|-----|---------|-----|--------|
| **Pour** **ce** | **que** | **Plaisance** | **est** | **morte** |
| Because | | Pleasure | is | dead |

Pour ce que Plaisance est morte
Ce may, suis vestu de noir;
C'est grand pitié de véoir
Mon coeur qui s'en desconforte.

| sə | mɛ | sɥi | vɛ ty | də nwa r |
|----|-----|------|-------|----------|
| **Ce** | **may,** **suis** | **vestu** | **de noir;** |
| This | May, am | dressed | in black; |

Je m'abille de la sorte
Que doy, pour faire devoir;
Pour ce que Plaisance est morte,
Ce may, suis vestu de noir.

| sɛ | grɑ̃ | pi tje | də | ve wa |
|----|------|--------|-----|-------|
| **C'est** | **grand** | **pitié** | **de** | **véoir** |
| It is | great | pity | to | see |

| rmɔ̃ | kœ | rki | sɑ̃ | de kɔ̃ fɔ rtə |
|------|----|-----|-----|-----------------|
| **Mon** | **coeur** | **qui** | **s'en** | **desconforte.** |
| My | heart | which | of it | grieves. |

| ʒə | ma bi jə | də | la | sɔ rtə |
|----|-----------|-----|-----|--------|
| **Je** | **m'abille** | **de** | **la** | **sorte** |
| I | dress | in | the | manner |

| kə | dwa | pu | rfɛ rə | də vwa r |
|----|-----|-----|---------|-----------|
| **Que** | **doy,** | **pour** | **faire** | **devoir;** |
| That | I must, | to | make | duty; |

| pu | rsə | kə | plɛ zɑ̃ | sɛ | mɔ rtə |
|----|-----|-----|----------|-----|--------|
| **Pour** | **ce** | **que** | **Plaisance** | **est** | **morte** |
| Because | | | Pleasure | is | dead, |

| sə | mɛ | sɥi | vɛ ty | də | nwa r |
|----|----|-----|-------|-----|-------|
| **Ce** | **may,** | **suis** | **vestu** | **de** | **noir.** |
| This | May, | am | dressed | in | black. |

| lə | tɑ̃ | sɛ | nu vɛ lə | pɔ rtə |
|----|-----|-----|-----------|--------|
| **Le** | **temps** | **ces** | **nouvelles** | **porte** |
| The | weather | these | news | brings |

| ki | nə | vø | de dɥi | ta vwa r |
|----|----|-----|---------|-----------|
| **Qui** | **ne** | **veut** | **déduit** | **avoir;** |
| That | not | wants | diversion | have; |

| mɛ | pa | rfɔ rsə | dy | plu vwa r |
|----|----|----------|-----|-----------|
| **Mais** | **par force** | | **du** | **plouvoir** |
| But | by | strength | of the | rain |

Le temps ces nouvelles porte
Qui ne veut déduit avoir;
Mais par force du plouvoir
Fait des champs clore la porte,
Pour ce que Plaisance est morte.

(*Claude Debussy Songs 1880–
1904.* New York: Dover, 1981)

⸻ ● ⸻

Because Pleasure is dead
This May, I am dressed in black;
It is a great pity to see
My heart grieve.

I dress in the manner
That befits, for duty's sake;
Because Pleasure is dead,
This May, I am dressed in black.

The weather brings these news
And does not want any diversion;
But because of the strong rain
It shuts the entrance to the fields,
Because Pleasure is dead.

fɛ    dɛ    ʃɑ̃      klɔ rə   la   pɔ rtə
**Fait des champs clore la porte,**
Makes of the fields    shut    the   door,

pu   rsə   kə   plɛ zɑ̃    sɛ   mɔ rtə
**Pour ce que Plaisance est morte**
Because      Pleasure   is   dead.

# —————— "Fêtes galantes" ——————
## *(Second series)*

**Date of composition:** *1904.*
**Date of publication:** *1904.*
**Publisher:** *A. Durand, Paris.*
**Dedicated to Madame Emma Bardac.**
**First Performance:** *23 June 1904 at Madame Edouard Colonne's musical Thursday.*
**Source:** *Paul Verlaine,* Fêtes galantes, *1869.*

   I. **"Les Ingénus"** (The Ingenuous).
  II. **"Le Faune"** (The Faun).
 III. **"Colloque sentimental"** (Sentimental Colloquy).

The second series of *Fêtes galantes* brought to an end an association of twenty years between Debussy and Verlaine; it had been thirteen years since Debussy had collected and published the first series. He dedicated this later volume to a talented and beautiful singer, Madame Emma Bardac, who was to become his wife; the dedication read very mysteriously in homage to the marvelous month of June spent with "a. l. p. m.", decoded afterward as his own little dear.[46] This second series, of three songs, differed from the first by its greater sobriety of style: Debussy was no longer experimenting but showing full maturity in poetic interpretation as well as mastery of musical means.

## I. **"Les Ingénus"**

In the world of the traditional French comedy, the *ingenue* is a naïve maiden. In Verlaine's poem, however, the *ingénus* are young men, and their seducers, awaited and encouraged, are young women. It is a silly, harmless game of peeps and blushes, a festival of whispered lures that leaves the men conquered but dismayed; truly how much of a game is left when, as dusk closes in on an unsettled season, maddening discourse begins. The wild carousel of intercepted legs and glimpses of pretty necks of the first two stanzas vanishes into the languor of closer encounter. So the maidens dream and the young men ponder, their hearts bewildered: No wonder they become the dupes of this game of glances.

The eighteenth-century setting of *Fêtes galantes* is missing in this poem: There are no serenaders, no velvet-clad beaux or libertine ladies, no fountains or marbles, no moonlight or nightingale. The poem is a personal recollection of the elation of a bright breezy day, full of laughter and teasing and frolicking under the trees when one is young, beautiful, and carefree. The charming story unwinds simply and spontaneously, but closes on the same Verlainian twist as in "En Sourdine": Ambiguous questions arise with the onset of evening, of a kind that the poet leaves indefinite.

Debussy has artfully transposed this little masterpiece, using a simplicity of means that enhances the ingenuousness of the young men. The slowing of the rhythm on the final line creates a depth of feeling: If the ingenuousness has been disturbed, it is not from youthful astonishment, but by intimations of futurity and a fearful glimpse of knowledge to come.

## le zɛ̃ ʒe ny
# Les Ingénus
# The Ingenuous

| lɛ | o | ta lɔ̃ | ly tɛ | ta vɛ | klɛ | lɔ̃ gə |
|---|---|---|---|---|---|---|
| **Les** | **hauts** | **talons** | **luttaient** | **avec** | **les** | **longues** |
| The | high | heels | struggled | with | the | long |

| ʒy pə |
|---|
| **jupes,** |
| skirts, |

| ɑ̃ | sɔ rtə kə | sə lɔ̃ | | lə | tɛ rɛ̃ | e |
|---|---|---|---|---|---|---|
| **En** | **sorte que,** | **selon** | | **le** | **terrain** | **et** |
| So | that, | depending on | | the | terrain | and |

| lə | vɑ̃ |
|---|---|
| **le** | **vent,** |
| the | wind, |

Les hauts talons luttaient avec les longues jupes,
En sorte que, selon le terrain et le vent,
Parfois luisaient des bas de jambes, trop souvent
Interceptés! et nous aimions ce jeu de dupes.

Parfois aussi le dard d'un insecte jaloux
Inquiétait le col des belles sous les branches,
Et c'étaient des éclairs soudains de nuques blanches
Et ce régal comblait nos jeunes yeux de fous.

| pa rfwa | lɥi zɛ | de | bɑ | də |
|---|---|---|---|---|
| **Parfois** | **luisaient** | **des** | **bas** | **de** |
| Sometimes | gleamed | some | bottoms | of |

| ʒɑ̃ bə | tro | su vɑ̃ |
|---|---|---|
| **jambes,** | **trop** | **souvent** |
| legs, | too | often |

| tɛ̃ tɛ rsɛ pte | e | nu | zɛ mjɔ̃ | sə | ʒø |
|---|---|---|---|---|---|
| **Interceptés!** | **et** | **nous** | **aimions** | **ce** | **jeu** |
| Intercepted! | and | we | enjoyed | this | game |

| də dy pə |
|---|
| **de dupes.** |
| of dupes. |

| pa rfwa | o si | lə | da | rdœ̃ | nɛ̃ sɛ ktə |
|---|---|---|---|---|---|
| **Parfois** | **aussi** | **le** | **dard** | **d'un** | **insecte** |
| Sometimes | also | the | sting | of an | insect |

| ʒa lu |
|---|
| **jaloux** |
| jealous |

| ɛ̃ ki e tɛ | lə | kɔ | ldɛ | bɛ lə | su |
|---|---|---|---|---|---|
| **Inquiétait** | **le** | **col** | **des** | **belles** | **sous** |
| Troubled | the | neck | of the | beauties | beneath |

| lɛ | brɑ̃ ʃə |
|---|---|
| **les** | **branches,** |
| the | branches, |

| e | se tɛ | dɛ | ze klɛ | rsu dɛ̃ | də |
|---|---|---|---|---|---|
| **Et** | **c'étaient** | **des** | **éclairs** | **soudains** | **de** |
| And | there were | some | flashes | sudden | of |

| ny kə | blɑ̃ ʃə |
|---|---|
| **nuques** | **blanches** |
| napes | white |

Le soir tombait, un soir
équivoque d'automne:
Les belles, se pendant rêveuses à
nos bras,
Dirent alors des mots si spécieux,
tout bas,
Que notre âme depuis ce temps
tremble et s'étonne.

*(Forty-three Songs for Voice
and Piano.* New York:
International, 1961)

———————●———————

The high heels struggled with the
long skirts,
So that, depending on the terrain
and the wind,
A lower leg occasionally
gleamed, too often
Intercepted!—and we enjoyed
this play of flirts.

Sometimes also the sting of some
jealous insect
Troubled the necks of the
beauties beneath the branches
And there were sudden flashes of
white napes
And this feast gratified our young
foolish eyes.

Evening fell, an equivocal
autumn evening:
The beauties, hanging on
dreamily to our arms,
Then, very softly, murmured
such specious words
That ever since our startled souls
have trembled.

e    sə   re ga   lkɔ̃ blɛ    no    ʒœ nə   zjø
**Et   ce   régal  comblait  nos   jeunes  yeux**
And  this  treat  filled      our   young   eyes

də  fu
**de  fous.**
of   fools.


lə   swa     rtɔ̃ bɛ    œ̃ swa     re ki vɔ kə
**Le   soir     tombait, un soir     équivoque**
The  evening  fell,      an  evening  equivocal

do tɔ nə
**d'automne:**
of autumn:


lɛ   bɛ lə    sə  pã dã    rɛ vø zə    za   no
**Les  belles,   se pendant rêveuses   à    nos**
The  beauties, hanging on  dreaming   to   our

bra
**bras,**
arms,


di rə    ta lɔ  rdɛ    mo     si  spe si jø   tu
**Dirent  alors  des    mots    si  spécieux,  tout**
Uttered  then   some   words   so  specious,  very

bɑ
**bas,**
softly,


kə   nɔ     trɑ mə  də pɥi  sə   tã
**Que  notre  âme    depuis  ce   temps**
That  our    soul    since    that  time

trã        ble  se tɔ nə
**tremble  et   s'étonne.**
trembles  and  wonders.

# II. "Le Faune"

The spiraling flight of time and the foreboding of ominous moments make up the main themes of this short octosyllabic poem. The serenity of the present hour contrasts with the mischievousness of the faun's laughter: What unfortunate sequel does he anticipate to the happiness of those who come to him and to the melancholy land of future disenchantment? The poem is one whole swirling sentence that leads to the desperate dance of vanishing time on a beat of insistent drums.

A flute pattern and drum rhythms dominate the accompaniment of Debussy's setting, drowning the vocal melody into subdued melancholy. As in Verlaine's poem, prevalence is given to the aging faun over the young lovers, and the continuous call of the drums underlines the pitiless passage of time and the transience of present happiness.

lə fo n
## Le  Faune
The  Faun

| œ | vjø | fo nə | də | tɛ rə | kyi tə |
|---|-----|-------|-----|-------|--------|
| **Un** | **vieux** | **faune** | **de** | **terre** | **cuite** |
| An | old | faun | of | terra | cotta |

| ri | to | sɑ̃ trə | dɛ | bu lɛ̃ grɛ̃ |
|----|-----|--------|-----|------------|
| **Rit** | **au** | **centre** | **des** | **boulingrins,** |
| Laughs | in the | center | of the | bowling greens, |

| pre za ʒɑ̃ | sɑ̃ | du | ty nə | syi tə |
|-----------|-----|-----|-------|--------|
| **Présageant** | **sans** | **doute** | **une** | **suite** |
| Foreboding | without | doubt | a | sequel |

| mɔ vɛ | za | sɛ | zɛ̃ stɑ̃ | sə rɛ̃ |
|-------|-----|-----|---------|--------|
| **Mauvaise** | **à** | **ces** | **instants** | **sereins** |
| Bad | to | these | moments | serene |

Un vieux faune de terre cuite
Rit au centre des boulingrins,
Présageant sans doute une suite
Mauvaise à ces instants sereins

Qui m'ont conduit et t'ont conduite,
-Mélancoliques pélerins,—
Jusqu'à cette heure dont la fuite
Tournoie au son des tambourins.

*(Forty-three Songs for Voice and Piano. New York: International, 1961)*

| ki | mɔ̃ | kɔ̃ dɥi | e | tɔ̃ |
|----|-----|---------|---|-----|
| **Qui** | **m'ont** | **conduit** | **et** | **t'ont** |
| Which | me have | led | and | you have |

| kɔ̃ dɥi tə | |
|------------|--|
| **conduite,** | |
| led, | |

| me lɑ̃ kɔ li kə | pe lə rɛ̃ |
|----------------|-----------|
| **—Mélancoliques** | **pélerins,—** |
| —Melancholy | pilgrims,— |

| ʒy ska | sɛ | tœ rə | dɔ̃ | la | fɥi tə |
|--------|-----|-------|-----|-----|--------|
| **Jusqu'à** | **cette** | **heure** | **dont** | **la** | **fuite** |
| To | this | hour | whose | the | flight |

| tu rnwa | o | sɔ̃ | de | tɑ̃ bu rɛ̃ |
|---------|---|-----|-----|-----------|
| **Tournoie** | **au** | **son** | **des** | **tambourins.** |
| Swirls | to the | sound | of the | tabors. |

An old terra-cotta faun
Laughs in the center of the bowling greens,
Presaging undoubtedly some ill sequel
To these serene moments

Which have led me and led you
—Melancholy pilgrims—
To this hour whose flight
Goes swirling to the sounding tabors.

# III.  "Colloque sentimental"

The last poem in the series of *Fêtes galantes* bears a despairingly ironic title, for it contains the most excruciating love exchange ever recorded by Verlaine. In a wintry scene of black night and frozen nature, the wandering "pilgrims" of "The Faun" have by now become stark figures of death. The illusory beauty, elegance, youthfulness, and romance of yesteryear vanish behind the cruelest game of words taking place here. Two lovers confront each other, one pleading and nostalgic, the other indifferent to entreaties. The memories of love then sink into a pitiless dance of time and death. With this poem Verlaine closes his series on a forlorn note: Love is transient, death triumphs over life, no ultimate fusion of souls is possible in eternity.

In his setting of "Colloque sentimental," Debussy respects the Verlainian division of the poem: The introduction describes the chilling scene very undramatically; the second part—or the lovers' dialogue—although melancholy in tone, is marked by a more animated rhythm and a change of key, and the third part reverts to the initial theme and key and dies away as the last nightingale call dwindles into silence. Debussy distinctly qualifies and opposes the lovers: the tone of the pleading inquiries becomes more urgent in every line, as happy moments are recalled, echoed by the descending nightingale theme of "En Sourdine"; the cold replies are spoken in a monotonous passionless tone and in a slower tempo. The cruelty of Verlaine's poem is rendered by Debussy with economy of means of the most suggestive kind. The beauty of the disheartening dialogue is enhanced by this simple treatment. There are no dramatic effects in Debussy's setting, and the poetic melancholy of the text is conveyed with subtlety and unerring taste.

# kɔ lɔ k  sã ti mã ta l
# **Colloque sentimental**
## Colloquy sentimental

| dã | lə | vjø | pa | rksɔ li tɛ | re | gla se |
|---|---|---|---|---|---|---|
| **Dans** | **le** | **vieux** | **parc** | **solitaire** | **et** | **glacé** |
| In | the | old | park | solitary | and | frozen |

| dø | fɔ rmə | (z)ɔ̃⁴⁷ | tu | ta lœ rə | pɑ se |
|---|---|---|---|---|---|
| **Deux** | **formes** | **ont** | **tout** | **à l'heure** | **passé.** |
| Two | forms | have | just | | passed. |

| lœ r | zjø | sɔ̃ | mɔ | re | lœ | rlɛ vrə |
|---|---|---|---|---|---|---|
| **Leurs** | **yeux** | **sont** | **morts** | **et** | **leurs** | **lèvres** |
| Their | eyes | are | dead | and | their | lips |

| sɔ̃ | mɔ lə |
|---|---|
| **sont** | **molles,** |
| are | limp, |

| e | lɔ̃ | nã tã | ta pɛ nə | lœ | rpa rɔ lə |
|---|---|---|---|---|---|
| **Et** | **l'on** | **entend** | **à peine** | **leurs** | **paroles.** |
| And | one | hears | barely | their | words. |

| dã | lə | vjø | pa | rksɔ li tɛ | re | gla se |
|---|---|---|---|---|---|---|
| **Dans** | **le** | **vieux parc** | | **solitaire** | **et** | **glacé** |
| In | the | old | park | solitary | and | frozen |

| dø | spɛ ktrə | (z)ɔ̃⁴⁷ | te vɔ ke | lə | pɑ se |
|---|---|---|---|---|---|
| **Deux** | **spectres** | **ont** | **évoqué** | **le** | **passé.** |
| Two | specters | have | evoked | the | past. |

Dans le vieux parc solitaire et glacé
Deux formes ont tout à l'heure passé.

Leurs yeux sont morts et leurs lèvres sont molles,
Et l'on entend à peine leurs paroles.

Dans le vieux parc solitaire et glacé
Deux spectres ont évoqué le passé.

—Te souvient-il de notre extase ancienne?
—Pourquoi voulez-vous donc qu'il m'en souvienne?

—Ton coeur bat-il toujours à mon seul nom?
Toujours vois-tu mon âme en rêve? Non.

—Ah! les beaux jours de bonheur indicible
Où nous joignions nos bouches!—C'est possible.

—Qu'il était bleu, le ciel, et grand l'espoir!
—L'espoir a fui, vaincu, vers le ciel noir.

tə      su vjɛ̃ ti      ldə  nɔ      trɛ ksta
—**Te    souvient-il de   notre extase**
—You    remember    of   our    ecstasy
zɑ̃ sjɛ nə
**ancienne?**
former?

pu rkwa     vu le    vu    dɔ̃      ki
—**Pourquoi voulez-vous donc    qu'il**
—Why        want    you   on earth it
lmɑ̃    su vjɛ nə
**m'en  souvienne?**
me it   remembers?

tɔ̃      kœ    rba ti    ltu ʒu      ra  mɔ̃
—**Ton   coeur bat-il    toujours à   mon**
—Your   heart beats it  still       at  my
sœ    lnɔ̃
**seul  nom?**
mere  name?

tu ʒu        rvwa ty    mɔ̃    na    mɑ̃  rɛ və
**Toujours vois-tu   mon   âme  en   rêve?**
Still        see  you  my    soul in   dream?
nɔ̃
—**Non.**
—No.

ɑ      lɛ     bo       ʒu     rdə bɔ nœ
—**Ah!  Les   beaux    jours de  bonheur**
—Ah!  The   beautiful days  of  happiness
rɛ̃ di si blə
**indicible**
inexpressible

Tels ils marchaient dans les
avoines folles,
Et la nuit seule entendit leurs
paroles.

(*Forty-three Songs for Voice
and Piano.* New York:
International, 1961)

————————————•————————————

In the old park, solitary and
frozen,
Two forms have just passed by.

Their eyes are dead and their lips
are limp,
And one barely hears the words
they say.

In the old park, solitary and
frozen,
Two specters have evoked the
past.

—Do you remember our old
ecstasy?
—Why on earth do you wish me
to remember it?

—Does your heart still beat
merely to my name?
Do you still see my soul in
dreams?—
No.

—Ah! The lovely days of
unspeakable happiness
When our lips met!—It is
possible.

| u | nu | ʒwa ɲɔ̃ | no | bu ʃə | | sɛ |
|---|---|---|---|---|---|---|
| **Où** | **nous** | **joignions** | **nos** | **bouches!** | | **—C'est** |
| When | we | joined | our | mouths! | | —It is |

| pɔ si blə |
|---|
| **possible.** |
| possible. |

| ki | le tɛ | blø | lə | sjɛ l | e | grɑ̃ |
|---|---|---|---|---|---|---|
| **—Qu'il** | **était** | **bleu,** | **le** | **ciel,** | **et** | **grand** |
| —How it | was | blue, | the | sky, | and | great |

| lɛ spwa r |
|---|
| **l'espoir!** |
| the hope! |

| lɛ spwa | ra | fɥi | vɛ̃ ky | | vɛ | rlə |
|---|---|---|---|---|---|---|
| **—L'espoir** | **a** | **fui,** | **vaincu,** | | **vers** | **le** |
| —The hope | has | fled, | vanquished, | toward | the |

| sjɛ | lnwa r |
|---|---|
| **ciel** | **noir.** |
| sky | black. |

| tɛ | li | lma rʃɛ | dɑ̃ | lɛ | za vwa nə |
|---|---|---|---|---|---|
| **Tels** | **ils** | **marchaient** | **dans** | **les** | **avoines** |
| Thus | they | walked | in | the | oats |

| fɔ lə |
|---|
| **folles,** |
| wild, |

| e | la | nɥi | sœ | lɑ̃ tɑ̃ di | lœ | rpa rɔ lə |
|---|---|---|---|---|---|---|
| **Et** | **la** | **nuit** | **seule** | **entendit** | **leurs** | **paroles.** |
| And | the | night | alone | heard | their | words. |

—How blue was the sky then and high our hope!
—Hope has fled, vanquished, toward the black sky.

Thus they walked through the wild oats
And the night alone heard the words they said.

# —————"Le Promenoir des deux —— Amants"
## (The Walk of the Two Lovers)

Date of composition: *1904 (I); 1910 (II, III).*
Date of publication: *1910.*
Publisher: *A. Durand, Paris.*
Dedicated to Emma Claude Debussy.
Source: *Tristan L'Hermite, "Le Promenoir des deux Amants," stanzas 1, 2, 4 (I); 14–16 (II); 22–24 (III). In Les Amours de Tristan, 1638.*

> I. **"Auprès de cette grotte sombre"** (Close to This Dark Grotto).
> II. **"Crois mon conseil, chère Climène"** (Take My Advice, Dear Climène).
> III. **"Je tremble en voyant ton visage"** (I Tremble When I See Your Face).

This long poem of twenty-eight verses is the most celebrated of Tristan L'Hermite's works and belongs to a lyrical tradition in poetry that goes back to Charles d'Orléans and extends to the Symbolists. The poem combines an impressionistic technique of juxtaposed sounds and visual effects with the use of symbols that associate nature and the human soul. Its irresistible charm allows one to forget some of its preciosity. This poem of seduction is divided into two parts of equal length: The poet begins by describing the rustic scene that he feels will be conducive to love; he then invites his beloved to join him and share the beauty of the moment.

Debussy chose the opening stanzas of the poem to set to music as "La Grotte," which he published along with two Charles d'Orléans rondels in 1904. He then set two more selections from the second part of the poem and combined them with "La Grotte" in 1910, under the title *Le Promenoir des deux Amants*. His choice of Tristan L'Hermite's poetry further emphasizes his inclination to a more classical style of composition. His three melodies catch the elegance of the poem and express it with delicate and mellow harmonies. Debussy could not but be sensitive to the effects of rippling waters, shimmering reflections, and whispering breezes, which played such a great part in his works.

The first performance was given on January 14, 1911, by the singer and pianist Jane Bathori, accompanied by Debussy himself.

# I. "Auprès de cette grotte sombre"

The beginning strophes of the poem that make up the first melody are very suggestive by their musicality, lyrical tone, and dreamlike atmosphere. Nature appears in its element most represented and celebrated in the early seventeenth century, water. Water, in its many forms, held the artists' imagination. Captive and dormant in mirroring ponds, gleaming and rippling in brooks, tumultuous in fountains, it reflected the wanderings of the Baroque soul between essence and appearance, reality and illusion.

Near the dark grotto, past where light and shadow struggle and water and pebbles contend, there is a secluded site perfectly suited to love, a still pond that awaits reflections. Here Narcissus[48] drowned for having loved himself to excess. Here the poet wishes to beguile his beloved, for it is a quiet, beautiful, and bewitching spot. Indeed this ideal place, secluded and sensuous as it is, stirs ambivalent feelings; dormant waters can be luring and treacherous, and unrest may lie under their deceptive stillness. The dreamy evocation of the sleeping waters withholds its mystery: What curbed desires may hide in the dark recesses of the poet's heart?

Debussy wrote a rich and mysterious song that Jane Bathori notes as one of his most beautiful. The accompaniment reveals the composer's taste for evocative effects and conveys a mellowness of harmonies that matches the musicality of the poem. Bathori recommends singing the melody slowly, but not too much so. The voice should be smooth and control the legato throughout.

o prɛ də sɛ tgrɔ tsɔ̃ br
# Auprès de cette grotte sombre
Close to this grotto dark

| o prɛ | də | sɛ tə | grɔ tə | sɔ̃ br |
|-------|-----|-------|--------|--------|
| **Auprès** | **de** | **cette** | **grotte** | **sombre** |
| Close | to | this | grotto | dark |

| u | lɔ̃ | rɛ spi | rœ̃ | nɛ | rsi | du |
|---|-----|--------|-----|-----|-----|-----|
| **Où** | **l'on** | **respire** | **un** | **air** | **si** | **doux,** |
| Where | one | breathes | an | air | so | soft, |

| lɔ̃ də | ly | ta vɛ | klɛ | ka ju |
|--------|-----|-------|-----|-------|
| **L'onde** | **lutte** | **avec** | **les** | **cailloux** |
| The water | struggles | with | the | pebbles |

| e | la | ly mjɛ | ra vɛ kə | lɔ̃ brə |
|---|-----|--------|----------|--------|
| **Et** | **la** | **lumière** | **avecque** | **l'ombre.** |
| And | the | light | with | the shade. |

| sɛ | flo | la se | də | le gzɛ rsi sə |
|-----|-----|-------|-----|---------------|
| **Ces** | **flots,** | **lassés** | **de** | **l'exercice** |
| These | waters, | weary | from | the exercise |

| ki | lzɔ̃ | fɛ | də sy | sə | gra vje |
|-----|------|-----|-------|-----|---------|
| **Qu'ils** | **ont** | **fait** | **dessus** | **ce** | **gravier,** |
| That they | have | done | over | this | gravel, |

| sə | rə po zə | dɑ̃ | sə | vi vje |
|-----|----------|-----|-----|--------|
| **Se** | **reposent** | **dans** | **ce** | **vivier** |
| Themselves | rest | in | this | pond |

| u | mu ry | to trə fwa | na rsi sə |
|---|-------|------------|-----------|
| **Où** | **mourut** | **autrefois** | **Narcisse. . .** |
| Where | died | once | Narcissus. . . |

Auprès de cette grotte sombre
Où l'on respire un air si doux,
L'onde lutte avec les cailloux
Et la lumière avecque l'ombre.

Ces flots, lassés de l'exercice
Qu'ils ont fait dessus ce gravier,
Se reposent dans ce vivier
Où mourut autrefois
Narcisse. . .

L'ombre de cette fleur vermeille
Et celle de ces joncs pendants
Paraissent estre là dedans
Les songes de l'eau qui
sommeille. . .

*(Claude Debussy Songs 1880–1904. New York: Dover, 1981)*

————————•————————

Close to this dark grotto
Where one breathes such soft air,
The water struggles with the pebbles
And the light with the shade.

These waters, weary from the activity
That they have had over this gravel,
Rest in this pond
Where once Narcissus died. . .

lɔ̃ brə     də sɛ tə   flœ    rvɛ rmɛ jə
**L'ombre**     **de cette fleur**    **vermeille**
The reflection of this     flower vermilion

e   sɛ lə   də sɛ    ʒɔ̃     pɑ̃ dɑ̃
**Et**   **celle**   **de ces**    **joncs**   **pendants**
And   that    of these   rushes   drooping

pa rɛ sə     tɛ trə   la də dɑ̃
**Paraissent estre   là–dedans**
Seem      to be   there inside

lɛ    sɔ̃ ʒə   də lo     ki    sɔ mɛ jə
**Les**   **songes**   **de l'eau**     **qui**   **sommeille.**
The   dreams   of the water   that   sleeps.

The reflection of this vermilion
flower
And of these drooping rushes
Seems to be therein
The dreams of the sleeping
water.

# II.  "Crois mon conseil, chère Climène"

Once the poet has extolled the seductiveness of the ideal site and depicted the reassuring nature that encloses it, he addresses his beloved and persuades her to follow him, in all trustfulness, to the waters of the pond. Since he is a court poet, he must woo her gallantly, and therefore he uses the tools of his trade—or, more precisely, seductive conceits: Climène's rosy cheeks and amber-scented breath have stirred up the gentle breeze that is transmuted into the sighs of charmed Zephyrus; Zephyrus, in turn, stands for the poet and his hidden feelings. By a reversed stylistic device, the commonplaces of the feminine blazon become Nature's attributes: Climène, and her lover after her, merge into nature, enveloped in an aura of sensuous stillness.

Debussy gave an engaging version of the madrigal-like triplet. After a soft and expressive opening that recounts the lover's enticing invitation, the song becomes lively as it depicts the enraptured Zephyrus and moves on fervidly in the lover's eulogy of his lady's beauty. All the nuances of the lover's entreaties and courtship come to light through rhythms and caressing harmonies.

krwa mɔ̃ kɔ̃ sɛj ʃɛ rklimɛn
## Crois mon conseil, chère Climène
Take my advice, dear Climène

| krwa | mɔ̃ | kɔ̃sɛj | ʃɛrə | klimenə | Crois mon conseil, chère |
|------|-----|--------|------|---------|--------------------------|
| **Crois** | **mon** | **conseil,** | **chère** | **Climène;** | Climène; |
| Take | my | advice, | dear | Climène; | Pour laisser arriver le soir, |
| | | | | | Je te prie, allons nous asseoir |
| pu | rlese | (r)arive[49] | lə | swar | Sur le bord de cette fontaine. |
| **Pour** | **laisser** | **arriver** | **le** | **soir,** | |
| To | let | come | the | evening, | N'ouis-tu pas soupirer Zéphire, |
| | | | | | De merveille et d'amour atteint, |
| zə | tə | pri | alɔ̃ | nu | za swa | Voyant des roses sur ton teint |
| **Je** | **te** | **prie,** | **allons** | **nous** | **asseoir** | Qui ne sont pas de son empire? |
| I | you | beg, | let us go | ourselves | sit | |

| rsy | rlə | bɔ | rdə | sɛ tə | fɔ̃ tɛ nə |
|-----|-----|------|-----|-------|-----------|
| **Sur** | **le** | **bord** | **de** | **cette** | **fontaine.** |
| On | the | margin | of | this | fountain. |

| nu i | ty | pɑ | su pi re | ze fi rə |
|------|-----|-----|----------|----------|
| **N'ouïs-tu** | **pas** | **soupirer** | **Zéphire,** | |
| Hear | you | not | sigh | Zephyrus, |

| də | mɛ rvɛ | je | da mu | ra tɛ̃ |
|-----|--------|-----|-------|--------|
| **De** | **merveille** | **et** | **d'amour** | **atteint,** |
| With | wonder | and | love | stricken, |

| vwa jɑ̃ | de | ro zə | sy | rtɔ̃ | tɛ̃ |
|---------|-----|-------|-----|------|-----|
| **Voyant** | **des** | **roses** | **sur** | **ton** | **teint,** |
| Seeing | some | roses | on | your | complexion, |

| ki | nə | sɔ̃ | pɑ | də | sɔ̃ | nɑ̃ pi rə |
|-----|-----|------|-----|-----|------|-----------|
| **Qui** | **ne** | **sont** | **pas** | **de** | **son** | **empire?** |
| Which | not | are | not | of | his | power? |

| sa | bu ʃə | dɔ dœ | rtu tə | plɛ nə |
|-----|-------|-------|--------|--------|
| **Sa** | **bouche** | **d'odeur** | **toute** | **pleine** |
| His | mouth | of perfume | all | full |

| a | su fle | sy | rnɔ trə | ʃə mɛ̃ |
|-----|--------|-----|---------|--------|
| **A** | **soufflé** | **sur** | **notre** | **chemin,** |
| Has | breathed | upon | our | path, |

| mɛ lɑ̃ | tœ̃ | nɛ spri | də | ʒa smɛ̃ |
|--------|-----|---------|-----|---------|
| **Mêlant** | **un** | **esprit** | **de** | **jasmin** |
| Mingling | an | exhalation | of | jasmine |

| a | lɑ̃ brə | də | ta | du | sa lɛ nə |
|-----|---------|-----|-----|-----|----------|
| **A** | **l'ambre** | **de** | **ta** | **douce** | **haleine.** |
| With | the amber | of | your | sweet | breath. |

Sa bouche d'odeur toute pleine
A soufflé sur notre chemin,
Mêlant un esprit de jasmin
A l'ambre de ta douce haleine.

(*Le Promenoir des deux
Amants.* Paris: Durand, n. d.)

———————•———————

Take my advice, dear Climène;
To await the falling of the
evening,
I beg you, let us go and sit
On the margin of this fountain.

Don't you hear Zephyrus sigh,
Stricken with wonder and love,
At seeing the roses of your
complexion,
On which he has no power?

His mouth, full of perfume,
Has breathed upon our path,
Mingling an exhalation of
jasmine
With the amber of your sweet
breath.

## III. "Je tremble en voyant ton visage"

Climène has complied with her lover's wishes. They are now bending over their reflections in the pond. Trembling at the sight of her face, the lover fears that the strength of his desire might frighten and destroy her. He therefore pleads that she not trust these treacherous waters too much, that is, that she not give in too easily to his passion, for they might both be shipwrecked in the adventure. Instead he asks her to bestow upon him some of her unsullied love by offering him water to drink from her hands; the offering will place him above the rest of mankind. The poet moves from apprehension to quietude, from passion to tenderness, a tenderness imposed but exalting.

Debussy's setting conveys with intensity the restrained feelings of passion, the struggle within the lover's soul, and the final assuagement. The intimacy of the lovers is most naturally and tenderly expressed by the dreamy texture of the accompaniment. The whole song is a murmur of enticing charm.

ʒə trɑ̃ blɑ̃ vwa jɑ̃ tɔ̃ vi za ʒ
## Je tremble en voyant ton visage
I tremble at seeing your face

| ʒə | trɑ̃ | | blɑ̃ | vwa jɑ̃ | tɔ̃ | vi za ʒə |
|----|------|----|------|---------|-----|----------|
| **Je** | **tremble** | **en** | **voyant** | **ton** | **visage** | |
| I | tremble | at | seeing | your | face | |

| flɔ te | ra vɛ kə | mɛ | de zi r |
|--------|----------|----|---------|
| **Flotter** | **avecque** | **mes** | **désirs,** |
| Float | with | my | desires, |

| tɑ̃ | ʒe | də | pœ | rkə | mɛ | su pi r |
|-----|----|----|----|-----|----|---------|
| **Tant** | **j'ai** | **de** | **peur** | **que** | **mes** | **soupirs** |
| So much | I have | of | fear | that | my | sighs |

Je tremble en voyant ton visage
Flotter avecque mes désirs,
Tant j'ai de peur que mes soupirs
Ne lui fassent faire naufrage

De crainte de cette aventure
Ne commets pas si librement
A cet infidèle élément
Tous les trésors de la Nature.

| nə | lҷi | fa sə | fɛ rə | no fra ʒə |
|----|-----|-------|-------|-----------|
| **Ne** | **lui** | **fassent** | **faire** | **naufrage** |
| Not | it | cause | make | wreck |

| də | krɛ̃ tə | də | sɛ | ta vɑ̃ ty r(ə) |
|----|--------|-----|-----|----------------|
| **De** | **crainte** | **de** | **cette** | **aventure** |
| For | fear | of | this | adventure |

| nə | kɔ mɛ | pɑ | si | li brə mɑ̃ |
|----|-------|-----|-----|------------|
| **Ne** | **commets** | **pas** | **si** | **librement** |
| Not | entrust | not | so | freely |

| a | sɛ | tɛ̃ fi dɛ | le le mɑ̃ |
|----|-----|-----------|-----------|
| **A** | **cet** | **infidèle** | **élément** |
| To | this | faithless | element |

| tu | lɛ | tre zɔ | rdə la | na ty rə |
|----|-----|--------|--------|----------|
| **Tous** | **les** | **trésors** | **de la** | **Nature.** |
| All | the | treasures | of the | Nature. |

| vø | ty | pa | rɛ̃ | du | pri vi lɛ ʒə |
|----|-----|-----|-----|-----|--------------|
| **Veux-tu,** | **par** | **un** | | **doux** | **privilège,** |
| Will | you, | by | a | sweet | privilege, |

| mə | mɛ | tro də sy | dɛ | zy mɛ̃ |
|----|-----|-----------|-----|--------|
| **Me** | **mettre** | **au-dessus** | **des** | **humains?** |
| Me | raise | above | of | humans? |

| fɛ | mwa | bwa | ro | krø | də tɛ | mɛ̃ |
|----|-----|-----|-----|-----|-------|-----|
| **Fais-moi** | **boire** | **au** | | **creux** | **de tes** | **mains,** |
| Make me | drink | in the | cup | of | your | hands, |

| si | lo | nɑ̃ | di su | pwɛ̃ | la | nɛ ʒə |
|----|-----|-----|-------|------|-----|-------|
| **Si** | **l'eau** | **n'en** | **dissout** | **point** | **la** | **neige.** |
| If | the water | of it | melt | not | the | snow. |

Veux-tu, par un doux privilège,
Me mettre au-dessus des humains?
Fais-moi boire au creux de tes mains,
Si l'eau n'en dissout point la neige.

(*Le Promenoir des deux Amants.* Paris: Durand, n. d.)

———————•———————

I tremble when I see your face
Floating with my desires,
So afraid I am that my sighs
May sink it.

For fear of this adventure
Do not commit so freely
To the care of this faithless element
All the treasures of Nature.

Will you, by a sweet privilege,
Raise me above mortals?
Let me drink from your cupped hands,
If the water does not melt their snow.

# –"Trois Ballades de François——— Villon"

## *(Three Ballads of François Villon)*

Date of composition: *May 1910.*
Date of publication: *1910.*
Publisher: *A. Durand, Paris.*
Source: *François Villon*, Le Testament, *1461.*

- I. "Ballade de Villon à s'amye" (Ballad of Villon to his beloved).
- II. "Ballade que Villon feit à la requeste de sa mère pour prier Nostre-Dame" (Ballad that Villon makes at the request of his mother to pray to Our Lady).
- III. "Ballade des femmes de Paris" (Ballad of the women of Paris).

The three ballads belong to Villon's major work, *The Testament*, which he wrote during his wandering years in and out of jail. What gives them a distinctive character and establishes their reputation in medieval poetry is their truthful and intimate accents. A ballad traditionally consists of three stanzas followed by a short envoy or appeal usually addressed to the "Prince" or leader of a poets' circle; each stanza ends with a one-line refrain.

In setting Villon's ballads to music, Debussy carried on his predilection for the medieval spirit and furthered his experiments with both the medieval modes and the harmonic techniques of his time.

# I. "Ballade de Villon à s'amye"

However flawless its form may be, this ballad is more contrived and less compassionate than the other two. The conventional theme of the battle of the sexes appears here, presented with a certain degree of crude cynicism.

In the Provençal tradition of courtly love that pervaded medieval French poetry, the beloved lady was a sacred and mysterious idol, merciless at times, yet holding always a promise of hope, life, and felicity. The perfect lover awaited her in thorough subservience and discretion; suffering was his usual lot, and whenever despair took hold of him, he would go into exile and die (or at least claim that he would). Thus began the myth of the martyr lover. This soon fossilized vision of human relationships was counteracted by a vein of realism from northern France: The poet lover allowed himself to rebel, snarl skeptically at the conventions of love, mock the aging beauty who had once refused him, and proclaim that women were cruel, greedy, and faithless creatures.

When Villon left Paris in 1456, he made it known that it was out of lovesickness, whereas it was truly to plot some burglary. He may have had some amorous relationship with a certain Martha, an allegedly wicked, coarse, and deceitful woman, for whom he bore a long grudge. Villon repeatedly lamented, wished for vengeance and death, and felt victimized until he regained his common sense.

The "Ballade à s'amye" was addressed to Charles d'Orléans, the poet prince, and written in the style in vogue in the medieval courts of love. The first stanza presents all the rhetorical clichés of the genre: The lady has beauty and charm but of the most treacherous kind, that wounds and breaks a lover's heart. In the second stanza, realism takes over and suppresses the lament: The stricken lover starts insulting his beloved in a harsh and revengeful tone. Why did he not run away, scream to arouse indignation, or rally help? Tragedy would have been lesser. Rightfully, as is proclaimed in the third stanza, revenge will take its natural course, for time will come when nothing is left of her beauty and youth. The poet's triumph is short and bitter though: How foolish is revenge when we are all human and mortal!

Anguish and regret are the moods indicated by Debussy at the beginning of his melody, to lament the cruelty and faithlessness of the beloved woman. The slow rhythm of the accompaniment expresses the poet's disillusion. In the second part, the anguish yields to increasing hysteria that conveys the intensity of the lover's anger. In the third part Debussy calls for a soft and melancholic expressiveness followed by irony. The piano's sudden silences establish the contrasting feelings of sarcasm and despair.

ba la də vi jɔ̃ a sa mi
# Ballade de Villon à s'amye
Ballad of Villon to his beloved

fo sə      bo te      ki      tɑ̃      mə ku tə      ʃɛ r
**Faulse beauté, qui tant me couste cher,**
False      beauty,    who     so       me  costs     dear,

ry      dɑ̃ ne fɛ      i pɔ kri tə      du sœ r
**Rude en effet, hypocrite doulceur,**
Cruel   in  fact,     deceitful        sweetness,

a mu      rdy rə ply      kə      fɛ      ra ma ʃe
**Amour dure, plus     que     fer,    à   mascher;**
Love      hard,  more    than    iron,   to  chew;

nɔ me      tə      pɥi      də ma dɛ fa sɔ̃      sœ r
**Nommer te      puis de ma deffaçon      soeur.**
Call       you     can     of  my  destruction   sister.

ʃa rmə      fe lɔ̃      la      mɔ      rdœ̃      po vrə
**Charme félon,      la  mort d'ung      povre**
Charm       felonious, the death of a       poor
kœ r
**cueur,**
heart,

ɔr gœ      jmy se      ki      ʒɑ̃      mɛ      to
**Orgueil mussé, qui gens      met     au**
Pride       hidden,  that  people  sends   to
mu ri r
**mourir,**
death,

Faulse beauté, qui tant me couste cher,
Rude en effet, hypocrite doulceur,
Amour dure, plus que fer, à mascher;
Nommer te puis de ma deffaçon soeur.
Charme félon, la mort d'ung povre cueur,
Orgueil mussé, qui gens met au mourir,
Yeulx sans pitié! ne veult droict de rigueur,
Sans empirer, ung povre secourir?

Mieulx m'eust valu avoir esté crier
Ailleurs secours, c'eust esté mon bonheur:
Rien ne m'eust sceu de ce fait arracher;
Trotter m'en fault en fuyte à deshonneur.
Haro, haro, le grand et le mineur!
Et qu'est cecy? mourray sans coup ferir,
Ou pitié peult, selon ceste teneur,
Sans empirer, ung povre secourir.

| jø | sã | pi tje | nə | vø | drwa | də |
|----|----|--------|-----|-----|------|-----|
| **Yeulx** | **sans** | **pitié!** | **ne** | **veult** | **droict** | **de** |
| Eyes | without | pity! | not | will | law | of |

| ri gœ r | | | | | | |
|---|---|---|---|---|---|---|
| **rigueur,** | | | | | | |
| rigor, | | | | | | |

| sã | zã pi re | œ̃ | po vrə | sə ku ri r | | |
|----|----------|----|--------|------------|---|---|
| **Sans** | **empirer,** | **ung** | **povre** | **secourir?** | | |
| Without | worsening, | a | poor | help? | | |

| mjø | my | | va ly | a vwa | rĕ te | |
|-----|----|----|-------|-------|-------|---|
| **Mieulx** | **m'eust** | | **valu** | **avoir** | **esté** | |
| Better | me would have | | been | have | gone | |

| kri je | | | | | | |
|--------|---|---|---|---|---|---|
| **crier** | | | | | | |
| call for | | | | | | |

| ra jœ | rsə ku | rsy | | te te | mɔ̃ | |
|-------|--------|-----|---|-------|-----|---|
| **Ailleurs** | **secours,** | **c'eust** | | **esté** | **mon** | |
| Elsewhere | help, | it would have | | been | my | |

| bɔ nœ r | | | | | | |
|---------|---|---|---|---|---|---|
| **bonheur:** | | | | | | |
| happiness: | | | | | | |

| rjɛ̃ | nə | my | | sy | də | sə |
|------|-----|----|----|----|-----|-----|
| **Rien** | **ne** | **m'eust** | | **sceu** | **de** | **ce** |
| Nothing | not | me would have | | known | from | this |

| fɛ | ta ra ʃe | | | | | |
|----|-----------|---|---|---|---|---|
| **fait** | **arracher;** | | | | | |
| reality | tear out; | | | | | |

Ung temps viendra, qui fera desseicher,
Jaulnir, flestrir, vostre espanie fleur:
J'en risse lors, se tant peusse marcher,
Mais las! nenny: Ce seroit donc foleur,
Vieil je seray; vous, laide et sans couleur.
Or, beuvez fort, tant que ru peult courir.
Ne donnez pas à tous ceste douleur
Sans empirer ung povre secourir.

Prince amoureux, des amans le greigneur,
Vostre mal gré ne vouldroye encourir;
Mais tout franc cueur doit, par Nostre Seigneur,
Sans empirer, ung povre secourir.

(*Trois Ballades de François Villon*. Paris: Durand, n.d.)

— • —

False beauty, who has cost me so dear,
Cruel really, deceitful sweetness,
Love harder than iron to be chewed;
I can call you sister of my ruin.
Felonious charm, the death of a poor heart,
Hidden pride, that sends people to death,
Pitiless eyes! Will not severe justice
Help a poor man instead of crushing him.

trɔ te      mã      fo      ã      fyi      ta
**Trotter   m'en   fault   en   fuite   à**
Run away I          must    in   flight   with

de zɔ nœ r
**deshonneur.**
disgrace.

a ro      a ro      lə      grã      e      lə      mi nœ r
**Haro,    haro,    le      grand   et     le      mineur!**
Shame,   shame,   the      loud    and    the     soft!

e      kɛ      sə si      mu rre      sã      ku
**Et     qu'est   cecy?     mourray   sans   coup**
And    what is   this?     will die  without blow

fe ri r
**ferir,**
striking,

u      pi tje      pø      sə lɔ̃            sɛ tə      tə nœ r
**Ou    pitié      peult,   selon           ceste      teneur,**
Or     pity       can,     according to    this       text,

sã            zã pi re      œ̃      po vrə      sə ku ri r
**Sans         empirer,     ung    povre       secourir.**
Without      worsening,   a      poor        help.

œ̃      tã      vjɛ̃ dra      ki      fə ra
**Ung    temps   viendra,    qui     fera**
A      time    will come,   that    will cause

de se ʃe
**desseicher,**
to dry up,

ʒo ni r      fle tri r      vɔ      tre pa ni      flœ r
**Jaulnir,    flestrir,     vostre   espanie        fleur:**
Yellow,     wilt,         your     full-bloomed   flower:

It would have been better for me
to go call
For help elsewhere, it would have
made me happier:
Nothing would have been able to
tear me out of this reality;
I must run away in flight with
disgrace.
Shame, shame, cry loud and soft!
And what is this? I will die
without striking a blow,
Or pity can, according to this
refrain,
Help a poor man instead of
crushing him.

A time will come that will cause
to wither,
Yellow, wilt your full-bloomed
flower:
I shall laugh then, if I can still
walk,
But alas! nay: It would then be
madness,
I shall be old; you ugly and
colorless.
Now, drink deep, as long as the
brook can run.
Do not give this grief to all,
Help a poor man instead of
crushing him.

Prince of love, the greatest of all
lovers,
I would not want to incur your
displeasure;
But every honest heart must, by
our Lord,
Help a poor man instead of
crushing him.

ʒɑ̃ ri sə lɔr sə tɑ̃ py sə
**J'en risse lors, se tant peusse**
I of it shall laugh then, if still can

ma rʃe
**marcher,**
walk,

mɛ lɑ s ne ni sə sə rɛ dɔ̃
**Mais las! nenny: Ce seroit donc**
But alas! nay: That would be then

fɔ lœ r
**foleur,**
madness,

vjɛ jʒə sə re vu lɛ de sɑ̃
**Vieil je seray; vous laide et sans**
Old I shall be; you ugly and without

ku lœ r
**couleur.**
color.

ɔ r by ve fɔ rtɑ̃ kə ry pø
**Or, beuvez fort, tant que ru peult**
Now, drink deep, as long as brook can

ku ri r
**courir.**
run.

nə dɔ ne pɑ za tu sɛ tə du lœ r
**Ne donnez pas à tous ceste douleur**
Don't give not to all this pain

sɑ̃ zɑ̃ pi re œ̃ po vrə sə ku ri r
**Sans empirer ung povre secourir.**
Without worsening a poor help.

prɛ̃		sa mu rø	dɛ	za mɑ̃	lə	grɛ ɲœr
**Prince	amoureux,	des	amans	le	greigneur,**
Prince		amorous,	of	lovers	the	greatest,

vɔ trə		ma	lgre	nə	vu drɛ		ɑ̃ ku ri r
**Vostre	mal	gré	ne	vouldroye	encourir;**
Your		ill	will	not	would		incur:

mɛ	tu	frɑ̃	kœ	rdwa	pa	rnɔ trə
**Mais	tout	franc	cueur	doit,	par	Nostre**
But	every	honest	heart	must,	by	Our
sɛ ɲœ r
**Seigneur,**
Lord,

sɑ̃		zɑ̃ pi re	œ̃	po vrə	sə ku ri r
**Sans	empirer,	ung	povre	secourir.**
Without	worsening,	a	poor	help.

## II. Ballade que Villon feit à la requeste de sa mère pour prier Nostre-Dame

Villon was an outcast, a thief, and possibly a murderer. He had much to be forgiven for. His violent yet tender soul was obsessed by its worthlessness and indulged in pains of remorse at the thought of dying. He prayed as all his contemporaries did, for he believed in God. God, however, was too awesome a figure to turn to for mercy. No better compassionate intercessor between the frightened medieval soul and God could be found than the Virgin Mary.

While waiting for his death sentence, Villon facetiously started bequeathing his trivial possessions until he paused in meditation: Now the time had come to commend his soul to God. The list of his sins was so long, however, that scruples seemed to hold him back: By what right could he pray for himself when he had sinned so much? The memory of his poor old mother, a simple and loving soul, then rose to the son's guilty conscience: She would beg the Virgin Mary to intercede for her son's salvation, since God's mercy rested on the humble and suffering.

The mother's prayer opens with the ritual salutations to Mary, as queen and mother, divine and human, generous and compassionate. May Mary's bounty deliver the worthless woman from suffering and welcome her humble ignorant soul in Heaven, for she is assuredly God's faithful servant! The prayer is touching and candid; Villon evokes his mother's naive faith with immense tenderness. Yet in her voice, another voice trembles; behind her call for mercy, an obscure and hidden distress looms that is greater than an old woman's poor little sins. Villon is praying with his mother, for himself, like a child: No solemn formulas, no bombastic doctrines, only the artless faith of the primitive soul haunted by popular stories and dogmas. Villon is praying, for he is a great sinner and he fears the damnation of Hell. This ballad is one of his most moving and artistic: Its simple means of expression gives a poignant sincerity to the repentant sinner's distress and enlightens the beauty of the search for human dignity through contrition.

Debussy's setting is pervaded with a medieval coloring that

enhances the beautiful simplicity of the prayer. The melodic line is humble, meditative, and perfectly controlled. In the third stanza touches of chromaticism in the accompaniment enrich the texture of the song while depicting the naive imagery of Hell and Paradise. The song is remarkably impregnated with a contemplative feeling, fervor, and respect for humility. Villon's envoy has not been incorporated.[50]

ba la dkə vi jɔ̃ fɛ a la rə kɛ
## Ballade que Villon feit à la requeste
Ballad that Villon makes at the request

tdə sa mɛ r pu rpri je nɔ trə dam
## de sa mère pour prier Nostre-Dame
of his mother to pray Our Lady

da mə    dy    sjɛ l      re ʒɑ̃ tə    tɛ ri ɛn (ə)
**Dame    du    ciel,       regente    terrienne,**
Lady     of    heaven,    regent     of the earth,

ɑ̃ pə rjɛ rə    dɛ    zɛ̃ fɛ rno    pa ly
**Emperière    des    infernaux    palux,**
Empress     of the    infernal    marshes,

rə sə ve    mwa vɔ    trɛ̃ blə    kre ti ɛ nə
**Recevez-moy, vostre    humble    chrestienne,**
Receive    me,    your    humble    Christian,

kə    kɔ̃ prɛ̃ sə    swa    ɑ̃ trə    vo    ze ly
**Que    comprinse    soye    entre    vos    esleuz,**
Let    included    be    among    your    elect

Dame du ciel, régente terrienne,
Emperière des infernaulx palux,
Recevez-moy, vostre humble chrestienne,
Que comprinse soye entre vos esleuz,
Ce non obstant qu'oncques riens ne valuz.
Les biens de vous, ma dame et ma maistresse,
Sont trop plus grans que ne suys pecheresse,
Sans lesquelz bien ame ne peult merir
N'avoir les cieulx, je n'en suis menteresse.
En ceste foy je vueil vivre et mourir.

sə nɔ nɔ pstɑ̃ kɔ̃ kə rjɛ̃ nə
**Ce non obstant qu'oncques riens ne**
This although that never anything was

va ly
**valuz.**
worth.

lɛ bjɛ̃ də vu ma da mə e ma
**Les biens de vous, ma dame et ma**
The goodness of you, my lady and my

mɛ trɛ sə
**maistresse,**
mistress,

sɔ̃ tro ply grɑ̃ kə nə sɥi
**Sont trop plus grans que ne suys**
Is much more great than am

pe ʃə rɛ sə
**pecheresse,**
sinner,

sɑ̃ lɛ kɛ lbjɛ̃ ɑ mə nə pø
**Sans lesquelz bien ame ne peult**
Without which goodness soul not can

me ri r
**merir**
merit

na vwa rlɛ sjø ʒə nɑ̃ sɥi
**N'avoir les cieulx, je n'en suis**
Nor have the heavens, I not am

mɑ̃ tə rɛ sə
**menteresse.**
liar.

A vostre Filz dictes que je suys sienne;
De luy soyent mes pechez aboluz:
Pardonnez-moy comme à l'Egyptienne,
Ou comme il feit au clerc Theophilus,
Lequel par vous fut quitte et absoluz,
Combien qu'il eust au diable faict promesse
Preservez-moy que je n'accomplisse ce!
Vierge portant sans rompure encourir
Le sacrement qu'on celebre à la messe.
En ceste foy je vueil vivre et mourir.

Femme je suis povrette et ancienne,
Qui riens ne sçay, oncques lettres ne leuz;
Au moustier voy dont suis paroissienne,
Paradis painct où sont harpes et luz,
Et ung enfer où damnez sont boulluz:
L'ung me faict paour, l'aultre joye et liesse.
La joye avoir fais-moy, haulte Déesse,
A qui pecheurs doibvent tous recourir,
Comblez de foy, sans faincte ne paresse.
En ceste foy je vueil vivre et mourir.

(*Trois Ballades de François Villon*. Paris: Durand, n.d.)

ɑ̃ sɛ tə fwa ʒə vø vi vre mu ri r
**En ceste foy je vueil vivre et mourir.**
In this faith I will live and die.

a vɔ trə fi s di tə kə ʒə sɥi sjɛ nə
**A vostre Filz dictes que je suys sienne;**
To your Son say that I am his;

də lɥi swa (ə) mɛ pe ʃe za bɔ ly
**De lui soyent mes pechez aboluz:**
By him be my sins cleared:

pa rdɔ ne mwa kɔ ma le ʒi psi ɛ nə
**Pardonnez-moy comme à l'Egyptienne,**
Forgive me as to the Egyptian,

u kɔ mi lfi to klɛ rte o fi ly s
**Ou comme il feit au clerc Theophilus,**
Or as he did to the clerc Theophilus,

lə kɛ lpa rvu fy ki te a psɔ ly
**Lequel par vous fut quitte et absoluz,**
Who by you was acquitted and absolved,

kɔ̃ bjɛ̃ ki ly to dja blə fɛ
**Combien qu'il eust au diable faict**
Although he had to the devil made
prɔ mɛ sə
**promesse.**
promise.

pre zɛ rve mwa kə ʒə na kɔ̃ pli sə sə
**Preservez-moy que je n'accomplisse ce!**
Save me that I not accomplish that!

Lady of Heaven, regent of the earth,
Empress of the infernal marshes,
Receive me, your humble Christian,
That I may be included among your elect,
Although I was never worth anything.
Your goodness, my lady and mistress
Is far greater than my sinfulness
Without which no soul can merit
Or gain Heaven, I am not lying.
In this faith will I live and die.

Say to your Son that I am his;
May my sins be abolished by him:
Let him forgive me as he forgave the Egyptian woman,[50a]
Or as he forgave the clerk Theophilus,[51]
Who was acquitted and forgiven by you,
Although he had made a pact with the devil.
Preserve me from doing the same!
O Virgin that bore without incurring blemish[52]
The sacrament that is celebrated at Mass.
In this faith will I live and die.

| vjɛ rʒə | pɔ rtã | sã | rɔ̃ py | rã ku ri r |
|---|---|---|---|---|
| **Vierge** | **portant** | **sans** | **rompure** | **encourir** |
| Virgin | bearing | without | rupture | incurring |

| lə | sa krə mã | kɔ̃ | se lɛ | bra la |
|---|---|---|---|---|
| **Le** | **sacrement** | **qu'on** | **celebre** | **à** **la** |
| The | sacrament | that one | celebrates | at the |

| mɛ sə |
|---|
| **messe.** |
| Mass. |

| ã | sɛ tə | fwa | ʒə | vø | vi | vre | mu ri r |
|---|---|---|---|---|---|---|---|
| **En** | **ceste** | **foy** | **je** | **vueil** | **vivre** | **et** | **mourir.** |
| In | this | faith | I | will | live | and | die. |

I am a poor old woman,
Who knows nothing; never could read a letter;
I see in the church of which I am a parishioner
A painted paradise with harps and lutes
And a hell where the damned are boiled:
One frightens me, the other brings me joy and gladness.
Give me joy, great Goddess,
To whom all sinners must turn,
Full of faith, without hypocrisy or sloth.
In this faith will I live and die.

| fa mə | ʒə | sɥi | po vrɛ | te | ã si ɛ nə |
|---|---|---|---|---|---|
| **Femme** | **je** | **suis** | **povrette** | **et** | **ancienne,** |
| Woman | I | am | poor | and | old, |

| ki | rjɛ̃ | nə | sɛ | ɔ̃ kə | lɛ trə | nə |
|---|---|---|---|---|---|---|
| **Qui** | **riens** | **ne** | **sçay,** | **oncques** | **lettre** | **ne** |
| Who | nothing | not | know, | never | letter | not |

| ly |
|---|
| **leuz;** |
| read; |

| o | mu tje | vwa | dɔ̃ | sɥi | pa rwa siɛ nə |
|---|---|---|---|---|---|
| **Au** | **moustier** | **voy** | **dont** | **suis** | **paroissienne,** |
| To | the church | see | of which | am | parishioner, |

| pa ra di | pɛ̃ | u | sɔ̃ | a rpə | ze | ly |
|---|---|---|---|---|---|---|
| **Paradis** | **painct** | **où** | **sont** | **harpes** | **et** | **luz,** |
| Paradise | painted | where | are | harps | and | lutes, |

e      œ̃    nɑ̃ fɛ   ru      dɑ ne    sɔ̃   bu ly
**Et    ung   enfer où      damnez  sont  boulluz:**
And a      hell    where  damned   are   boiled:

lœ̃       mə   fɛ    pœ     rlo trə   ʒwa   e
**L'ung     me   faict  paour,  l'autre   joye  et**
The one    me   gives  fear,      the other  joy   and

li ɛ sə
**liesse.**
gladness.

la     ʒwa    a vwa   rfɛ    mwa   o tə     de ɛ sə
**La     joye    avoir   fais- moy,  haulte  Déesse,**
The   joy     have    make me,    great   Goddess,

a      ki     pe ʃœ     rdwa və   tu      srə ku ri r
**A      qui    pecheurs  doibvent  tous    recourir,**
To   whom  sinners    must        all     turn,

kɔ̃ ble    də    fwa    sɑ̃       fɛ̃ tə      nə
**Comblez   de    foy,   sans      faincte   ne**
Filled     with  faith,  without  hypocrisy  or

pa rɛ sə
**paresse.**
sloth.

ɑ̃     sɛ tə    fwa    ʒə    vø      vi      vre   mu ri r
**En    ceste   foy    je    vueil  vivre   et    mourir.**
In    this    faith   I    will   live    and   die.

# III. "Ballade des femmes de Paris"

Women were the victims of the medieval train of thought on the sexes: They were deceitful, vicious, coquettish, mercenary, in short, sources of misery. Their best and worst weapon was their tongue, by which they were able to make demands, dissemble, and be the eventual ruin of men. Parisian women, in particular, were known for their consummate verbal skills: They would hold sessions at churches and homes, street corners, markets, and wash-houses; the fishwives were notorious for their brawls, and their reputation did not abate with time. In this third ballad, Villon enumerates the cleverest talkers in the world, from ancient to modern times, from Florence to Spain, and concludes his list with the Parisians: They of all deserve the prize for the greatest eloquence. The brilliant procession of women moves along at a brisk tempo as if accompanied by fifes and drums. Yet, contrary to the prevalent medieval scorn for the fair sex's astonishing gift, Villon does not stigmatize women with contempt and aversion. After all, love and women are not to him as vital concerns as Death and Hell. He rather enjoys watching them gab and quarrel, and gracefully devotes to them this mischievous ballad.

Debussy gives a witty, lively, and colorful rendering of the poem. The song brings out the continuous chatter of the women, places triumphant emphasis on the refrain, and conveys Villon's irony. The vocal part requires fast and accurate diction.

## ba la de fa mdə pa ri
## Ballade des femmes de Paris
## Ballad of the women of Paris

| kwa | kɔ̃ | tjɛ̃ | bɛ lə | lɑ̃ ga ʒjɛ rə |
|-----|-----|------|-------|----------------|
| **Quoy** | **qu'on** | **tient** | **belles** | **langagières** |
| Although | one | considers | fine | talkers |

flɔ rɑ̃ ti nə      ve ni sjɛ nə
**Florentines, Veniciennes,**
Florentines,  Venetians,


a se        pu       rɛ trə   mɛ sa ʒjɛ rə
**Assez     pour    estre    messaigières,**
Enough    to       be       messengers,


e        mɛ mə mɑ̃     lɛ     zɑ̃ sjɛ n(ə)
**Et      mesmement   les    anciennes;**
And      likewise         the    old;


mɛ       swa      lɔ̃ ba rdə       rɔ me nə
**Mais,    soient   Lombardes,    Romaines,**
But,      be they  Lombards,     Romans,


ʒə nə vwa zə    a    mɛ      pe ri l
**Genevoises,   à    mes    périls,**
Genoese,        at   my     risks,


pje mɔ̃ tɛ zə     sa vwa zjɛ nə
**Piemontoises, Savoysiennes,**
Piedmontese,    Savoyards,


i        lnɛ       bɔ      bɛ k     kə     də   pa ri
**Il       n'est     bon     bec      que    de   Paris.**
There   not is    sharp   tongue   but    in   Paris.


də  bo      pa rle    tjɛ nə     ʃa je rə
**De  beau    parler    tiennent   chayères,**
Of   fine    speech    hold       chairs,


sə   di   tɔ̃      na pɔ li tɛ nə
**Ce   dit- on     Napolitaines,**
So    say  they   Neapolitans,


Quoy qu'on tient belles langagières
Florentines, Veniciennes,
Assez pour estre messaigières,
Et mesmement les anciennes;
Mais, soient Lombardes, Romaines,
Genevoises, à mes perils,
Piemontoises, Savoysiennes,
Il n'est bon bec que de Paris.

De beau parler tiennent chayères,
Ce dit-on Napolitaines,
Et que sont bonnes cacquetières
Allemandes et Bruciennes;
Soient Grecques, Egyptiennes,
De Hongrie ou d'aultre païs,
Espaignolles ou Castellannes,
Il n'est bon bec que de Paris.

Brettes, Suysses, n'y sçavent guères,
Ne Gasconnes et Tholouzaines;
Du Petit-Pont deux harangères
Les concluront, et les Lorraines,
Anglesches ou Callaisiennes,
(Ay-je beaucoup de lieux compris?)
Picardes, de Valenciennes. . .
Il n'est bon bec que de Paris.

Prince, aux dames parisiennes,
De bien parler donnez le prix;
Quoy qu'on die d'Italiennes,
Il n'est bon bec que de Paris.

(*Trois Ballades de François Villon.* Paris: Durand, n.d.)

e     kə   sɔ̃   bɔ nə    ka kə tjɛ rə
**Et   que  sont  bonnes  cacquetières**
And   that  are   good    chatterers

a lə mɑ̃ də    ze   bry sjɛ nə
**Allemandes  et   Bruciennes;**
Germans       and  Prussians;

swa     grɛ kə      e ʒi psjɛ nə
**Soient  Grecques,  Egyptiennes,**
Be they  Greeks,     Egyptians,

də    ɔ̃ gri   u    do trə   pe i
**De    Hongrie  ou   d'aultre  païs,**
From  Hungary  or   other    land,

ɛ spa ɲɔ lə    u    ka stɛ la nə
**Espaignolles  ou   Castellannes,**
Spaniards      or   Catalans,

i    lnɛ    bɔ̃    bɛ k    kə   də  pa ri
**Il   n'est  bon   bec     que  de  Paris.**
There not is  sharp  tongue  but  in  Paris.

brɛ tə     sɥi sə    ni   sa və    gɛ rə
**Brettes,  Suysses, n'y  sçavent  guères,**
Bretons,  Swiss,    not  know     barely,

nə      ga skɔ      ne   to lu zɛ nə
**Ne      Gasconnes  et   Tholouzaines;**
Neither  Gascons    and  Toulousans;

dy      pə ti pɔ̃      dø    a rɑ̃ ʒɛ rə
**Du      Petit-Pont  deux  harangères**
From the Petit-Pont   two   fishwives

Although one considers as fine talkers
Florentines, Venetians,
Enough to be good bearers of news,
And likewise the old women;
Yet, be they from Lombardy, Rome,
Genoa, Heaven forbid,
Piedmont, Savoy,
There is no sharper tongue than in Paris.

Of fine speech professorships are held
So they say by the Neapolitans,
One also says that good chatterers are
The Germans and the Prussians;
Be they Greeks, Egyptians,
From Hungary or other lands,
Spaniards or Catalans,
There is no sharper tongue than in Paris.

The Bretons, the Swiss are barely proficient,
Neither are the women from Gascony or Toulouse;
Two fishwives from the Petit-Pont[53]
Will have the last word over those from Lorraine,
England or Calais,
(Have I included enough places?)
Picardy, Valenciennes. . .
There is no sharper tongue than in Paris.

lɛ    kɔ̃ kly rɔ̃    e    lɛ    lɔ rɛ nə
**Les    concluront,  et   les   Lorraines,**
Them  will conclude, and   the   Lorrainers,

ɑ̃ glɛ ʃə    zu    ka lɛ zjɛ nə
**Anglesches  ou   Callaisiennes,**
English      or    Calaisians,

e ʒə    bo ku    də    ljø    kɔ̃ pri
**(Ay-je  beaucoup de   lieux  compris?)**
(Have I  many     of   places included?)

pi ka rdə    də    va lɑ̃ sjɛ nə
**Picardes,  de    Valenciennes. . .**
Picards,    from   Valenciennes. . .

i    lnɛ    bɔ̃    bɛ k    kə    də    pa ri
**Il   n'est  bon   bec    que   de   Paris.**
There not is sharp  tongue but   in   Paris.

prɛ̃ s    o    da mə    pa ri zjɛ nə
**Prince,  aux   dames   parisiennes,**
Prince,  to the  ladies  Parisian,

də    bjɛ̃    pa rle    dɔ ne    lə    pri
**De  bien   parler    donnez  le    prix;**
Of   fine   speech    give    the   prize;

kwa    kɔ̃    di    di ta li ɛ nə
**Quoy   qu'on  die   d'Italiennes,**
Whatever they  say   of Italians,

i    lnɛ    bɔ̃    bɛ k    kə    də    pa ri
**Il   n'est  bon   bec    que   de   Paris.**
There not is sharp  tongue but   in   Paris.

Prince, to the Parisian ladies,
Give the prize for fine speech;
Whatever may be said of the
Italians,
There is no sharper tongue than
in Paris.

# ——"Trois Poèmes de Stéphane Mallarmé"

## (Three Poems of Stéphane Mallarmé)

Date of composition: *Summer 1913.*
Date of publication: *1913.*
Publisher: *Durand & Cie, Paris.*
Source: *Stéphane Mallarmé*, Poésies complètes, *1887.*
Dedicated to the memory of Stéphane Mallarmé, and in homage to Madame E. Bonniot (née G. Mallarmé).

   I. "Soupir" (Sigh).
  II. "Placet futile" (Futile Entreaty).
 III. "Éventail" (Fan).

Thirty years or so after "Apparition" and nineteen years after the *Prélude à l'après-midi d'un Faune,* Debussy was again inspired by Mallarmé's poetry. This Mallarmé cycle—which was to be the last of Debussy's song cycles—was composed in memory of the poet, then dead for fifteen years, and dedicated to the poet's daughter. The three poems have in common a complex syntactical structure that opens the door to a variety of interpretations. They also share a recreated, fleeting world in which everything is allusive, a "precious" vocabulary and virtuosity of sounds. Considering the occasional abstruseness of the texts, one can imagine how ill at ease the composer must have been; it might explain why the musical language he chose remains very close to traditional forms. The melodic line of the vocal part is merely suggested, whereas the harmonic progressions of the accompaniment are attuned to the elliptical nature of the texts.

# I. "Soupir"

"Soupir" was written by Mallarmé in 1864 and first published in the *Parnasse Contemporain* (Contemporary Parnassus) of 1866. This autumnal reverie of ten lines, made up of one long involuted sentence, focuses on a single metaphor that seems taken after Baudelaire's *Jet d'eau* (The Fountain): As the water in a fountain soars toward the sky, the soul of the poet rises toward the poet's beloved. All the declining attributes of autumn are present and form almost untranslatable metaphors: The beloved's forehead is splashed with freckles of russet; her eyes have lost their steady direction and now wander; the sky is turning softer and paler; the jet of water remains white; the sun exhales its last rays above the still waters; dying leaves are swept away by the wind. The spiraling movement of the sentence ascends and descends, in harmony with the movement of the poet's soul that first soars, then loses its flame and abates at dusk, disintegrated and melancholy. The sighing fountain that a weary Azure turns down, falls again languorous and resigned in the basins. The anemic autumnal sun cannot beget ardor; its last feeble yellow ray strikes the end of desire.

The highly involved grammatical structure of the poem demanded of the composer some elucidating, which Debussy did by using variations in textures and rhythms. The melodic line borders on the recitative and calls for appropriate breathing to clarify the meaning of the text.

su pi r
## Soupir
Sigh

| mɔ̃ | nɑ mə vɛ | rtɔ̃ | frɔ̃ | u | rɛ v |
|---|---|---|---|---|---|
| **Mon** | **âme** | **vers** | **ton** | **front où** | **rêve,** |
| My | soul | toward | your | brow where | dreams, |

| o | kɑ lmə | sœ r |
|---|---|---|
| **ô** | **calme** | **soeur,** |
| O | calm | sister, |

| œ̃ | no tɔ nə | ʒɔ̃ ʃe | də | tɑ ʃə | də |
|---|---|---|---|---|---|
| **Un** | **automne** | **jonché** | **de** | **taches** | **de** |
| An | autumn | strewn | with | freckles | of |

| ru sœ r |
|---|
| **rousseur** |
| russet |

| e | vɛ | rlə | sjɛ | lɛ rɑ̃ | də | tɔ̃ |
|---|---|---|---|---|---|---|
| **Et** | **vers** | **le** | **ciel** | **errant** | **de** | **ton** |
| And | toward | the | heaven | wandering | of | your |

| nœ | jɑ̃ ʒe li kə |
|---|---|
| **oeil** | **angélique** |
| eye | angelic |

| mɔ̃ tə | kɔ mə | dɑ̃ | zœ̃ | ʒa rdɛ̃ |
|---|---|---|---|---|
| **Monte,** | **comme** | **dans** | **un** | **jardin** |
| Soars, | as | in | a | garden |

| me lɑ̃ kɔ li kə |
|---|
| **mélancolique,** |
| melancholy, |

| fi dɛ lə | œ̃ | blɑ̃ | ʒɛ | do | su pi rə |
|---|---|---|---|---|---|
| **Fidèle,** | **un** | **blanc** | **jet** | **d'eau** | **soupire** |
| Faithful, | a | white | jet | of water | sighs |

| vɛ | rla zy r |
|---|---|
| **vers** | **l'Azur!** |
| toward | the Azure! |

| vɛ | rla zy | ra tɑ̃ dri | dɔ ktɔ brə | pɑ |
|---|---|---|---|---|
| **Vers** | **l'Azur** | **attendri** | **d'Octobre** | **pâle** |
| Toward | the Azure | tender | of October | pale |

| le | py r |
|---|---|
| **et** | **pur** |
| and | pure |

| ki | mi | ro | grɑ̃ | ba sɛ̃ | sa |
|---|---|---|---|---|---|
| **Qui** | **mire** | **aux** | **grands** | **bassins** | **sa** |
| Which | mirrors | in the | great | basins | its |

| lɑ̃ gœ | rɛ̃ fi ni(ə) |
|---|---|
| **langueur** | **infinie** |
| languor | infinite |

Mon âme vers ton front où rêve,
ô calme soeur,
Un automne jonché de taches de rousseur
Et vers le ciel errant de ton oeil angélique
Monte, comme dans un jardin mélancolique,
Fidèle, un blanc jet d'eau soupire vers l'Azur!
Vers l'Azur attendri d'Octobre pâle et pur
Qui mire aux grands bassins sa langueur infinie
Et laisse, sur l'eau morte où la fauve agonie
Des feuilles erre au vent et creuse un froid sillon,
Se traîner le soleil jaune d'un long rayon.

(*Trois Poèmes de Stéphane Mallarmé.* Paris: Durand, n.d.)

| e | lɛ sə | sy | rlo | mɔ | rtu | la |
|---|---|---|---|---|---|---|
| **Et** | **laisse, sur** | **l'eau** | **morte** | **où** | | **la** |
| And | lets, | on | the water | dead | where | the |

| fo | va gɔ ni |
|---|---|
| **fauve** | **agonie** |
| tawny | death agony |

| dɛ | fœ jə | ɛ | ro | vɑ̃ | e | krø |
|---|---|---|---|---|---|---|
| **Des** | **feuilles** | **erre** | **au** | **vent** | **et** | **creuse** |
| Of the | leaves | roams | in the | wind | and | ploughs |

| zœ̃ | frwa | si jɔ̃ |
|---|---|---|
| **un** | **froid** | **sillon,** |
| a | cold | furrow, |

| sə | tre ne | lə | sɔ lɛ | jʒo nə | dœ̃ | lɔ̃ |
|---|---|---|---|---|---|---|
| **Se** | **traîner** | **le** | **soleil** | **jaune** | **d'un** | **long** |
| Itself | drag | the | sun | yellow | of a | long |

| rɛ jɔ̃ |
|---|
| **rayon.** |
| ray. |

My soul, toward your brow
where dreams, O calm sister,
An autumn strewn with russet
freckles
And toward the wandering
heaven of your angelic eye,
Soars, as in a melancholy garden
A faithful white fountain sighs
toward the Azure!
Toward the tender Azure of pale
and pure October
Which mirrors in the great basins
its infinite languor
And lets, on the dead water
where the tawny death agony
Of leaves roams in the wind and
ploughs a cold furrow,
The yellow sun trail a long drawn
out ray.

# II. "Placet futile"

This early love poem of Mallarmé's was first published in 1862 when the young poet traveled to London with his future wife. It is addressed to an imaginary lady and, written in sonnet form, recalls the style of seventeenth- and eighteenth-century gallant poetry. Under the guise of a court abbé, the poet sues for his lady's favor in "precious" terms. He first wishes to be Hebe painted on the Sèvres cup, who comes alive every time the lady's lips touch the cup. The futility of his entreaty becomes humiliating, and, rejecting formality in the second stanza, he lets out his resentment, for he is not a petty plaything nor a prop for her little games. The lady, though not indifferent, will not look at her suitor who, soon regretting his anger, marvels at her magnificent blonde hair. He then begs her to choose him as the shepherd of her smiles, the sole keeper of her content. But the more pressing his entreaties, the less hopeful he becomes. The poem ends in preciosity as it started: By his artistic discourse, the poet conceals the deception of defeated wooing under a playful artificiality. The sonnet is elegant, of discreet sensuousness, and somewhat icy in its subtle irony and formal beauty.

Both Debussy and Fauré set it to music. Debussy chose a slow minuet tempo that enhances the elegant exactness of the text. Ornaments bring out the graceful charm of the imagery.

pla sɛ  fy ti l
**Placet  futile**
Entreaty  futile

| | | | | | |
|---|---|---|---|---|---|
| prɛ̃ sɛ sə | a | ʒa lu ze | lə | dɛ stɛ̃ | dy |
| **Princesse!** | **à** | **jalouser** | **le** | **destin** | **d'une** |
| Princess! | by | envying | the | fate | of a |
| ne be | | | | | |
| **Hébé** | | | | | |
| Hebe | | | | | |

Princesse! à jalouser le destin
d'une Hébé
Qui point sur cette tasse au baiser
de vos lèvres,
J'use mes feux mais n'ai rang
discret que d'abbé
Et ne figurerai même nu sur le
Sèvres.

| ki | pwɛ̃ | sy | rsɛ tə | tɑ | so | be ze |
|----|------|-----|--------|----|-----|-------|
| **Qui** | **poind** | **sur** | **cette** | **tasse** | **au** | **baiser** |
| Who | appears | on | this | cup | from | the kiss |

| də vo | le vrə |
|-------|--------|
| **de vos** | **lèvres,** |
| of your | lips, |

| ʒy zə | mɛ | fø | mɛ | ne | rɑ̃ | di skrɛ |
|-------|-----|-----|-----|-----|------|---------|
| **J'use** | **mes** | **feux** | **mais** | **n'ai** | **rang** | **discret** |
| I waste | my | ardor | but | have | rank | modest |

| kə | da be |
|----|-------|
| **que** | **d'abbé** |
| only | of abbé |

| e | nə | fi gy rə re | mɛ mə | ny | sy | rlə |
|---|-----|-------------|-------|-----|-----|-----|
| **Et** | **ne** | **figurerai** | **même** | **nu** | **sur** | **le** |
| And | not | will figure | even | nude | on | the |

| sɛ vrə |
|--------|
| **Sèvres.** |
| Sèvres. |

| kɔ mə | ʒə | nə | sɥi | pɑ | tɔ̃ | bi ʃɔ̃ |
|-------|-----|-----|-----|-----|------|--------|
| **Comme** | **je** | **ne** | **suis** | **pas** | **ton** | **bichon** |
| As | I | not | am | not | your | lapdog |

| ɑ̃ ba rbe |
|-----------|
| **embarbé,** |
| bearded, |

| ni | la | pa sti jə | ni | dy | ru ʒə | ni | ʒø |
|----|-----|-----------|----|-----|-------|-----|-----|
| **Ni** | **la** | **pastille,** | **ni** | **du** | **rouge,** | **ni** | **jeux** |
| Nor | the | pastille, | nor | some | rouge, | nor | games |

| mjɛ vrə |
|---------|
| **mièvres** |
| dainty |

Comme je ne suis pas ton bichon embarbé,
Ni la pastille, ni du rouge, ni jeux mièvres
Et que sur moi je sais ton regard clos tombé,
Blonde dont les coiffeurs divins sont des orfèvres!

Nommez-nous. . . toi de qui tant de ris framboisés
Se joignent en troupeaux d'agneaux apprivoisés
Chez tous broutant les voeux et bêlant aux délires,

Nommez-nous. . . pour qu'Amour ailé d'un éventail
M'y peigne flûte aux doigts endormant ce bercail,
Princesse, nommez-nous berger de vos sourires.

(*Trois Poèmes de Stéphane Mallarmé.* Paris: Durand, n.d.)

———————————— ● ————————————

Princess! Envious of the fate of Hebe[54]
Who appears on this cup from the kiss of your lips,
I waste my ardor but I hold only the modest rank of abbé
And will not figure, even nude, on the Sèvres porcelain.[55]

As I am not your bearded lapdog,
Nor a pastille, nor rouge, nor dainty games
And as I am aware of your shut eyes directed upon me,
Blonde of whom the divine hairdressers are goldsmiths!

| e | kə | sy | rmwa | ʒə | se | tɔ̃ | rə ga |
|---|---|---|---|---|---|---|---|
| **Et** | **que** | **sur** | **moi** | **je** | **sais** | **ton** | **regard** |
| And | as | on | me | I | know | your | glance |

| rklo | tɔ̃ be |
|---|---|
| **clos** | **tombé,** |
| shut | fallen, |

| blɔ̃ də | dɔ̃ | | lɛ | kwa fœ | | rdi vɛ̃ | sɔ̃ |
|---|---|---|---|---|---|---|---|
| **Blonde** | **dont** | | **les** | **coiffeurs** | | **divins** | **sont** |
| Blonde | of whom | the | hairdressers | | divine | | are |

| dɛ | zɔ rfɛ vrə |
|---|---|
| **des** | **orfèvres!** |
| some | goldsmiths! |

| nɔ me | | nu | | twa | də ki | | tɑ̃ |
|---|---|---|---|---|---|---|---|
| **Nommez-nous.** | | **..** | **toi** | **de** | **qui** | | **tant** |
| Name | | us... | you | of | whom | so many |

| də | ri | | frɑ̃ bwa ze |
|---|---|---|---|
| **de** | **ris** | | **framboisés** |
| of | laughters | raspberry-flavored |

| sə | | ʒwa ɲə | tɑ̃ | tru po | | da ɲo |
|---|---|---|---|---|---|---|
| **Se** | | **joignent** | **en** | **troupeau** | | **d'agneaux** |
| Themselves | unite | in | flock | | of lambs |

| za pri vwa ze |
|---|
| **apprivoisés** |
| tame |

| ʃe | tu | sbru tɑ̃ | | lɛ | vœ | | e | bɛ lɑ̃ |
|---|---|---|---|---|---|---|---|---|
| **Chez** | **tous** | **broutant** | | **les** | **voeux** | | **et** | **bêlant** |
| Of | all | browsing | | the | desires | and | bleating |

| to | de li rə |
|---|---|
| **aux** | **délires,** |
| at the | transports, |

Name us. . . you whose countless raspberry-scented laughters Gather in a flock of tame lambs To browse on our desires and bleat on our transports,

Name us. . . so that Love with his fan-shaped wing May portray me, flute in hand, putting this sheepfold to sleep, Princess, name me as shepherd of your smiles.

nɔ me        nu        pu    rka mu        re le
**Nommez-nous. . . pour qu'Amour ailé**
Name   us. . .      so       that Love          winged
dœ̃        ne vɑ̃ taj
**d'un      éventail**
with a   fan

mi        pɛ ɲə    fly    to    dwa
**M'y       peigne flûte aux doigts**
Me there paints   flute   in      fingers
ɑ̃ dɔ rmɑ̃         sə    bɛ rka j
**endormant     ce    bercail,**
putting to sleep this  sheepfold,

prɛ̃ sɛ sə    nɔ me      nu      bɛ rʒe    də  vo
**Princesse, nommez-nous berger     de  vos**
Princess,    name     us      shepherd of  your
su ri rə
**sourires.**
smiles.

# III. "Éventail"

Many of Mallarmé's poems were occasional short pieces composed in homage to friends and acquaintances. He wrote as many as eighteen "Éventails." In those days the fan was an important accessory of a woman's dressing; on it gallant verse was often inscribed. The fan of this poem of 1884, entitled "Autre éventail, de Mademoiselle Mallarmé" (Other fan of Miss Mallarmé), belonged to Geneviève Mallarmé, the poet's only daughter.

This unusual fan addresses the young dreamer directly and beseeches her to hold it in such a way that pure delight may arise. The girl's hand holds it bound on one end, fluttering on the other, thus shifting volumes and masses of air. Space, fictitiously recreated by the fan's motion, blurs contours and becomes vertiginous: There is no steadfast direction to this unremitting flutter; space sways like a huge kiss without destination or purpose. Then the fan comes to a stop as the girl, sinking deeper into her reverie, folds it. The play is now over: The girl's dreams, which had been on the threshold of action while fluttering with the fan wing, are closed once more within the intimate shelter of their chaste paradise; likewise, the attempted laughter dies on her lips and buries itself in the folded fan.

The last stanza enlarges on the maiden's inner paradise: Magnified and embellished, the fan becomes a glorious scepter from the distant pink shores of nonexistence. Standing out against the golden sunset of the imagination, it rests, motionless, against the illuminating glow of the girl's bracelet. The dreamer's flight into the recreated space of fantasy is now spiritualized and immobilized into contemplation.

# e vɑ̃ ta j
# Éventail
## Fan

o  rɛ vø zə   pu    rkə   ʒə  plɔ̃ ʒə
**O  rêveuse, pour  que   je  plonge**
O  dreamer, so     that  I   plunge

o     py    rde li sə   sɑ̃    ʃə mɛ̃
**Au   pur   délice     sans   chemin,**
Into  pure  delight    without  path,

sa ʃə      pa   rœ̃  sy pti   l mɑ̃ sɔ̃ ʒə
**Sache,    par  un   subtil   mensonge,**
Contrive,  by   a    subtle   deceit,

ga rde   mɔ̃    nɛ lə   dɑ̃    ta    mɛ̃
**Garder  mon   aile   dans   ta    main.**
Keep     my    wing   in     your  hand.

y nə    frɛ ʃœ    rdə   kre py sky lə
**Une   fraîcheur  de    crépuscule**
A      freshness  of    twilight

tə    vjɛ̃    (t)a  ʃa kə  ba tə mɑ̃
**Te    vient   à     chaque battement**
You   comes  at    each    beat

dɔ̃    lə   ku     pri zɔ nje   rə ky lə
**Dont  le   coup   prisonnier  recule**
Whose the  stroke prisoned    drives away

lɔ ri zɔ̃     de li ka tə mɑ̃
**L'horizon   délicatement.**
The horizon  delicately.

O rêveuse, pour que je plonge
Au pur délice sans chemin,
Sache, par un subtil mensonge,
Garder mon aile dans ta main.

Une fraîcheur de crépuscule
Te vient à chaque battement
Dont le coup prisonnier recule
L'horizon délicatement.

Vertige! voici que frissonne
L'espace comme un grand baiser
Qui, fou de naître pour personne,
Ne peut jaillir ni s'apaiser.

Sens-tu le paradis farouche
Ainsi qu'un rire enseveli
Se couler du coin de ta bouche
Au fond de l'unanime pli!

(*Trois Poèmes de Stéphane
Mallarmé*. Paris: Durand, n.d.)

———————•———————

O dreamer, so that I may plunge
Into pure pathless delight,
Contrive, by subtle deceit,
To hold my wing in your hand.

A twilight freshness
Comes to you at each flutter
Whose imprisoned stroke pushes
back
The horizon delicately.

vɛ rti ʒə   vwa si   kə    fri sɔ nə
**Vertige!** **Voici** **que** **frissonne**
Vertigo!   See    how   shivers

lɛ spa sə   kɔ      mœ̃ grɑ̃   be ze
**L'espace** **comme** **un** **grand** **baiser**
The space  like    a   great  kiss

ki    fu    də   nɛ trə    pu    rpɛ rsɔ nə
**Qui,** **fou** **de** **naître** **pour** **personne,**
Which,  mad  to   be born   for   no one,

nə     pø    ʒa ji    rni   sa pe ze
**Ne** **peut** **jaillir** **ni** **s'apaiser.**
Neither can   spring up  nor   abate.

sɑ̃    ty    lə   pa ra di   fa ru ʃə
**Sens- tu** **le** **paradis** **farouche**
Feel  you   the  paradise   chaste

ɛ̃ si   kœ̃    ri    rɑ̃ sə və li
**Ainsi** **qu'un** **rire** **enseveli**
Like   a    laughter  buried

sə ku le   dy     kwɛ̃    də ta    bu ʃə
**Se couler** **du**    **coin**   **de ta**   **bouche**
Flow    from the  corner  of your  mouth

o fɔ̃     də  ly na ni mə     pli
**Au fond** **de** **l'unanime**    **pli!**
Down   of   the unanimous  fold!

lə   sɛ ptrə  dɛ    ri va ʒə   ro zə
**Le** **sceptre** **des**   **rivages** **roses**
The  scepter  of the  shores   pink

Vertigo! See how space
Shivers like an immense kiss
Which, mad to be born for no one,
Can neither spring up nor abate.

Do you feel the chaste paradise
Which like a buried laughter
Flows from the corner of your mouth
Deep down into the unanimous fold!

The scepter of pink shores
Stagnating on golden evenings, this it is,
This white furled flight you rest
Against the fire of a bracelet.

sta ɲɑ̃        sy  rlɛ swa        rdɔ r    sə   lɛ
**Stagnants sur les soirs       d'or,   ce  l'est,**
Stagnant    on  the  evenings of gold, this it is,

sə   blɑ̃   vɔ   lfɛ rme  kə   ty   po zə
**Ce   blanc  vol   fermé  que  tu   poses**
This white flight shut        that you place

kɔ̃ trə   lə   fø   dœ̃    bra sə lɛ
**Contre le   feu  d'un  bracelet.**
Against the  fire of a    bracelet.

# ——"Noël des enfants qui n'ont – plus de maisons"
## *(Christmas Carol of the Homeless Children)*

**Date of composition:** *December 1915.*
**Date of publication:** *1916.*
**Publisher:** *Durand & Cie, Paris.*
**First performance:** *Paris, the Sorbonne, 9 April 1916.*

This last song of Debussy's was written, text and music, on the eve of the first operation performed against the cancer that was to take his life two years later. The song was prompted by Debussy's patriotic feelings and inspired by the invasion of Northern France by the German armies during World War I. Such circumstances explain the style of the poem and the tone of the melody.

The poem was written in the name of a child who recounts the destruction of his familiar world: It is Christmas time, and nothing is left of the warmth of his home. Not only was his house burned down, but his father is at war and his mother is dead. The victimized child raises his voice to accuse the enemy and, in his naive way, begs that there be no Christmas for the Germans. Then the prayer becomes of a more universal scope and pleads not only for the starving French children but for children from other suffering lands. It ends advocating a return to some normalcy by victory.

The economy and simplicity of the words call for a subdued interpretation: One must remember that it is a child speaking. The naive patriotism, however, should not be understated, for it represents Debussy's direct appeal to justice, dignity, and compassion. The song had its first performance at a special concert in the main amphitheater of the Paris University, given to promote friendship between France and other countries.

nɔ ɛ lde zɑ̃ fɑ̃ ki
## Noël des enfants qui
Christmas carol of the children who
nɔ̃ ply də me zɔ̃
## n'ont plus de maisons
not have any more of houses

nu       na vɔ̃      ply        də   me zɔ̃
**Nous n'avons plus       de   maisons!**
We    not have  any more  of   houses!

lɛ     zɛ nə mi   (z)ɔ̃ tu              pri
**Les   ennemis  ont   tout           pris,**
The   enemies  have  everything  taken,

          tu          pri      tu          pri
          **tout       pris,   tout       pris,**
          everything  taken,  everything  taken,

          ʒy ska    nɔ trə   pə ti   li
          **jusqu'à  notre    petit   lit!**
          even      our      little   bed!

i      lzɔ̃    bry le   le kɔ       le   nɔ trə
**Ils   ont   brûlé   l'école     et   notre**
They  have  burned  the school  and  our
mɛ         tro si
**maître    aussi.**
teacher    too.

Nous n'avons plus de maisons!
Les ennemis ont tout pris, tout
pris, tout pris, jusqu'à notre petit
lit!
Ils ont brûlé l'école et notre
maître aussi.
Ils ont brûlé l'église et monsieur
Jésus-Christ
Et le vieux pauvre qui n'a pas pu
s'en aller!

Nous n'avons plus de maisons.
Les ennemis ont tout pris, tout
pris, tout pris, jusqu'à notre petit
lit!
Bien sûr! papa est à la guerre,
Pauvre maman est morte!
Avant d'avoir vu tout ça.
Qu'est-ce que l'on va faire?
Noël! petit Noël! n'allez pas chez
eux, n'allez plus jamais chez eux,
Punissez-les!

i        lzɔ̃    bry le    le gli        ze     mə sjø
**Ils    ont    brûlé    l'église    et    monsieur**
They    have    burned    the church    and    mister

ʒe zy    kri
**Jésus–Christ**
Jesus Christ

e    lə    vjø    po vrə    ki    na    pɑ    py
**Et    le    vieux    pauvre    qui    n'a    pas    pu**
And    the    old    poor        who    has    not    been able

sɑ̃    na le
**s'en    aller!**
to    escape!

nu    na vɔ̃    ply        də me zɔ̃
**Nous    n'avons    plus        de    maisons.**
We    not have    any more    of    houses.

lɛ    zɛ nə mi    (z)ɔ̃    tu        pri
**Les    ennemis    ont    tout        pris,**
The    enemies    have    everything    taken,

tu            pri        tu            pri
**tout        pris,        tout        pris,**
everything    taken,    everything    taken

ʒy ska    nɔ trə    pə ti    li
**jusqu'à    notre    petit    lit!**
even    our    little    bed!

bjɛ̃ syr    pa pa    ɛ    ta    la    gɛ rə
**Bien sûr!    papa    est    à    la    guerre,**
Of course!    Papa    is    at    the    war,

Vengez les enfants de France!
Les petits Belges, les petits
Serbes, et les petits Polonais
aussi!
Si nous en oublions, pardonnez-
nous
Noël! Noël! surtout, pas de
joujoux,
Tâchez de nous redonner le pain
quotidien.

Nous n'avons plus de maisons!
Les ennemis ont tout pris, tout
pris, tout pris, jusqu'à notre petit
lit!
Ils ont brûlé l'école et notre
maître aussi.
Ils ont brûlé l'église et monsieur
Jésus-Christ
Et le vieux pauvre qui n'a pas pu
s'en aller!
Noël! écoutez-nous, nous
n'avons plus de petits sabots:
Mais donnez la victoire aux
enfants de France!

(Paris: Durand, n.d.)

———————————•———————————

We have no more homes!
The enemies have taken
everything, taken everything,
taken everything, even our little
beds!
They have burned the school and
our teacher too.
They have burned the church and
Mr. Jesus Christ
And the poor old man who was
unable to escape!

po vrə    ma mɑ̃    ɛ    mɔ rtə
**Pauvre   maman   est   morte!**
Poor      Mama     is    dead!

avɑ̃    da vwa    rvy    tu    sa
**Avant   d'avoir   vu    tout   ça.**
Before   having    seen   all    that.

kɛ        skə    lɔ̃    va    fɛ rə
**Qu'est-ce   que   l'on   va    faire?**
What is it    that   one    will   do?

nɔ ɛl       pə ti    nɔ ɛl              na le pɑ
**Noël!      petit    Noël!              n'allez pas**
Christmas!   dear     Father Christmas!   don't go
ʃe     zø
**chez   eux,**
to      them,

         na le      ply    ʒa mɛ    ʃe     zø
         **n'allez   plus   jamais   chez   eux,**
         don't go   more   ever     to     them,

py ni se    le
**Punissez-les!**
Punish      them!

vɑ̃ ʒe    le    zɑ̃ fɑ̃    də    frɑ̃ sə
**Vengez   les   enfants   de    France!**
Avenge    the   children   of    France!

lɛ    pə ti    bɛ lʒə    lɛ    pə ti    sɛ rbə
**Les   petits   Belges,   les   petits   Serbes**
The    little    Belgians,  the   little    Serbs

We have no more homes.
The enemies have taken
everything, taken everything,
taken everything, even our little
beds!
Of course! Papa is away at war,
Poor Mama died
Before seeing all this.
What are we going to do?
Christmas! Dear Father
Christmas, don't go to them,
don't ever go back to them,
Punish them!

Avenge the children of France!
The little Belgians, the little
Serbians, and the Polish children
too!
If we omit any, forgive us.
Christmas! Christmas! above all,
no toys,
Try to give us back our daily
bread.

We have no more homes!
The enemies have taken
everything, taken everything,
taken everything, even our little
beds!
They have burned the school and
our teacher too.
They have burned the church and
Mr. Jesus Christ
And the poor old man who was
unable to escape!

Christmas! hear us, we have no
little clogs left:
But give the victory to the
children of France!

e le pəti pɔlɔnɛ osi
**et les petits Polonais aussi!**
and the little Poles too!

si nu zã nubli jɔ̃ pardɔne nu
**Si nous en oublions, pardonnez–nous.**
If we any omit, forgive us.

nɔɛl nɔɛl syrtu pɑ də
**Noël! Noël! surtout, pas de**
Christmas! Christmas! above all, not any
ʒuʒu
**joujoux,**
toys,

tɑʃe də nu rədɔne lə pɛ̃
**Tâchez de nous redonner le pain**
Try to us give back the bread
kɔtidjɛ̃
**quotidien.**
daily.

nu navɔ̃ ply də mezɔ̃
**Nous n'avons plus de maisons!**
We not have any more of houses!

lɛ zɛnəmi (z)ɔ̃ tu pri
**Les ennemis ont tout pris,**
The enemies have everything taken,

tu pri tu pri
**tout pris, tout pris,**
everything taken, everything taken,

ʒyska nɔtrə pəti li
**jusqu'à notre petit lit!**
even our little bed!

i lzɔ̃ bry le le kɔ̃ le nɔ trə mɛ
**Ils ont brûlé l'école et notre maître**
They have burned the school and our teacher
tro si
**aussi.**
too.

i lzɔ̃ bry le le gli ze mə sjø
**Ils ont brûlé l'église et monsieur**
They have burned the church and mister
ʒe zy kri
**Jésus–Christ**
Jesus Christ

e lə vjø po vrə ki na pa py
**Et le vieux pauvre qui n'a pas pu**
And the old poor who has not been able
sɑ̃ na le
**s'en aller!**
to escape!

nɔ ɛl e ku te nu nu na vɔ̃
**Noël! écoutez-nous, nous n'avons**
Christmas! hear us, we not have
ply də pə ti sa bo
**plus de petits sabots:**
any more of little clogs:

mɛ dɔ ne la vi ktwa ro zɑ̃ fɑ̃ də
**Mais donnez la victoire aux enfants de**
But give the victory to the children of
frɑ̃ sə
**France!**
France!

# APPENDIX A

## Correspondences between Spelling and Sound

The following list does not claim to be exhaustive, since it is based only on the texts of Debussy's songs. It is arranged in alphabetical order and divided into two categories: vowels (including diphthongs) and consonants. It can be used as a cross-reference for the IPA transcriptions of the songs.

## I. Vowels

| Spelling | Letter position | Pronunciation | Examples |
|----------|----------------|---------------|----------|
| a | initial, central, final | ʋa/ | avril, tard, chantera |
| a | + final consonant, silent or sounded | ʋa/ | éclats, par |
| | except in some words | ʋav | hélas, passe |
| à | in all positions | ʋa/ | là, déjà |
| â | in all positions | ʋa/ | câline, âme |
| aa | | ʋav | Graal |
| ai, aî | in all positions | ʋɛv | aimons, paraît |
| ai, aî | in vocal harmonization | ʋev | aimé, gaîté |
| ai | in future and past definite endings | ʋev | baissai |
| -aie, aient | ` | ʋɛv | paie, semblaient |
| ail, aill, | in some words | ʋajv | bataille |
| | in other words | ʋajv | ailleurs |
| aim, ain | +silent or sounded C | ʋɛɪv | mainte |
| am, an, | + vowel | ʋa/ | années, |
| amm, ann | | or /av | flamme |
| aoû | | ʋuv | août |
| -ase | | ʋaz(ə)v | extase |
| au | | ʋov | automne |
| | | or /ɔv | aurore |
| ay | | ʋɛjv | rayon |
| | except | ʋɛɪv | paysage |
| e | 1. *initial* + final silent C | ʋɛv | tu es, il est |
| | except: et | ʋev | |
| | + m, n + C | ʋaɪv | entends |
| | + m, n + vowel (in prefixes) | ʋaɪv | enivrait |
| | + mn, nn + vowel | ʋaɪv | ennui |
| | + double C | ʋev | effeuille |
| | + two C | ʋɛv | estoc |
| | 2. *central* | | |
| | + final pronounced C except n | ʋɛv | cet, hiver, bel |
| | + final silent C, usually f, r, z, d | ʋev | clef, chez, pied, léger |
| | + one C | ʋəv | premier, sereine |
| | + two C | ʋɛv | vermeil |
| | + double C | ʋɛv | cette |

| | | | |
|---|---|---|---|
| | except in some words | vev | dessein |
| | except in some words | va/ | femme, solennel |
| | + m, n + C | vaɪv | temps, cependant |
| | 3. final⁵⁷ | vəv | le, ne |
| é | | vev | étoiles, blés |
| ée(s)⁵⁸ | | vev | vallée |
| è | | vɛv | mère |
| ê | | vɛv | rêve |
| ë | central position | vev | Noël |
| eai | | vɛv | songeais |
| ean | | vaɪv | présageant |
| eau | | vov | beau |
| ei | | vev | sereine |
| eil, eill | | vɛjv | soleil, pareille |
| ein | | vɛɪv | dessein |
| -en | usually | vaɪv | cependant |
| | sometimes in final position | vɛɪv | rien |
| en- | in prefix + vowel | vaɪnv | enivrait |
| -enne | | vɛnv | antienne |
| -ent | verb ending | vəv | échangent |
| -eoi | | vwav | asseoir |
| -er | | vev | premier |
| | | or vɛv | cher |
| -es | final | vəv | vestes |
| est | verb form | vɛv | n'est-ce pas |
| -et | final | vɛv | regret |
| et | conjunction et 'and' | vev | |
| eu | initial, central + silent C | vøv | feu |
| eu | initial, central + pronounced C | vœv | heure |
| eu | in forms of verb avoir | vyv | eu, eut |
| euil, euill | | vœjv | feuille |
| -ez | | vev | allez |
| i | | viv | image |
| î | | viv | île |
| ï | | viv | ouïs |
| ï | between two vowels | vjv | Naïades |
| -ie⁵⁹ | final | vi(ə)v | songerie |
| i | + vowel, in same syllable⁶⁰ | vjv | violes, cieux |
| | + vowel in same syllable and preceded by a consonant cluster | vijv | prier, destrier |
| | in forms of verb rire 'laugh' | vijv | riant |
| -il | final after a vowel | vjv | soleil |
| -ill | between vowels, including mute e | vjv | bataille |
| | after consonant | vijv | fille |
| | except in a few words | vilv | ville |
| im, in | + Consonant, or final | vɛɪv | impérissables, coquin |
| -is | final (plural form) | viv | épis |
| | final, in a few words | visv | iris, Tircis |
| o | + final silent C | vov | flot |
| | + pronounced C, except s, m, n | vɔv | forêt, d'or |

| ô | | vov | ô, nôtre |
|---|---|---|---|
| obs- | | vɔpsv | obscure |
| oë | | vɔɛv | Noël |
| oeil | | vœjv | oeil |
| oeu | + pronounced C | vœv | coeur |
| | final or with silent C | vøv | voeu |
| oi | | vwa/ | soir |
| | or /2av | | croire |
| om, on | + C, or final | vɔɪv | colombe, bon |
| omm, onn | | vɔmv vɔnv | bonne |
| ou, oû, où | | vuv | pour, goûteʀ, où |
| -oue | | vuv | houe |
| -oy- | | vwajv | croyaiɬ |
| | | | |
| u | | vyv | azur |
| û | | vyv | mûreɬ |
| u | + vowel[61] | vɥv | nuiʈ, tueur |
| | + vowel, preceded by consonant | | |
| | clusters: | vyv | cruelɭe, blueʈɬ |
| | after c, q, g + vowel | v v | cɥeillir, qɥi, gɥère |
| ua | in certain words | vwav | aquarelle |
| -ue- | in verb forms | vyv | tueʀa |
| -ue | final[62] | vy(ə)v | retenue |
| ueil | | vœjv | cɥeilľir |
| -um | final | vœɪv | parfum |
| un | + C or final | vœɪv | défunʈɬ, un |
| -us | final | vyv | perduɬ |
| | in Latin words | vysv | Angélus |
| | | | |
| y | initial | vjv | yeuʈ |
| | central, final | viv | lyre |
| ym, yn | + C or final | vɛɪv | nympheɬ |

## II. Consonants

| b | | vbv | brise |
|---|---|---|---|
| bb | | vbv | abbé |
| -b | + s, t | vpv | subtil |
| c | + a, o, u | vkv | vaincu, corʈɬ |
| | + e, i | vsv | indiċible, douceurɬ |
| | final, generally | vkv | bec, donc |
| | + C | vkv | cruelɭe, insecte |
| ç | + a, o, u | vsv | ça |
| cc | | vkv | acclamé |
| ch | | vʃv | archeʈ |
| | in words of Greek origin | vkv | choeur |
| cq | | vkv | doncqɥeɬ |
| d | | vdv | onde |
| | in liaison | vtv | m'apɥrend à |
| | final | v v | pieɖ, fonɖ |
| -ds | final | v v | j'entenɖɬ |

| | | | |
|---|---|---|---|
| **f** | | vfv | forêt |
| | final | vfv | soif |
| **ff** | | vfv | souffle |
| **g** | + a, o, u or C except n | vgv | galop, gage |
| | + e, i | vʒv | gerbe |
| | final | v v | sang, long |
| **ge** | + a, o, u | vʒv | pigeon |
| **gn** | | vɲv | signaux |
| **gu** | | vgv | déguisement |
| **h** | | v v | haie, déshérité |
| | preceded by c | vkv or /ʃv | chrétien, chemin |
| **j** | | vʒv | jets |
| **l** | | vlv | lits, angélus |
| **ll** | | vlv | colline |
| | preceded by i | vjv or /»v | fille, ville |
| **l** | final | vlv | avril, linceul |
| **m** | | vmv | main, charme |
| | final; see nasal sounds | v v | nom |
| **mm** | | vmv | immense |
| **mn** | | vnv | automne |
| **n** | | vnv | nature |
| **n** | final, see nasal sounds | v v | garçon |
| | final in liaison | vnv | s'en iront |
| **nn** | | vnv | Egyptiennes |
| **p** | | vpv | épées |
| | final | v v | trop, coup |
| **ph** | | vfv | séraphins |
| **pp** | | vpv | apparition |
| **qu** | | vkv | coquet |
| | except in | vkwv | aquarelle |
| **qu'** | | vkv | qu'un, jusqu'à |
| **r** | | vrv | rêve, soupir |
| | final: first conjugation endings and suffixes –er, –ier: | v v | frôler, vivier, léger |
| | final, in some words | vrv | hiver, cher |
| | final, in liaison | vrv | chanter à la fois |
| **rr** | in future and conditional forms | vrrv | mourrai, mourrais |
| **s** | | vsv | songes, destrier |
| | between vowels | vzv | pose |
| | final | v v | dedans, sous |
| | final in a few words | vsv | jadis, hélas |
| | final in plural forms | v v | arbres |
| | final in liaison | vzv | les âmes |
| **sc** | + e, i | vsv | sceptre |
| | + a, o, u | vskv | Scaramouche |
| **ss** | | vsv | essaim |
| **–st** | final | v v | Jésus-Christ, est |
| **t** | | vtv | tête |
| | + suffix –ience | vsv | patience |
| | + i + vowel | vsv | insatiables |
| | | or /sv | chrétienne, antienne |
| | final | v v | et, flot |

| | | | |
|---|---|---|---|
| | final in liaison | *vtv* | vient éclore |
| **th** | | *vtv* | Hyacinthies |
| **tt** | | *vtv* | Brettes |
| **v** | | *vvv* | rêve |
| **x** | + vowel | *vgzv* | exhale, exil |
| | otherwise | *vksv* | extase |
| | final | *v v* | voix |
| | final in a small number of words | *vksv* | syrinx |
| | final in plural forms | *v v* | yeux |
| | final in liaison | *vzv* | aux yeux |
| **z** | | *vzv* | zéphyr, azur |
| | final | *v v* | tournez |

# Chronology

## Claude Debussy and His Time

The chronological sequence of years covers the entire span of Debussy's life. The list of songs includes those both published and unpublished, the published songs being italicized. For the various song series, the titles of individual melodies do not appear in this diagram. Biographical entries are limited to the most important facts. Debussy's other works consist only of his published musical works. The data from the contemporary artistic and intellectual events are those exclusively relevant or influential on Debussy's life and musical career.

| Year | Songs | Life | Other Works | Artistic and Intellectual Events | Political Events |
|------|-------|------|-------------|----------------------------------|------------------|
| 1862 | | Aug. 22: born at St. Germain-en-Laye. | | Baudelaire, *Petits Poèmes en Prose* Leconte de Lisle, *Poèmes barbares* | IInd Empire, Napoleon III |
| 1864 | | | | Offenbach, *La Belle Hélène* | |
| 1865 | | | | Manet, *Olympia* | |
| 1866 | | | | Massenet, *Poèmes d'avril* Manet, *Le Déjeuner sur l'herbe* First "Parnasse Contemporain" | |
| 1867 | | | | Gounod, *Roméo et Juliette* Death of Baudelaire Paris Exhibition of the Pre-Raphaelites | |
| 1868 | | | | Monet, *Argenteuil-sur-Seine* | |
| 1869 | | | | Verlaine, *Fêtes Galantes* Death of Berlioz | |
| 1870 | | | | Verlaine, *La Bonne Chanson* Mussorgsky, *The Nursery*, 1868–1872 | Franco-Prussian War Sedan Defeat Fall of IInd Empire |
| 1871 | | Piano lessons, Mme. Mauté. | | 2nd "Parnasse Contemporain" Founding of *Société Nationale de Musique* | Paris uprisings of the Commune |
| 1872 | | Enters the Paris Conservatoire. | | Bizet, *L'Arlésienne* Monet, *Impression: soleil levant* Mussorgsky, *Boris-Godunov* | |
| 1873 | | | | Rimbaud, *Une Saison en enfer* | Prussians leave France |
| 1874 | | | | Impressionists' 1st exhibition at Nadar's Verlaine, *Romances sans paroles* | MacMahon, President IIIrd Republic |
| 1876 | | First public appearance. | | Bayreuth, The *Ring* Mallarmé, *L'Apres-midi d'un faune* Mussorgsky, *Songs and Dances of Death* (1875–77) | Elections: Republican victory |

| Year | Songs | Life | Other Works | Artistic and Intellectual Events | Political Events |
|------|-------|------|-------------|----------------------------------|------------------|
| 1877 | | | | Wagner, *Parsifal*<br>Saint-Saëns, *Samson et Dalila* | |
| 1878 | | | | Paris World Exhibition: Four<br>concerts of Russian music<br>conducted by Rimsky-Korsakov | |
| 1879 | c.1879 Ballade à la<br>lune<br>Madrid, Princesse<br>des Espagnes | Pianist for Mme.<br>Wilson-Pelouze. | | Massenet, *Poèmes d'amour*<br>C. Franck, *Les Béatitudes*<br>Tchaikovsky, *Eugene Onegin* | |
| 1880 | *Nuit d'étoiles*<br>Caprice<br>c.1880 *Fleur des<br>blés*<br>Rêverie | Pianist, Mme. von<br>Meck.<br>Visits Interlaken,<br>Arcachon, Rome,<br>Naples, Fiesole.<br>Composition class of<br>Guiraud. | Danse bohémienne<br>Symphonie en si | Concerts Colonne: Tchaikovsky,<br>*4th Symphony*<br>Death of Flaubert<br>Tennyson, *Ballads*<br>First gatherings at Mallarmé's<br>Renoir, *Le Déjeuner des Canotiers* | |
| 1881 | Souhait<br>Zéphyr | Visits Moscow,<br>Vienna.<br>Accompanies Mme.<br>Moreau-Sainti's<br>class.<br>Meets Blanche<br>Vasnier. | | Verlaine, *Sagesse*<br>Death of Mussorgsky<br>Offenbach, *Contes d'Hoffmann* | Legislative elections |
| c.1881 | Les Roses<br>Séguidille<br>*Pierrot*<br><br>*Aimons-nous et<br>dormons*<br>Rondel chinois<br>Tragédie<br>*Jane* | Pianist at the "Chat<br>Noir." | | | |
| 1882 | Fantoches<br>O floraison divine<br>des lilas<br>Fête galante<br>Flots, palmes,<br>sables<br>*En sourdine*<br>(1st v.)<br>*Mandoline*<br>Rondeau<br>Pantomime<br>*Clair de lune*<br>(1st v.) | 2nd journey to<br>Russia, Austria.<br>Accompanies choral<br>group.<br>1st public appearance<br>as a composer. | Printemps<br>Triomphe de<br>Bacchus<br>Intermezzo | Bourget, *Les Aveux* | |
| c.1882 | *Beau soir*<br>La Fille aux<br>cheveux de lin<br>Sérénade | | | | |
| 1883 | Coquetterie<br>posthume<br>Chanson<br>espagnole<br>Romance<br>Musique<br>*Paysage<br>sentimental* | 2nd Prix de Rome<br>(*Le Gladiateur.*<br>Cantata). | Invocation | | War in Tonkin |

| Year | Songs | Life | Other Works | Artistic and Intellectual Events | Political Events |
|---|---|---|---|---|---|
| c.1883 | L'Archet<br>Chanson triste<br>Fleur des eaux<br>Eglogue | | | | |
| 1884 | *Voici que le<br>printemps*<br>*Apparition*<br>Romance d'Ariel<br>Regret | 1st Prix de Rome | L'Enfant prodigue | Huysmans, *A Rebours*<br>Massenet, *Manon*<br>C. Franck, *Variations<br>Symphoniques* | Berlin International<br>Conference |
| 1885 | Chevaux de bois<br>(1st version) | Rome, Villa Medici.<br>Fiumicino, at Count<br>Primoli's.<br>Meets Franz Liszt. | | La Revue Wagnérienne<br>Mallarmé, *Prose des Esseintes*<br>H. de Régnier, *Les Lendemains*<br>J. Laforgue, *Les Complaintes* | |
| c.1885 | Barcarolle | | | | |
| 1886 | *Romance*<br>*Les Cloches* | | | Death of Liszt<br>Moréas, *Les Cantilènes*<br>Symbolist Manifesto<br>Last Impressionist Exhibition | Boulanger, War<br>minister |
| 1887 | *Ariettes oubliées*<br>(1885–87) | Returns to Paris. | Printemps | 1st French translation of Shelley's<br>works<br>1st Paris performance of *Lohengrin*<br>Mallarmé, *Poèmes*<br>Symbolist meetings: Librairie de<br>l'Art Indépendant<br>Death of Laforgue | Presidency of Sadi-<br>Carnot |
| 1888 | | Bayreuth: *Parsifal*<br>and *Meistersinger*.<br>Friendship with<br>Godet. | Two Arabesques<br>La Damoiselle êlue | | Wilhelm II, Kaiser<br>Boulangist Movement |
| 1889 | *Cinq Poèmes de<br>Baudelaire*<br>(1887–89) | Member, Société<br>Nationale de<br>Musique.<br>2nd trip to Bayreuth:<br>*Tristan.*<br>Paris World<br>Exhibition.<br>Frequents taverns.<br>Friendship with Satie<br>and R. Peter.<br>c.1889: relationship<br>with Gaby<br>Dupont. | Pétite Suite<br>Fantaisie for piano<br>and orchestra | Paris World Exhibition (Russian<br>music, Japanese and Annamite<br>Art) | End of Boulangism |
| 1890 | *La Belle au bois<br>dormant* | Starts frequenting<br>Mallarmé's salon. | Fantaisie<br>Ballade slave<br>Tarantelle Syrienne<br>Suite Bergamasque<br>Piano pieces | M. Denis, Illustrations of *Sagesse*<br>H. de Régnier, *Poèmes anciens et<br>romanesques*<br>O. Wilde, *Picture of Dorian Gray*<br>Fauré, *Cinq mélodies*<br>c.1890: Satie, *Trois Morceaux en<br>forme de poire*<br>Symbolist Theatre | |
| 1891 | *Les Angélus*<br>*Fêtes Galantes* (1st<br>series)<br>*Trois mélodies* | Emotional crisis.<br>Friendship with<br>Mourey. | Marche écossaise<br>Mazurka | Monet, *The Waterlilies*<br>Death of Banville<br>1st Nabis Exhibition | |

| Year | Songs | Life | Other Works | Artistic and Intellectual Events | Political Events |
|---|---|---|---|---|---|
| 1892 | *Proses Lyriques* | Friendship with Chausson and H. Lerolle. | | Maeterlinck, *Pelléas et Mélisande* Fauré, *La Bonne Chanson* | |
| 1893 | | Meets Oscar Wilde. Visits Maeterlinck. Begins *Pelléas et Mélisande*. Meets Pierre Louÿs. | String Quartet | Paris Opera: *Lohengrin, Das Rheingold, Die Walküre* 1st performance of Maeterlinck's *Pelléas et Mélisande* | Ceremonies of the Franco-Russian Alliance in Paris |
| 1894 | | Brussels: 1st concert of his works. Broken engagement to Thérèse Roger. | Prélude à l'après-midi d'un faune | Brussels, Exhibition of Impressionist Paintings and Art Nouveau, Libre Esthétique Gallery Paris, Turner Exhibition | Assassination of President Sadi-Carnot |
| 1895 | | Taverne Weber, Reynold's Bar. | | P. Louÿs, *Chansons de Bilitis* Monet, *La Cathédrale de Rouen* | |
| 1896 | | | Pour le Piano | Death of Verlaine 1st Mussorgsky song recital in Paris | Paris visit of Czar Nicholas II |
| 1897 | *Chansons de Bilitis* (1897–98) | Gaby's attempted suicide. | Orchestration of Satie's Three Gymnopédies | Gide, *Les Nourritures terrestres* | |
| 1898 | | Debts and despair. Conducts choir at the Fontaines. Rupture with Gaby. | | Ravel, *Habanera* Death of Mallarmé Zola, *J'accuse* | Dreyfus case Death of Bismarck |
| 1899 | *Berceuse pour la tragédie de la mort* *Nuits Blanches* (1899–1902) | Death of Chausson. Marries Rosalie Texier. | Nocturnes | Ravel, *Pavane pour une Infante défunte* Paris performance of R. Strauss' *Also sprach Zarathustra* | |
| 1900 | | | | | Dreyfus case: 2nd verdict Boer War |
| 1901 | | Music critic, *La Revue Blanche*. | *Lindaraja* | *Death of Toulouse-Lautrec* | |
| 1902 | | 1st journey to London. | Pelléas et Mélisande | Ravel, *Jeux d'eau* | Combes Ministry Defeat of the Boers |
| 1903 | *Dans le Jardin* | Awarded the Legion of Honor. 2nd journey to London. Paris, Concert of his works. Meets Emma Bardac. | Danse sacrée, Danse profane D'un cahier d'esquisse Première Rapsodie Estampes | Death of Gauguin Schönberg, *Pelleas und Melisande* Exhibition of Oriental Art | |
| 1904 | *Trois Chansons de France* *Fêtes Galantes* (2nd series) 1904–10: *Le Promenoir des deux Amants.* I | June: leaves Lilly Debussy. Summer with E. Bardac. Lilly's attempted suicide. | La Mer L'Isle joyeuse Masques | Monet, *Vues de Londres* Puccini, *Madame Butterfly* Colette, *Dialogue de Bêtes* | Russo-Japanese War |

| Year | Songs | Life | Other Works | Artistic and Intellectual Events | Political Events |
|------|-------|------|-------------|----------------------------------|------------------|
| 1905 | | Divorced from Lilly. Contract with Durand; journey to Eastbourne, London. Birth of daughter, Emma-Claude. | Le Roi Lear Images I | Paris Autumn Salon: the Fauves Monet, *Nymphéas* | Separation of Church and State Triple Alliance (Germany, Austria-Hungary, Italy) |
| 1906 | | Meets J. Toulet. Meets R. Strauss. | | Claudel, *Partage de Midi* Death of Cézanne | |
| 1907 | | Conducts in Brussels. Summer near Dieppe. | Images II | 1st Paris performance of R. Strauss' *Salomé* Ravel, *Histoires Naturelles* | Triple Entente (France, Russia, Great Britain) |
| 1908 | | Marries Emma Bardac. Conducts in London. | Children's Corner Trois Chansons de Charles d'Orléans | Ravel, *Gaspard de la nuit* | |
| 1909 | | First signs of cancer. Conservatory, member of the advisory board. Meets Diaghilev. | Hommage à Haydn | Maeterlinck, *L'Oiseau bleu* | Hollweg, German Chancellor |
| 1910 | Le Promenoir des deux Amants, II, III | Meets Mahler, Stravinsky. Journey to Vienna and Budapest. | Première Rapsodie 12 Préludes I La plus que lente Petite Pièce | Munich Festival of French Music Stravinsky, *L'Oiseau de feu* 1st Paris performance of Mahler's *2nd Symphony* | |
| 1911 | | Conducts in Turin. Debts. | Images Le Martyre de Saint Sébastien | New Directions in Cubism Strauss, *Der Rosenkavalier* Stravinsky, *Petrushka* | Franco-German incident at Agadir |
| 1912 | | Last meeting with P. Louÿs. | 12 Préludes II Jeux Syrinx | Ravel, *Daphnis et Chloé* Diaghilev's production of *L'Après-Midi d'un Faune* | 1st Balkan War |
| 1913 | 3 Poèmes de Stéphane Mallarmé | Journey to Russia. | La Boîte à joujoux | Apollinaire, *Alcools* Proust, *Du côté de chez Swann* 1st complete edition of Mallarmé's Poems Stravinsky, *Le Sacre du Printemps* | |
| 1914 | | Journeys in Europe. Leaves Paris for Angers. | Berceuse héroïque 6 Epigraphes antiques | Eluard, *Poèmes* M. de Falla, *La Vida Breve* | Sarajevo assassination Franco-German War Battle of the Marne |
| 1915 | Noël des enfants | Edits Chopin's works. Productive summer in Normandy. Operation. | En Blanc et noir Elégie 12 Etudes I, II Sonata for cello and piano Sonata for flute, viola and harp | Ravel, *Piano trio* | |
| 1916 | | Edits Bach's Sonatas | Sonata for violin and piano | Cocteau, *Poésies* Freud, *Introduction to Psychoanalysis* | Battle of Verdun Battle of the Somme |

| Year | Songs | Life | Other Works | Artistic and Intellectual Events | Political Events |
|---|---|---|---|---|---|
| 1917 | | Charity concert of his works | Ode à la France | Death of Degas<br>Valéry, *La Jeune Parque*<br>Paris, Concerts of French Music<br>Dadaist movement | Russian Revolution<br>Clemençeau<br>Government |
| 1918 | | March 25: dies in Paris.<br>March 28: buried at Père Lachaise Cemetery. | | | Germano-Russian Treaty<br>March 29: German bombardment of Paris |

# APPENDIX C

## Catalogue of Songs

The songs are entered in chronological order after François Lesure's and Margaret Cobb's authoritative Catalogues of Debussy's works. The List presents the entire collection of published songs for solo voice and piano accompaniment.

| Date of composition | Song Title | Poet | Date of publication | Publisher | Dedication |
|---|---|---|---|---|---|
| 1880 | Nuit d'étoiles | Banville | 1882 | Société artistique d'édition d'estampes et de musique | Mme. Moreau-Sainti |
| c.1880 | Fleur des blés | André Girod | 1891 | Vve Girod | Mme. E. Deguingand |
| 1881 | Zéphyr | Banville | 1932 | Schott | |
| c.1881 | Pierrot | Banville | 1.5.1926 | *Revue Musicale* | Mme. Vasnier |
| c.1881 | Aimons-nous et dormons | Banville | 1933 | Presser | Paul Vidal |
| c.1881 | Jane | Leconte de Lisle | 1982 | Presser | Mme. Vasnier |
| 1882 | En sourdine (1st version) | Verlaine | 1944 | Elkan-Vogel | Mme. Vasnier |
| 1882 | Mandoline | Verlaine | 1.9.1890 | *Revue Illustrée* | Mme. Vasnier |
| 1882 | Rondeau | Musset | 1932 | Schott | Alexandre von Meck |
| 1882 | Pantomime | Verlaine | 1.5.1926 | *Revue Musicale* | Mme. Vasnier |
| 1882 | Clair de lune (1st version) | Verlaine | 1.5.1926 | *Revue Musicale* | Mme. Vasnier |
| c.1882 | Beau soir | Bourget | 1891 | Vve Girod | |
| 1883 | Paysage setimental | Bourget | 15.4.1891 | *Revue Illustrée* | Mme. Vasnier |
| 1884 | Voici que le printemps | Bourget | 1907 | Société nouvelle d'éditions musicales | Mme. Vasnier |
| 1884 | Apparition | Mallarmé | 1.5.1926 | *Revue Musicale* | Mme. Vasnier |
| 1885–87 | Ariettes oubliées: Verlaine 1. C'est l'extase 2. Il pleure dans mon coeur 3. L'ombre des arbres 4. Chevaux de bois 5. Green 6. Spleen | Verlaine | 1888 (separately) 1903 | Vve Girod Fromont | Mary Garden |
| 1887–89 | Cinq poèmes de Baudelaire 1. Le Balcon 2. Harmonie du soir 3. Le Jet d'eau 4. Recueillement 5. La Mort des amants | Baudelaire | 1890 | Librairie de l'Art Indépendant | Etienne Dupin |
| 1890 | La Belle au bois dormant | Vincent Hyspa | 1902 | Société Nouvelle d'éditions musicales | |

| | | | | | |
|---|---|---|---|---|---|
| 1891 | Les Angélus | Le Roy | 1891 | Hamelle | |
| 1891?<br>1903? | Dans le Jardin | Paul Gravollet | 1905 | Hamelle | |
| 1886?<br>1891? | Deux Romances:<br>1. Romance<br>2. Les Cloches | Bourget | 1891 | Durand | |
| 1891 | Fêtes Galantes I:<br>1. En sourdine (2nd version)<br>2. Fantoches (2nd version)<br>3. Clair de lune (2nd version) | Verlaine | 1903 | Fromont | Mme. Robert Godet<br>Mme. Lucien Fontaine<br>Mme. Arthur Fontaine |
| 1891 | Trois Mélodies:<br>1. La Mer est plus belle<br>2. Le Son du cor s'afflige<br>3. L'échelonnement des haies | Verlaine | 1901 | Hamelle | Ernest Chausson<br>Robert Godet<br>Robert Godet |
| 1892–93 | Proses Lyriques:<br>1. De Rêve<br>2. De Grève<br>3. De Fleurs<br>4. De Soir | Debussy | 1895 | Fromont | Vidal Hocquet<br>Raymond Bonheur<br>Mme. Ernest Chausson<br>Henry Lerolle |
| 1897–98 | Chansons de Bilitis:<br>1. La Flûte de Pan<br>2. La Chevelure<br>3. Le tombeau des Naïades | Pierre Louÿs | 1899 | Fromont | Mme. M. V. Peter |
| 1904 | Trois Chansons de France:<br>1. Rondel: Le Temps<br>2. La Grotte<br>3. Rondel: Pour ce que<br>    Plaisance | Charles d'Orleans<br>Tristan L'Hermite<br>Charles d'Orleans | 1904 | Durand | Mme. S. Bardac |
| 1904 | Fêtes Galantes II:<br>1. Les Ingénus<br>2. La Faune<br>3. Colloque sentimental | Verlaine | 1904 | Durand | Mme. S. Bardac |
| 1904–10 | Le Promenoir des deux<br>Amants:<br>1. Auprès de cette grotte<br>    sombre (1904)<br>2. Crois mon conseil (1910)<br>3. Je tremble en voyant ton<br>    visage (1910) | Tristan L'Hermite | 1910 | Durand | Emma Claude Debussy |
| 1910 | Trois Ballades de François<br>Villon:<br>1. Ballade de Villon à s'amye<br>2. Ballade que Villon feit à la<br>    requeste de sa mère<br>3. Ballade des femmes de Paris | François Villon | 1910 | Durand | |
| 1913 | Trois Poèmes de Stéphane<br>Mallarmé:<br>1. Soupir<br>2. Placet futile<br>3. Éventail | Mallarmé | 1913 | Durand | In memory of<br>S. Mallarmé<br>In homage to Mme.<br>E. Bonniot |
| 1915 | Noël des enfants qui n'ont plus<br>de maisons | Debussy | 1916 | Durand | |

# *Notes*

# Notes

[1] As in popular songs or musical comedies.

[2] A vowel sound is represented in spelling by one or more vowels. See Appendix A, pp. 293–297.

[3] Some orthoepists (Grammont, Martinon) place it next to /œ/, others (Martinet) next to /ø/. According to Martinet's statistics, more than half of the French-speaking population polled pronounce it almost like /ø/. André Martinet, *La Prononciation du français contemporain*, pp. 69–70.

[4] A slight modification of the vowel sounds has been noticed among French singers, due to the voice register or else his or her geographical origin. This modification occurs particularly in the nasal sounds and the closed vowel sounds, in a high range: Nasal sounds are denasalized and closed vowels opened. Diphthongization, however, never takes place.

[5] Examples are all taken from Debussy's songs. This precludes other existent spellings.

[6] In some words, -ill- is pronounced /il/. Example: *ville* /vi lə/.

[7] These symbols will not appear in the IPA transcriptions of the poems.

[8] Marie Krysinska wrote free verse. Debussy tried his hand at free verse in his *Proses Lyriques*.

[9] From a letter to Durand (1908), quoted by Lockspeiser in *Debussy: His Life and Mind*, II, p. 197.

[10] This includes two versions of "Clair de lune" and "En Sourdine," published at different times.

[11] The same setting of Tristan L'Hermite's "La Grotte" appeared twice.

[12] No biographical data on André Girod have been recorded at the *Bibliothèque Nationale* under this name; the catalogue of the Music Department shows another poem by Girod, "Histoire d'Automne" (Autumn story), adapted to music by Alexandre Georges in 1922.

[13] Two more settings were to be composed in 1886 and published.

[14] Romanticism in France lasted approximately from 1820 until 1845.

[15] Entitled "Nuit d'étoiles" by Debussy.

[16] See Laforgue's influence on Debussy, Chapter II, p. 27.

[17] A literary doctrine prevalent in the last third of the nineteenth century, it described man and his environment as the products of specific biological, social, and economic laws.

[18] The text of "Chevaux de bois" came from the *Sagesse* poem.

[19] The title, borrowed from Mendelssohn, refers to songs in which the melody is important, not the words.

[20] "Richard Wagner and *Tannhauser*" (1861).

[21] See Baudelaire's sonnet "Correspondances."

[22] Stefan Jarocinski, Introduction to the album of the complete recordings of Debussy's songs.

[23] Gravelot and Gravelet are other given versions of Gravollet.

[24] In an article from the *Revue Musicale*, quoted by Jarocinski in his Introduction to the album of the complete recordings of Debussy's songs.

[25] There is disagreement among musicologists on the date of composition of "Nuit d'étoiles"; it has been variously dated between 1876 and 1880.

[25a] 1. The last line of each refrain is repeated.
      2. Second quatrain and refrain omitted by Debussy:

> Dans les ombres de la feuillée,
> Quand tout bas je soupire seul,
> Tu reviens, pauvre âme éveillée,
> Toute blanche dans ton linceul.

> Nuit d'étoiles
> Sous tes voiles
> Sous ta brise et tes parfums,
> Triste lyre
> Qui soupire,
> Je rêve aux amours défunts.     (Banville)

[26] *bois* can be pronounced /bwa/ or /bwɑ/. See Robert, *Dictionnaire alphabétique et analogique de la langue française*.

[26a] "Ah Ah—", added by Debussy.

[26b] First stanza, line 5:

> N'effleurera ta tête blonde     (Debussy)
> Ne courbera ta tête blonde     (Banville)

[26c] Changes in text:
      1. Refrains 2, 3, 4:

> Deux beaux yeux m'ont brisé le coeur     (Debussy)
> Deux beaux yeux m'ont blessé le coeur     (Leconte de Lisle)

2. Third quatrain:
    J'irai puiser ma mort prochaine    (Debussy)
    J'aurai puisé ma mort prochaine    (Leconte de Lisle)

[26d] Last quatrain of Verlaine's poem:

> Et quand, solennel, le soir
> Des chênes noirs tombera,
> Voix de notre désespoir,
> Le rossignol chantera.

Debussy's variant and addition:

> Et quand, solennel, le soir
> Des chênes tombera,
> Voix de notre désespoir
> Le rossignol chantera.
> Voix de notre désespoir
> Le rossignol chantera.

[27] Added by Debussy.
[27a] Tircis, Aminte, and Damis were shepherd figures in Pastorals. Clitandre is the lover in the Commedia dell'arte.
[27b] Changes in text:

1. 2nd stanza:

> Ainsi s'endort la fleur d'églantier.    (Debussy)
> Ainsi s'endort une fleur d'églantier.    (Musset)

2. 3rd stanza, 2nd line:
    . . . son printemps virginal    (Debussy)
    . . . son bouquet printanier    (Musset)

[27c] Added by Debussy:

1. 1st stanza: last two lines
2. 3rd stanza: 4th line
3. 4th stanza: last line and melisma

[28] Melisma and last line added by Debussy.
[28a] A bergamasquer is an inhabitant of the city of Bergamo, Italy; a bergamasque was an eighteenth-century dance from Bergamo.
[29] Setting influenced by Russian compositions, most likely Borodin's.
[29a] Last line of poem:

> Qui pâlissait au fond de la pâle vallée.    (Debussy)
> Que nous vîmes au fond de la pâle vallée.    (Bourget)

[30] "long exil": the linking sound between the two words is normally /k/, but may sound awkward in this musical context; it should therefore be sung very lightly and close to a /g/.
[31] "épaule gauche il": if breathing is necessary, sing /e po lə go ʃ il/.
[32] "prolonge une": if breathing is necessary, sing /pro lɔ̃ ʒə y nə/.
[32a] Last line of poem: Repeat of "étoiles parfumées," added by Debussy.
[33] Charles-Simon Favart (1710–92) was an author of comedies and light operas and a protégé of Louis XV's favorite, Mme. de Pompadour.
[33a] Verlaine wrote two versions of "Chevaux de bois"; one appeared in *Romances sans paroles*, the other in *Sagesse*. Debussy's selection comes from *Sagesse*.
[33b] Pierre Bernac suggests not pronouncing the final /ə/ in order to take a breath.
[34] 2nd stanza, last line:

> O le bruit de la pluie!    (Debussy)
> O le chant de la pluie!    (Verlaine)

[34a] Last line of poem: Repeat of "noyées," added by Debussy.

[35] Stanzas 5 and 6 of Verlaine's poem, omitted by Debussy:

> Tournez au son de l'accordéon
> Du violon, du trombone fous,
> Chevaux plus doux que des moutons, doux
> Comme un peuple en révolution.
>
> Le vent fouettant la tente, les verres,
> Les zincs et le drapeau tricolore,
> Et les jupons, et que sais-je encore?
> Fait un fracas de cinq cents tonnerres.   (*Sagesse*)

[35a] La gerbe épanouie
>    En mille fleurs,
> Où Phoebé réjouie
>    Met ses couleurs,
> Tombe comme une pluie
>    De larges pleurs.   (Baudelaire)

[36] 1886 is the date suggested by Margaret Cobb, based upon a letter of 1886 that Debussy wrote to M. Vasnier in which he mentioned Bourget's melodies. These melodies would be "Romance" and "Les Cloches." The same date is given by Pierre Bernac.

[37] Three melismas added by Debussy in stanzas 1, 3, 4.

[37a] Same as above.

[38] Scaramouche and Pulcinella are buffoons from the Commedia dell'arte.

[39] A character in the Italian comedy who has also been associated with Pantaloon, Columbine's father.

[40] Medicinal plants.

[41] According to Vallas and Jarocinski.

[42] In Greek mythology, Hyacinthus was a handsome boy of whom Apollo was passionately fond. One day, Apollo accidentally killed him with a discus.

[43] A satyr was a woodland god or demon, often having the pointed ears, legs, and short horns of a goat.

[44] The Naiads were nymphs living in and presiding over brooks, springs, and fountains.

[45] Since "La Grotte" is the same song as "Auprès de cette grotte sombre," it is presented hereafter as part of *Le Promenoir des deux Amants*, pp. 250–257.

[45a] 2nd stanza:

> Il n'y a beste ne oiseau
> Qui en son jargon ne chante ou crye:
> Le temps a laissé son manteau
> De vent, de froidure et de pluye.   (Charles d'Orléans)

[46] Debussy used to address his wife, Emma, as "la petite mienne" (my own little dear). The phrase was inspired by a poem by Laforgue.

[47] Optional liaisons. Bernac finds it "more singable with the liaison and more expressive without." *The Interpretation of French song*, p. 186.

[48] In Greek mythology, Narcissus was the handsome son of the river god Cephisus. The gods punished him for having spurned Echo's love by making him fall in love with his own reflection.

[49] /ra ri ve/: the first /r/, being a linking consonant sound, must be sounded very lightly and softly.

[50] Villon's envoy:

> Vous portastes, digne Vierge, princesse,
> Jesus regnant qui n'a ne fin ne cesse,
> Le Tout Puissant, prenant nostre faiblesse,
> Laissa les cieulx et nous vint secourir,
> Offrit a mort sa très chiere jeunesse
> Nostre Seigneur tel est, tel le confesse:
> En ceste foy je vueil vivre et mourir.

[50a] Saint Mary the Egyptian was a courtesan from Alexandria who had implored the Virgin Mary's intercession.

[51] Theophilus, a clerk from Asia Minor (6th century), sold his soul to the devil, but, remorseful, begged the Virgin Mary to retrieve his contract from the Devil, which she did.

[52] Reference to the Immaculate Conception of the Virgin Mary.

[53] The *Petit-Pont* was a Paris bridge.

[54] Hebe, goddess of youth and spring, filled the cups of the gods with nectar.

[55] Sèvres porcelain made in Sèvres, a suburb of Paris.

[56] For this reason, the optional liaisons should be omitted.

[57] See *schwa*, p. 9.
[58] See *schwa*, p. 9.
[59] See *schwa*, p. 9.
[60] In keeping with the metrical structure of the verse, Debussy ascribed three notes to *violon* in "Harmonie du soir." Normally pronounced /vjɔ lɔ̃/, *violon* must be sounded here /vi jɔ lɔ̃/.
[61] In some cases, Debussy ascribed two notes to keep with the metrical structure of the verse. Example: *suavité*, normally pronounced /sɥa vi te/ must be sounded /sy a vi te/.
[62] See *schwa*, p. 9.

# Bibliography

Abraham, Claude. *Tristan L'Hermite*. Boston: Twayne Publishers, 1980.

Bathori, Jane. *Sur l'Interprétation des Mélodies de Claude Debussy*. Paris: Les Editions ouvrières, 1953.

Bernac, Pierre. *The Interpretation of French Song*. New York: Norton, 1970.

Bonnaud, Dominique. "Vincent Hyspa," in *L'Esprit Montmartrois*. Joinville-le-Pont: Carlier, 1938.

Bornecque, Jacques-Henry. *Verlaine par lui-même*. Paris: Seuil, 1966.

————. *Lumières sur les 'Fêtes galantes'*. Paris: Nizet, 1969.

Brereton, Geoffrey. *An Introduction to the French Poets*. London: Methuen, 1956.

Carter, A. E. *Paul Verlaine*. New York: Twayne Publishers, 1980.

Clive, H. P. *Pierre Louÿs*. Oxford: Clarendon Press, 1978.

Cobb, Margaret. *The Poetic Debussy*. Boston: Northeastern University Press, 1982.

Delattre, Pierre. *Principes de phonétique française*. 2d ed. Middlebury, Vt.: Middlebury College, 1951.

Dietschy, Marcel. *La Passion de Claude Debussy*. Neufchâtel: A la Baconnière, 1962.

Dumesnil, Maurice. *Claude Debussy, Master of Dreams*. New York: Ives Washburn, 1940.

Fouché, Pierre. *Traité de Prononciation française*. Paris: Klincksieck, 1956.

Fowlie, Wallace. *Mallarmé*. Chicago: University of Chicago Press, 1953.

Gourdet, Georges. *Debussy*. Paris: Hachette, 1970.

Grubb, Thomas. *Singing in French*. New York: Schirmer Books, 1979.

Jarocinski, Stefan. *Debussy, Impressionism and Symbolism*. Trans. R. Myers. London: Eulenburg Books, 1976.

————. *Debussy and his Poets* (Introduction to the complete recordings of Claude Debussy's melodies). Le Plessis Robinson: Blanchard, 1980. EMI 2C 165–16.371/4.

Jullian, Philippe. *Esthètes et Magiciens*. Paris: Librairie Académique Perrin, 1969.

————. *The Symbolists*. Trans. Mary Anne Stevens. London: Phaidon Press, 1973.

Le Roy, Georges. *Grammaire de Diction française*. Paris: La Pensée moderne, 1967.

Le Roy, Grégoire. *La Chanson du pauvre*. Paris: Société du Mercure de France, 1907.

Lesure, François. *Claude Debussy, Textes et Documents inédits*. Paris: Société française de musicologie, 1962.

————. *Catalogue de l'oeuvre de Claude Debussy*. Genève: Editions Minkoff, 1977.

————. *Claude Debussy—Lettres (1884–1918)*. Paris: Hermann, 1980.

Lockspeiser, Edward. *Debussy: His Life and Mind*. 2 vols. New York: MacMillan, 1962.

Maes, Pierre. "Grégoire Le Roy." *Epîtres*, 24, No. 39, March 1951, pp. 4–10.

Martinet, André. *La Prononciation du Français contemporain*. Genève: Droz, 1971.

Nichols, Roger. *Debussy*. London: Oxford University Press, 1972.

Richard, Jean-Pierre. *Univers imaginaire de Mallarmé*. Paris: Seuil, 1961.

Robert, Paul. *Dictionnaire alphabétique et analogique de la Langue française*. Paris: Société du Nouveau Littré, Le Robert, 1967.

Samazeuilh, G. "La 1ère Version inédite de 'En Sourdine' avec facsimile." In *Inédits sur Claude Debussy*. Paris: Collection Comoedia Charpentier, 1942.

Seroff, Victor. *Debussy, Musician of France.* New York: Putnam, 1956.
Siciliano, Italo. *François Villon et les Thèmes poétiques du Moyen-Age.* Paris: Nizet, 1971.
Souffrin, Eileen-Margaret. *Les Stalactites de Théodore de Banville.* Paris: Didier, 1942.
————. "Debussy, lecteur de Banville." *Revue de Musicologie,* 46, 1960, pp. 200–222.
Valdman, Salazar and Charbonnaux. *A Drillbook of French Pronunciation.* 2d ed. New York: Harper & Row, 1964.
Vallas, Léon. *Claude Debussy et son temps.* Paris: Albin Michel, 1958.
Vienne, Lucie de. *Nouveau Traité de Diction française.* Paris: La Pensée moderne, 1967.
Wenk, Arthur B. *Claude Debussy and the Poets.* Berkeley and Los Angeles: University of California Press, 1976.

**Editions of Debussy's songs:**
"Aimons-nous et Dormons." Bryn Mawr: Presser, 1933.
*"Calmes dans le demi-jour (En sourdine)*: Philadelphia: Elkan-Vogel, 1944.
*Claude Debussy. Songs 1880–1904,* ed. Rita Benton. New York: Dover, 1981.
*Forty-three Songs for Voice and Piano,* ed. Sergius Kagen. New York: International, 1961.
"Jane." Bryn Mawr: Presser, 1982.
"Noël des enfants qui n'ont plus de maisons." Paris: Durand, n.d.
*Promenoir des deux Amants (Le).* Paris: Durand, n.d.
*Quatre Chansons de jeunesse.* Paris: Jobert, 1969.
"Rondeau." In *Debussy et ses Mélodies, oeuvres complètes.* n.p.: Zen-on, 1982.
*Trois Ballades de François Villon.* Paris: Durand, n.d.
*Trois Poèmes de Stéphane Mallarmé.* Paris: Durand, n.d.
"Zéphyr." Mainz: Schott & Eschig, 1932.

# Index of Titles

Aimons-nous et dormons, 61
Angélus, Les, 164
Apparition, 99
Ariettes oubliées, 104
Auprès de cette grotte sombre, 251
Balcon, Le, 130
Ballade de Villon à s'amye, 258
Ballade des femmes de Paris, 271
Ballade que Villon feit à la requeste de sa mère, 265
Ballades de François Villon, Trois, 258
Beau soir, 87
Belle au Bois dormant, La, 159
Calmes dans le demi-jour (En sourdine), 69
C'est l'extase langoureuse, 106
Chansons de Bilitis, Les, 221
Chansons de France, Trois, 234
Chevaux de bois, 115
Chevelure, La, 226
Clair de lune (first version), 83
Clair de lune (Fêtes galantes, first series), 184
Cloches, Les, 174
Colloque sentimental, 246
Crois mon conseil, chère Climène, 254
Dans le jardin, 167
De Fleurs, 210
De Grève, 205
De Rêve, 200
De Soir, 215
Echelonnement des haies, L', 196
En sourdine (Calmes dans le demi-jour), 69, 177
En sourdine (Fêtes Galantes, first series), 177
Éventail, 283
Fantoches, 181
Faune, Le, 244
Fêtes Galantes, first series, 177

Fêtes Galantes, second series, 240
Fleur des blés, 52
Flûte de Pan, La, 221
Green, 122
Harmonie du soir, 138
Il pleure dans mon coeur, 109
Ingénus, Les, 240
Jane, 65
Jet d'eau, Le, 143
Je tremble en voyant ton visage, 256
Mandoline, 73
Mélodies, Trois, 188
Mer est plus belle, La, 188
Mort des Amants, La, 155
Noël des enfants qui n'ont plus de maisons, 287
Nuit d'étoiles, 47
Ombre des arbres, L', 112
Pantomime, 80
Paysage sentimental, 90
Pierrot, 58
Placet futile, 279
Poèmes de Charles Baudelaire, Cinq, 129
Poèmes de Stéphane Mallarmé, Trois, 275
Pour ce que Plaisance est morte, 237
Promenoir des deux Amants, Le, 250
Proses Lyriques, 199
Recueillement, 150
Romance, 171
Romances, Deux, 171
Rondeau, 76
Son du cor s'afflige, Le, 193
Soupir, 275
Spleen, 126
Temps a laissié son manteau, Le, 234
Tombeau des Naïades, Le, 230
Voici que le printemps, 94
Zéphyr, 56

# Index of First Lines

Aimons-nous et dormons, 62
Ame évaporée et souffrante, L', 172
Auprès de cette grotte sombre, 252
Bon Pierrot, que le foule contemple, Le, 58
Calmes dans le demi-jour, 70,178
C'est l'extase langoureuse, 106
Ciel d'hiver, si doux, si triste, si dormant, Le, 91
Cloches chrétiennes pour les matines, 165
Crois mon conseil, chère Climène, 254
Dame du ciel, régente terrienne, 266
Dans l'ennui si désolément vert, 211
Dans le vieux parc solitaire et glacé, 247
Dimanche sur les villes, 216
Donneurs de sérénades, Les, 74
Echelonnement des haies, L', 197
Faulse beauté, qui tant me couste cher, 260
Feuilles s'ouvraient sur le bord des branches, Les, 175
Fut-il jamais douceur de coeur pareille, 77
Hauts talons luttaient avec les longues jupes, Les, 241
Il m'a dit: "Cette nuit, j'ai rêvé . . ., 227
Il pleure dans mon coeur, 109
Je pâlis et tombe en langueur, 66
Je regardais dans le jardin, 168
Je tremble en voyant ton visage, 256
Long des blés que la brise, Le, 53
Long du bois couvert de givre . . ., Le, 230
Lorsqu'au soleil couchant les rivières sont roses, 88
Lune s'attristait. Des séraphins en pleurs, La, 100
Mère des souvenirs, maîtresse des maîtresses, 131
Mer est plus belle, La, 189
Mon âme vers ton front où rêve, calme soeur, 275
Nous aurons des lits pleins d'odeurs légères, 156
Nous n'avons plus de maisons, 287
Nuit a des douceurs de femme, La, 201
Nuit d'étoiles, 47
Ombre des arbres dans la rivière embrumée, L', 113
O rêveuse, pour que je plonge, 284
Pierrot, qui n'a rien d'un Clitandre, 81
Pour ce que Plaisance est morte, 237
Pour le jour des Hyacinthies . . ., 222
Princesse! à jalouser le destin d'une Hébé, 279
Quoy qu'on tient belles langagières, 271
Roses étaient toutes rouges, Les, 127
Scaramouche et Pulcinella, 182
Si j'étais le Zéphyr ailé, 57
Sois sage, ô ma Douleur, et tiens-toi plus tranquille, 151
Son du cor s'afflige vers les bois, Le, 194
Sur la mer les crépuscules tombent, 206
Temps a laissié son manteau, Le, 235

Tes beaux yeux sont las, pauvre amante, 144
Tournez, tournez, bons chevaux de bois, 117
Trous à son pourpoint vermeil, Des, 160
Vieux faune de terre cuite, Un, 244
Voici des fruits, des fleurs, des feuilles et des branches, 123
Voici que le printemps, ce fils léger d'Avril, 94
Voici venir les temps où vibrant sur sa tige, 139
Votre âme est un paysage choisi, 84, 185

# General Index

Analytical Cubism, 31
ANNUNZIO, Gabriele d', 42
Art Nouveau Movement, 24, 210
*Aveux, Les* (Bourget), 35, 171, 174
BACHELET, Alfred, 115
BAILLY, Léon, 27, 129
"Ballade à la lune" (Musset), 35
Ballets Russes, 30
BANVILLE, Théodore de, 25, 33, 34–5, 47, 56, 58
BARDAC-DEBUSSY, Emma, 30, 45, 240, 308
BARON, Emile, 26
BATHORI, Jane, 251
BAUDELAIRE, Charles, translator of Poe, 25, 40; and Verlaine, 37, 40; and Wagner, 40–1;
    and Symbolism, 40; relationship with Jeanne Duval, 130, 150; with Madame Sabatier, 138.
Bayreuth, 24, 28, 29, 40, 129, 193
BELFORT, May, 28
BONHEUR, Raymond, 26, 205
BONNIOT, Mme. E. (née Geneviève Mallarmé), 275, 283
BORODIN, Alexander, 159
BOUCHER, François, 38
BOURGET, Paul, 27, 33, 34, 35–6, 87, 90, 171, 174
BRAQUE, Georges, 31
Brasserie Pousset, 28, 41
BURNE-JONES, Edward, 24
BURNS, Robert, 37, 65
CAPLET, André, 43
CARAN D'ACHE, 27
*Cariatides, Les* (Banville), 35, 38
CARRIERE, Eugène, 28
CHABRIER, Emmanuel, 28
*Chansons de Bilitis, Les* (Louÿs), 41–2
*Chanson du Pauvre, La* (Le Roy), 164
Chat Noir, Le, 27, 36
CHAUSSON, Ernest, 28, 129, 210
CHAUSSON, Mme. Ernest, 210
CLAUDEL, Paul, 29
COLETTE, Sidonie-Gabrielle, 28
Comédie Française, The, 43
Commedia dell'arte, 38, 73, 80

Commune, The (1871), 23
Conservatoire, The Paris, 26, 29, 34, 37
COURBET, Gustave, 24
Cubism, 31
CYRANO DE BERGERAC, Savinien, 112
DAUDET, Léon, 27
DEBURAU, Jean-Gaspard, 58, 80
DEBUSSY, Achille-Claude, his teachers, 29, 37; goes to Rome, 25, 122; as accompanist, 36,
    47; his early songs, 34; Banville's influence, 26, 36; Bourget's influence, 25, 35–6, 171; travels
    with the Von Mecks, 29, 69, 73, 76, 159; his readings, 25; his protectors, 29; his friends, 26,
    28, 30; at *Chat Noir*, 27, 41; at Paris cafés, 27–8; travels to Bayreuth, 28, 29, 40, 129; and
    Richard Wagner, 28, 41, 129, 143, 155; at *Librairie de l'Art Indépendant,* 27; in salons, 28, 29;
    relationship with Mme. Vasnier, 27, 29, 34, 36, 40, 47; friendship with P. Louÿs, 26, 29, 30,
    33, 41–2; inspired by Verlaine, 37, 40, 240; as composer of songs, 33; Baudelaire's influence,
    40, 210; and Mallarmé, 29, 45, 100, 275; his publishers, 30; Russian influences, 94, 307; poetic
    inspiration, 31, 33; and contemporary music, 28, 30, 31; relationship with Emma Bardac, 30,
    45, 240; his later songs, 42–3; and French poetry, 46; reaction to World War I, 31.
Decadents, The, 27, 200
DEGAS, Edgar, 28, 29
DEGUINGAND, Mme. E., 52
DENIS, Maurice, 26
DERAIN, André, 31
DIAGHILEV, Serge, 30
DUKAS, Paul, 33
DUPARC, Henri, 28, 33
DUPIN, Etienne, 129
DUPONT, Gabrielle, 42
DURAND, Jacques, 30
Ecole romane, 42
FAVART, Charles-Simon, 104, 307
Faubourg St. Germain, 28
FAURÉ, Gabriel, 28, 33
Fauves, The, 31
*Fêtes galantes* (Verlaine), 36, 69
FLAUBERT, Gustave, 25
*Fleurs du mal, Les* (Baudelaire), 40, 210
FONTAINE, Lucien, 28
FONTAINE, Mme. Arthur, 184
FONTAINE, Mme. Lucien, 181
Footitt & Chocolat, 28
FORAIN, Jean-Louis, 29
FRANCK, César, 28
Franco-Prussian War (1870–1), 23
*Frissons, Les* (Gravollet), 43, 167
Gamelan(g), The 24, 184
GARDEN, Mary, 104
GAUGUIN, Paul, 29
GAUTIER, Théophile, 25, 38, 138
GEORGES, Alexandre, 306
GIDE, André, 27, 28, 41
GIROD, André, 33, 52, 306

GODET, Robert, 29, 177, 193, 196
GODET, Mme. Robert, 177
GONCOURTS, The, 27, 38
GRAMMONT, Maurice, 306
*Grand Testament, Le* (Villon), 44, 258
GRAVOLLET, Paul, 33, 43, 167
GUIRAUD, Ernest, 26, 29
HARTMANN, Georges, 30
HÉRÉDIA, José Maria de, 25, 29, 41
HOCQUET, Vital, 200
HUGO, Victor, 45, 115, 138
HUYSMANS, Joris Karl, 27
HYSPA, Vincent, 33, 41, 159
Impressionists, The, 24
Impressionism, 30
Industrial Revolution, The, 23
INDY, Vincent d', 28, 43
KAHN, Gustave, 29
KEATS, John, 24
KRYSINSKA, Marie, 27, 306
LAFORGUE, Jules, 36, 199, 215
LANCRET, Nicolas, 38
LAVIGNAC, Albert, 29
LECONTE DE LISLE, Charles, 25, 33, 36–7, 45, 65
LEROLLE, Henry, 215
LE ROY, Grégoire, 34, 41, 164
Librairie de l'Art Indépendant, 27, 41, 129
LOCKSPEISER, Edward, 31
LOUŸS, Pierre, 26, 27, 29, 41–2, 46
MAETERLINCK, Maurice, 29, 41, 42, 210
MAHLER, Gustav, 30, 31
MALLARMÉ, Stéphane; in *Parnasse Contemporain,* 25; Tuesday gatherings, 25, 29, 37, 41, 46; poems set to music by Debussy, 33; life, 42, 99, 275; importance and originality, 45–6.
MANET, Edouard, 28, 215
Manifesto of the Symbolists (1886), 25
MARTINET, André, 306
MASSENET, Jules, 33, 34, 104
MATISSE, Henri, 31
MAUCLAIR, Camille, 29
MAURRAS, Charles, 29
MAUTÉ-VERLAINE, Mathilde, 38, 39
MAUTÉ, Antoinette, 37
MECK, Nadezhda von, 29, 69, 73, 76
MECK, Alexander von, 56, 76
MENDELSSOHN-BARTHOLDY, Felix, 306
MERRILL, Stuart, 29
MONET, Claude, 29, 215
Montmartre (Paris), 27
MORÉAS, Jean, 26, 27, 29, 43
MOREAU, Gustave, 26
MOREAU-SAINTI, Mme., 36, 37, 52
MORICE, Charles, 27

MORISOT, Berthe, 29
MORRIS, William, 24
MOUREY, Gabriel, 29
MUSSET, Alfred de, 34, 35, 76
Naturalism, 25, 36, 43
NIJINSKY, Vaslav, 30
Nouveau Cirque, 28
Opera (Paris), 27
ORLEANS, Charles d', 33, 42, 43, 234–5, 237, 250, 259
Paris Autumn Salon (1905), 31
*Parnasse Contemporain, Le,* 25, 275
Parnassian Movement, 25, 34, 38, 43
*Parsifal* (Wagner), 24, 200
*Pelléas et Mélisande* (Debussy), 29, 41–2, 199
PETER, René, 28, 29
PETER, Mme. René, 221
PICASSO, Pablo, 31
POE, Edgar Allen, 25, 29, 40, 42
*Poèmes antiques, Les* (Leconte de Lisle), 37
Positivism, 23
*Prélude à l'après-midi d'un faune* (Debussy), 30, 46, 275
Pre-Raphaelites, 24, 25, 41, 99
Prix de Rome, 40
*Promenoir des deux amants, Le* (Tristan L'Hermite), 44
PROUST, Marcel, 27
PUVIS DE CHAVANNES, Pierre, 26
Rationalism, 24
RAVEL, Maurice, 43
Realism, 24
REDON, Odilon, 26, 28, 29
RÉGNIER, Henri de, 27, 28, 29, 199
REISSIGER, 47
RENOIR, Auguste, 28, 29
Reynold's Bar, 28
RIMBAUD, Arthur, 37, 38–9, 104–5, 109, 112, 115
RIMSKY-KORSAKOV, Nadezhda, 24
*Rite of Spring, The* (Stravinsky), 30
ROBERT, Paul, 27
RODENBACH, Georges, 29
RODIN, Auguste, 28
*Romances sans paroles* (Verlaine), 38
Romantics, 25, 34, 43, 193
Rome, 26, 27, 40
ROSSETTI, Dante Gabriel, 42
ROUAULT, Georges, 31
*Sagesse* (Verlaine), 38, 39
Salon Officiel (1863), 24
SATIE, Erik, 41
SCHOENBERG, Arnold, 31
Scientism, 23
Second Empire (1852–70), 23, 25
*Serres Chaudes* (Maeterlinck), 210

SHAKESPEARE, William, 42
SHELLEY, Percy Bysshe, 27
Société Nationale de Musique, 28
*Stalactites, Les* (Banville), 35
STEINLEN, Théophile-Alexandre, 27
STEVENS, Alfred, 28
STRAUSS, Richard, 30, 31
STRAVINSKY, Igor, 30, 31
SWEDENBORG, Emmanuel, 25
SWINBURNE, Algernon Charles, 24, 29
Symbolism, 25, 30, 34, 188
Symbolists, 24, 26, 29, 30, 35, 43, 199, 250
SYMONS, Arthur, 29
Taverne Weber, 27
TENNYSON, Alfred Lord, 24
TEXIER, Rosalie, 30, 42
Third Republic (1871–1945), 23
TINAN, Jean de, 29
TOULOUSE-LAUTREC, Henri de, 28
*Tristan und Isolde* (Wagner), 150
TRISTAN L'HERMITE, 33, 42, 44–5
Trocadéro, 24
TURNER, J. M. W., 205
Vachette Café, 27
VALÉRY, Paul, 29, 31
VALLAS, Léon, 159
VAN DONGEN, Cornelius Kees, 31, 226
VASNIER, Blanche, 29, 34, 36, 40, 47
VASNIER, Eugène, 26, 308
VERLAINE, Paul, in *Parnasse Contemporain,* 25; and Watteau, 38; and Mallarmé, 29; poems
    set to music by Debussy, 33; influence on Debussy, 37, 40; and Parnassians, 37; relationship
    with Rimbaud, 37, 38–9, 104–5, 109, 112, 115, 196; poetic production 37–8; and Banville, 38;
    relationship with Mathilde, 38, 39, 196; inspired by Commedia dell'arte, 38; in England,
    38–9, 109, 122, 188, 196.
VIDAL, Paul, 43, 61
VIÉLÉ-GRIFFIN, Francis, 29, 199
Villa Medici (Rome), 26, 34, 40, 104, 122
VILLIERS DE L'ISLE ADAM, P.A.M., 27, 29
VILLON, François, 33, 42, 43–4, 258–9, 265, 271
Wagnerian Review, The, 24
WAGNER, Richard, 24, 25, 30, 40, 41, 42, 44
WATTEAU, Antoine, 25, 38, 73
WEBER, Karl Maria, 47
WHISTLER, Paul, 27
WIDOR, Charles-Marie, 43
WILDE, Oscar, 27, 41
WILLETTE, Adolphe, 27
World Exhibition (1867), 24
World Exhibition (1889), 24, 138
World War I (1914–18), 31, 287
YSAÏE, Eugène, 28
ZOLA, Emile, 25